KLARTEXT

Dieses Projekt wurde
cofinanziert von der
EUROPÄISCHEN UNION

3. überarbeitete Auflage Mai 2008
1. Auflage Juni 2000
Satz und Gestaltung: Achim Nöllenheidt
Druck: Griebsch & Rochol Druck GmbH & Co. KG, Hamm
© Klartext Verlag, Essen 2008
Alle Rechte vorbehalten
ISBN 978-3-88474-815-7
www.klartext-verlag.de

TOUR THE RUHR

The English Language Guide

by

Roy Kift

Acknowledgements

I should like to thank all those who have assisted me during the various editions of this book, most especially Dr. Ludger Claßen of Klartext Verlag who took up the idea so readily and Achim Nöllenheidt for his many weeks of work on the layout, Mr. Jürgen Steiner and all his staff at Ruhrgebiet Tourismus GmbH for generously supporting the project, not forgetting Peter Neumann, Peter Blinne and Hans Oehl at the Verkehrsverbund Rhein-Ruhr for their advice and assistance in helping me to test the public transport network. During my travels countless people welcomed me into their establishments, gave me their time and supplied me with valuable information and guidance. I am very grateful to all of them, especially to Caroline Tillmann-Schumacher at the Ludwig Gallery in Oberhausen, Robert Laube who accompanied me on long crawls round the bars in Dortmund and the Bermuda Triangle, Rheinhold Hegemann who took time out to acquaint me with Recklinghausen, Ms. Yue Tutt who was invaluable in helping me to discover a lot of restaurants and Juliana von Hodenberg who took me on an unforgettable walk through the parklands in the north of Herne. Needless to say the local tourist offices throughout the region were immensely useful in providing me with basic information and advice, most particularly in Dortmund, Gelsenkirchen, Essen and Duisburg. My two daughters, Martha and Paula were invaluable in testing the family-fun venues and provided me with a wealth of enthusiastic and critical comments. Despite the pressures of her own work, my wife Dagmar was ever ready to arrange her timetable where possible in order to allow me as much free time as possible. And when everything looked like coming to a hopeless impasse my stepmother Hildegard Höher came to the rescue as always. Lastly, thanks to Bärbel Gross, Pitt Herrmann, Oliver Wittke, Doris Kunzmann, Hermann Rogenhagen, Axel Hillebrand, Richard Noice, Ingo Hinze, Klaus and Ursula Rürup, Roger Kettler, Nandakumar Deshpande, Professor Toshi Katayosi, Karen Hasler and all my friends at the American Women's Circle and the British Women's Club in Düsseldorf, for providing me with tips and comments for the various editions either personally or in writing. Keep in touch!

Symbols used in the book

✪ Top Twelve Highlight

🏴 has basic

🏴 🏴 comprehensive English information

☺ has something for all the family

♿ has a handicapped toilet and is for the most part accessible by wheelchair

♿ ♿ caters comprehensively for handicapped visitors

And lastly you'll be seeing the following symbol in almost every chapter:

⚓ does not mean 'ideal mooring facilities for seafarers'.
Be patient and it'll all become clear in chapter 12.
(I bet you look it up straightaway).

Introduction: third edition

This book was born of desperation. I'll tell you how it happened.

About fifteen years ago I moved from Berlin to the Ruhr area with heavy heart. I had never been remotely near the area. Nonetheless I knew everything there was to know about it: it was ugly, dirty, and awful. So my German friends had told me. They'd never been there either. But since my wife had been offered a good job in Dortmund and her chances of getting anything remotely similar were somewhat thinner than winning the national lot-

tery, we decided to turn our backs on the big-city lights and head out into the benighted wastelands of the Ruhr. Apart from one major problem I've not regretted a minute of it. The problem? Trying to persuade my friends and relations to pay me a visit. Either, like me, they knew nothing of the area; or they were convinced that its best – indeed only – features of interest were the roads leading out of it. As if to confirm this, there was not a single guide in

English to tell them about the region. The only solution, I decided, was to write one myself. I couldn't have made a better decision. For within three years two print-runs hade sold out completely and this edition will be the third updated guide in the space of ten years. During this time I have discovered that my readers consist not only of English-speaking visitors and other non-German speaking foreigners, but also of Germans who want to polish up their English and at the same time learn a little bit more about the Ruhrgebiet through English eyes. Indeed reactions have been so positive and so many things have changed in the area that I've now been forced to revise and enlarge the book twice to keep pace with developments. The area, which has been selected to be the European Capital of Culture for 2010 has a lot more new attractions, and I've had time to cover many of the old ones which I missed in the first edition, as well as eat my way through a few more restaurants!

My intention is to acquaint you with the many highlights in the area, help you to master the difficulties of getting around in a country whose language you probably don't understand, and point you in the right direction to enable you to make further discoveries for yourself in one of the most fascinating areas in Germany. Despite its five million or so inhabitants it's not London and it's not New York. It's not even Berlin, thank God. And it's most definitely not Majorca, although it also has plenty of fine places for you to laze around in the sun. The Ruhr area is for people with a healthy curiosity who are looking for a holiday with a difference. Nobody in their right mind would claim the region is an Elysium of unmitigated beauty but it's a million times greener and cleaner than its reputation. And best of all, the people are some of the friendliest I have met.

In compiling the information in the book I have done my best to be as accurate and up-to-date as possible. Things change so quickly that it is impossible to be 100% up-to-date. Even as I write the VRR public transport system has given notice of a radical review of their zoning and pricing system and this will be bound to impinge on my current accuracy. That said, should you notice any errors or omissions or disagree with my judgements, do as many other readers have done and send me an email with your suggestions. The address is at the end of the last chapter. With the exception of one or two restaurants, I am recommending nothing in this book unless I have been there personally. In particular I have checked all venues to see how well they cater for English-speaking visitors since I don't want you to waste your money on something you can't understand.

Ruhrgebiet Tourismus GmbH
info@ruhrgebiettouristik.de
www.ruhrgebiettouristik.de

Where possible I've also tried to take account of the needs of families and wheelchair people in my assessments, the more so because many of the physical hurdles met by wheelchair people also apply to adults with prams. And if the weather's bad, I shall be suggesting a few places where you'll still be able to have a wonderful time. So don't believe what anybody – and that includes me – tells you about the Ruhrgebiet. Find out for yourself. I can promise you, you're in for some pleasant surprises.

Lastly, if you're planning to move around the area staying in different places overnight, need tickets for concerts or are looking for day trips or package tours, do it the easy way and contact the Ruhrgebiet Tourismus office in Essen. This is the official organisation responsible for co-ordinating tourism in the region and can provide you with information on the area as a whole or fit you up with a holiday to suit your every wish.

PS: In case you haven't already guessed, the word 'gebiet' in Ruhrgebiet, is German for 'area'. It's pronounced 'g-beat' ('g' as in 'gazette').

1. Taking the Lid off the Pott

It's a funny thing about the Ruhrgebiet. Not a single German from outside the region would ever want to live there. And no-one who lives there wants to move out. What is it that makes the 'Pott' or 'Ruhrpott' (as the Germans call it) so unattractive to outsiders and so loved amongst its own inhabitants? Superficially the region seems to be little more than a conglomeration of run-down industrial towns in search of a future, with nothing to offer except beer and football. This was once the area where King Coal reigned supreme, the industrial heart of Germany whose 'montan' (coal and steel) industries powered Germany to its post-war economic miracles. The Pott may have gone off the boil in the 60s and 70s but thanks to bold initiatives in the region it's beginning to heat up again. The legacy of filth and pollution left by decades of heavy industry has been largely cleaned up, revealing a surprising amount of beautiful countryside. Most gratifyingly, the industrial monuments which were once the very centre of people's everyday existence have not only been preserved, but restored in the form of on-site museums, artistic venues and community centres as a living tribute to the men and women whose blood, sweat and tears transformed the region into the powerhouse of Germany – even for a time, of Europe.

Before I go any further I should like to take you on a short excursion into the past. Not because I'm a fan of history, but because I think it'll help you to get a better feel for the region and how you relate to it as you're looking around. And here's the first surprise: over the last two thousand years foreigners like you and me have left a considerable mark on the area. Around the time of Christ the Romans, having conquered France (or Gaul, as it was called in my schoolbooks) tried to get a foothold on the lower reaches of the Rhine. They even built a road from Southern Germany along the left bank of the river all the way up to Xanten, just north of Duisburg where they arrived around 200 BC and shortly afterwards set up a large military camp. The Franks, a local Germanic tribe, were none too pleased about being colonised and finally got their revenge when they destroyed the town in 351 AD, thereby unwittingly laying the basis for the town's major tourist attraction many centuries later – the Roman archaeological park. In 775 the next prominent foreigner arrived in the area. The French Emperor Charlemagne, having decided to enlarge his Empire, established a fortress in Hohensyburg, south of present-day Dortmund, with a breathtaking view over the river Ruhr. From here he was able to extend his influence along the river,

Xanten, Roman ruins

westwards to the Rhine and eastwards to the mouth of the river Möhne. (In the 20th century the Möhne was dammed up into a reservoir. The dam became the target for British bombers in the 2nd World War in their efforts to flood the Ruhr area and ruin the German war effort. Did you ever see 'The Dam Busters', a stirring old film from the 50s starring Richard Todd, Kenneth More and a stiff-lipped Alsatian? Or was it Kenneth More who was stiff-lipped? Anyway, that's the Möhne dam and it's still a lovely place for a day trip).

Back to Charlemagne: soon there was a string of royal courts, castles and moated fortresses dotted across the region, around which grew the first settlements like Dortmund and Essen. These were linked by a major trade route, the so-called 'Hellweg', whose name lives on in many of the towns and cities you will be visiting. In turn the 'Hellweg' joined up with a network of north-south trading routes, most importantly to the River Ruhr. On the southern borders of the river the land turns mountainous and here the trade in ironware from local ore was of primary significance for economic development. The area north of the river – the present-day Ruhrgebiet – had originally been covered in forests. But as it was cleared to make way for hamlets and farmsteads the land, loamy near the river valley, sandier and more marshy further north, was gradually turned over to agriculture. Rural transformation was accompanied by the arrival of Christian missionaries,

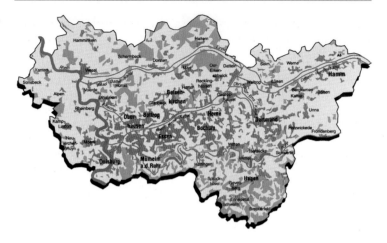

Towns, forests and rivers

mainly from England and Holland. They set up churches in Mülheim, Dinslaken, Duisburg (Meiderich) and Dorsten. Major abbeys followed in Broich (Mülheim), Werden (on the river bank south of Essen) and in Essen itself. The monks too began to take over the land for cultivation. As early as the 12th century deposits of coal were discovered along the southeast borders of the river valley near present-day Lethmathe, whose caves can still be visited. At this point the seams were practically on the surface and here open-cast mining began.

Mining in today's Ruhr area did not begin until much later. There is a simple explanation for this. As the seams proceed northwards into the heart of the Ruhrgebiet they get increasingly deeper. Beyond a certain depth coal is only accessible by sinking shafts into the earth. And since deep-shaft mining can only be achieved by harnessing steam-power to pump out water, the region had to wait for the discoveries of the English to give it the impulse required to develop from a backward rural area to a roaring centre of industrial production. With the arrival of railway communications and the development of the iron and steel industries in Dortmund, Essen and Oberhausen, mining became big business and the fulcrum of industrial production moved inexorably north of the river during the 19th and 20th centuries. I am told that the very same coal seam continues under the North Sea right into Northern England but I haven't had time to follow it. Yet.

Because of its connections with the Rhine – and by extension Holland – at Duisburg, the Ruhr was the leading industrial transportation waterway at the start of the 19th century. But within a hundred years it had lost its significance to man-made canals as mining moved northwards. Indeed if you look at a map, the course of the River Ruhr is practically identical with the southern perimeters of the Ruhr region, whereas the industrial heartlands are bisected by the Rhine-Herne canal. This leads from Duisburg to Henrichenburg, north-west of Dortmund, where it joins up with the Dortmund-Ems canal which was built to facilitate the import of iron ore from Sweden and give the Germans a trading outlet to their own coast. (Cycling enthusiasts will be delighted to learn that there are excellent new bicycle trails the length of both canals). Further northwards the region is traversed by the River Lippe and the Wesel-Datteln canal. Americans might be interested to know that Wesel was the birthplace of Peter Minuit, who in 1626 set up a town called New Amsterdam at the mouth of the Hudson river. The town was later renamed New York.

The history of the Ruhr area is intimately bound up with the great names of iron and steel, Leopold Hoesch (Dortmund), Friedrich Thyssen (Duisburg), and Alfred Krupp (Essen). But foreigners also played a significant role. In Oberhausen, where large deposits of ore were discovered, the French and Belgians moved in very early to build up zinc production. And one of the legendary coal entrepreneurs in the region around Gelsenkirchen was an Irishman, William Mulvany. Mulvany was originally a water engineer who tried to counter the disastrous effects of the potato famine in Ireland (1845-9) by instituting a massive drainage programme. When this failed due to the resistance of the landowners, Mulvany was made a scapegoat and sent into compulsory early retirement. It was 1853 and he was 46 years old. A year later he was contacted by an Irishman living in Brussels and invited to take over the management of some coal mines in the Ruhr area where the industry was enjoying its first boom period. Mulvany was astounded by the potential of the area and its latent riches. He moved to Germany in 1855 with his family and immediately began work on the first truly

William Thomas Mulvany,
ca. 1870

Erin Trading Estate, Castrop-Rauxel

modern pit in the region. The Hibernia Pit (Latin for Ireland) in Gelsenkirchen was genuinely revolutionary. Before then all pits had been protected against the intrusion of water by bricks. But thanks to the work of an English engineer called Coulson, Hibernia was the first pit whose shafts were fitted with steel tubbings, as the rings were called. The pit was up and running by 1856. This was followed a year later by the Shamrock Pit in nearby Herne. In 1864 Mulvany moved on to new challenges. He was not only one of the prime movers behind the decision to build the Rhine-Herne canal, but also founded the Prussian Mining and Iron Works Company whose President he became. One of his first

acts was to build the Erin Pit in Castrop-Rauxel on the northern border of Dortmund (Erin is Celtic for Ireland). And later his company was responsible for the Hansa and Zollern pits in Dortmund (→ ch. 9) as well as the Vulcan Steel Mills in Duisburg. By this time the area was seething with English and Irish mining specialists, officers and workers who had been lured abroad by Mulvany. Not more than a stone's throw away from the Erin pit, Mulvany bought himself a villa, Schloss Goldschmieding which now houses a gourmet restaurant and a fine park hotel. And just down the road from where I now live, the newly opened Erin Trading Estate – complete with Mulvany Centre and Erin pithead tower – has been completely re-landscaped in the style of the Irish countryside.

Mulvany was one of those who threw up his collieries wherever he could, and the region between Essen and the Rhine-Herne canal was soon a chaos of pits and pit-workers' housing. For where there was a mine, housing followed. Within decades villages exploded into cities, irrespective of the lack of basic urban provisions like roads, water supplies and sanitation systems. The result was that the little river running through the middle of the area, the Emscher, soon became a stinking, disease-filled cesspool. (To call it 'polluted' would be a compliment). 150 years later this area is known as the Emscher Park Region and people actually cycle along the river bank for pleasure. And without gas masks!

Demand for coal not only swallowed up the land it swallowed the available workers. Soon there were not enough locals to meet the demands of industrial production and foreigners began to pour in by their thousands from the hunger-stricken regions in and around present-day Poland. For them riches were a couple of rooms, a job and a vegetable garden with a pig or a goat. Prosperity was by no means guaranteed, however. There were many economic booms throughout the 19th century but these were accompanied by equally disastrous economic depressions as the roller coaster of capitalist growth took on its own uncontrolled momentum. Nonetheless immigration continued and by 1914 there were around 300,000 Polish-speaking inhabitants in the area around Gelsenkirchen, with their own network of churches, banks, clubs and unions.

The influence of foreigners on the region continued in a different way at the end of the Great War. In the 1918 Treaty of Versailles the allies demanded huge financial reparations from the Germans. Because of the appalling economic climate the

The Emscher today

Germans failed to meet these and were ordered instead to make payments in coal and wood. In its role as Germany's industrial power-house the Ruhr area once again became the centre of contention. Tensions came to a head in 1923. When the required deliveries were not forthcoming, an occupation force of 100,000 French and Belgian soldiers marched in to try to raise production by coercion. Needless to say they achieved the opposite as the locals met the military with passive resistance. A year later, seeing that their action was useless the foreigners agreed to withdraw. But the damage had been done. The economic crisis grew worse, and Adolf Hitler came to power on the wave of an anti-foreigner nationalist backlash. Ironically enough it was Hitler himself who was directly responsible for the next wave of foreign immigration. During the Second World War the Nazis brought in no less than 1.9 million prisoners-of-war from occupied areas in Russia and the East as compulsory labour to man the factories and pits in the Ruhr and release German workers to die at the front. The POWs were accompanied by an astounding 5.7 million civilian workers from abroad, of whom 1.7 million came from Poland and 2.8 million from Russia. With the defeat of Nazi Germany in 1946 the country's administration was carved up between the Americans, the French, the Russians and the British, who were responsi-

ble for the Ruhr. For the next fifty years there were British garrisons based in Dortmund and other towns in the area, many of whose soldiers married local women and stayed on. Even I, the least military-looking person you could imagine, am continually asked by strangers whether I used to "belong to the military". (I don't think they would have taken me even if I'd wanted to).

British citizens are now very much a minority in the Pott, even if our influence can still be seen in the design of inner-city parks and urban garden-cities. With the onset of the German economic miracle in the 50s 'guest workers' began to be recruited in their thousands to take over the dirtiest and most poorly paid work from the Germans. Italians comprised the largest group in the first wave and by 1960 they totalled more than 100,000. These were followed by workers from Spain, Greece, Turkey and the former Yugoslavia. The end of the 1950s witnessed the first great crisis in the coal and steel industries and the Ruhr area, which was almost completely reliant on the two for its prosperity, began to suffer. Since then both industries have declined even further and the area has been in a state of radical transformation from an industrial society to a community devoted to the service and leisure sectors. Today Turkish workers are the largest foreign group in the area. Indeed many of them have now set up their own businesses and entered middle-class professions in order to move up the social ladder. And finally, in the decade following the collapse of communism in 1989, there was a marked wave of immigration by German-speaking Russians. Despite their own economic problems the locals have generally been tolerant, even welcoming, towards the newcomers from abroad. Could this be because many of them have not forgotten their own family history? Within days of our arrival in Dortmund from Berlin I was sharing a beer on the doorstep of our house with my neighbour, a coal miner and son of a Polish worker and a German woman. This openness was brought home to me again during the 1999 Kosovo conflict. Not only were the authorities in the region quick to give asylum to thousands of exiles. The local population responded to the appalling suffering of those who had been hounded out of home and country, with gifts of money, televisions, bicycles and toys for the kids as well as free concerts and invitations to join them in their own social centres.

The down-to-earth, working-class side to the Ruhr with its warm-hearted village neighbourliness still remains. The inhabitants of the Ruhrgebiet are fiercely proud of their region, but nonetheless still cling defiantly to their very local identity: parish and suburb even more than town or district. Indeed, until recently, there has been almost a tribal resistance to administrative agglomeration in an area which is now the third largest urban conurbation in Europe – after London and Paris. Structural transformation has set in strongly. A strata of young, middle-class, educated entrepreneurs, academics and high-tech specialists has begun to make itself felt in the area and a new and fascinating Ruhrgebiet is emerging along the axis from Duisburg to Dortmund: ultra-modern and forward-looking, steely, even brassy in character. Despite its above-average level of unemployment, the Ruhr area is defiantly confident and able to compete with the rest of the country in enterprise, entertainment, shopping facilities, transport, sport and leisure at the start of the new millennium. There is a huge dynamic potential in the area and the first signs of this are beginning to emerge with the selection of the Ruhr metropolitan area, as it is officially known, as the European Capital of Culture 2010. With some luck the RUHR.2010 festivities should eventually lead to the area breaking free of the encrusted administrative shackles which have held it fast for the last two hundred years. Cities, towns, districts and parishes must dare to throw aside their individual interests and unite as one. Just imagine! The United Cities of the Ruhr, the largest metropolis in Germany and one of the top five cities in the world! Now there's a vision worth pursuing ...

2. Travelling the Area

One of the main problems for tourists anywhere is getting acquainted with the transport system. This is all the more difficult if you can't understand the language. But if you'll spend a couple of minutes reading this chapter before you start your travels you'll be in a good position to **save a lot of time, bother and money**.

The Ruhr area has around five and a half million inhabitants which makes it one of the world's largest industrial conurbations. But unlike, say, London or Berlin it has no obvious centre since it consists of a great many towns, each of which is jealously proud of its individuality. Because the area is central to the health of the German economy these towns are connected by a huge web of motorways. This might make you think that the best way to get around is by car. And in many ways it is. But if you've lived in the area for some time, as I have, you will know that the region's main artery, the A 40 (**A** stands for Autobahn = motorway) with its adjoining motorways, can jam up within seconds. Now there are some people who enjoy spending their lives stranded in a stinking line of non-moving metal staring at a faceless concrete landscape. Not me. And anyway, if you're on holiday nobody's forcing you to rush everywhere.

Thankfully the area has an good network of public transport run by the **<u>V</u>erkehrsverbund <u>R</u>hein-<u>R</u>uhr**

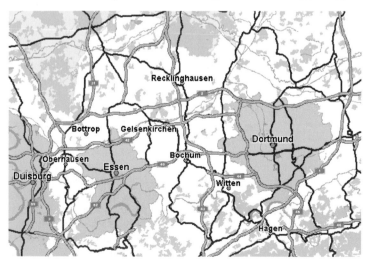

or Rhine-Ruhr Traffic Association. Since this is a mouth-and-a-half-full of a word we'll adopt the local abbreviation and call it the **VRR** from now on. Much of the network has been modernised in the last few years to cater for prams and wheelchair users. In many cases the VRR is even faster than travelling by car and will get you into the middle of a town without the hassle and expense of finding somewhere to park. If you know how to exploit this to its best you'll soon discover that the best way to experience the constantly changing face of the area and rub elbows with the locals is to travel by public transport. You certainly won't get that from hurtling along a motorway behind a juggernaut searching desperately for the right exit.

Thus, whilst not ignoring the needs of car drivers, I shall concentrate on providing you with the information to be able to do as I did while I was researching this book: to travel the area by 'public taxi' as the most relaxing means of transport. As a bonus, it is also the most environmentally-friendly. Nonetheless on my journeys I have discovered that there are some places which are far easier to reach by car. Wherever this is the case I shall tell you, in the hope of spurring the VRR to come up with a better alternative in the near future.

One last tip for hardened drivers. We all know that one of the most off-putting aspects of travelling by public transport is the time spent waiting for a connection between two routes, or timing a bus to get to the train on time. Since there are so many Park and Ride stations on the network, I often avoid this problem by driving to the nearest station from which I can get a direct train to my destination. This works best, of course, if it's not in the middle of town where you usually have to pay parking fees.

Public transport

The cheapest and most convenient ticket

The Ruhr area is the third largest urban conurbation in Europe and its transportation system is accordingly complex. It is run by a single public authority, the VRR, which is responsible for buses, trams and the regional railway service. Once you have **a ticket** it **is equally valid for bus, tram and train** (underground and overground). Depending on the length of your journey there are three* basic price levels – A, B and C. An 'A' ticket will <u>always</u> cover all journeys within the town you start your journey and even – <u>sometimes</u> – just over the border into an adjoining town. A 'B' ticket will cover your town and the immediately adjacent towns. A 'C' ticket enables you to travel the whole network**. These tickets are sold in three categories: the single-journey ticket (*EinzelTicket*); the four-journey ticket (*4er Ticket*) which is available for four single journeys and works out around 20% cheaper than buying four separate *Einzeltickets;* and the day ticket.

It is probably in your interest to **buy a day ticket if you intend to travel back and forth a lot**. This comes in two variations. The first is for one person only and is called a TagesTicket (day ticket). The second type of day ticket, called a Gruppenticket (group ticket), will save you even more money providing you are travelling in a group of at least three people. Indeed, **up to five people can travel all day backwards and forwards at will on one *Gruppenticket***.

Finally, if public transport is your principal means of getting around

the region whilst you're staying here it might be worth your while to buy a local time-table-plus-map for the town you're staying in (*Stadtfahrplan*), which costs about 1€ and also contains detailed information on connections to the other main towns in the area. If you only need details on all forms of rail connections, the 'Fast Traffic Time-Table' (*Verbundfahrplan Schnellverkehr*) will cost about the same again.

*actually there's a fourth basic ticket. The short-journey ticket (Kurzstrecke, vending machine code 0010) is the cheapest of the lot but it only covers three stops, which makes it useless for most tourist purposes. The VRR also offers weekly and monthly tickets but, in my opinion, the most convenient ticket for tourists in terms of price and flexibility is the day ticket.

**If you are reading this after autumn 2008, you will have noticed that the VRR has introduced a "D" ticket for the whole network, thereby splitting "B" and "C" zones even further. Sorry!

Kift's insider tip for day tickets

If you are travelling back and forth a lot during the day, buy a day ticket rather than separate tickets per journey. There are two basic sorts of day ticket: the *Tagesticket* and the *Gruppenticket*. If you are travelling alone or with only one other person it is more economical to buy one *Tagesticket* per person than a *Gruppenticket*. Both categories can also be bought as 4er tickets. These can be used on four separate occasions; say, four separate day's travel for one person, or two separate days travel for two persons on the 4er *Tagesticket*; or four separate day's travel for the group with a 4er *Gruppenticket*. Needless to say the 4er tickets work out cheaper, but don't forget to stamp them before starting your journey.

How to buy your ticket

You can buy tickets at VRR Service Centres, any shops showing the VRR sign in their windows – these tend to be newsagents and kiosks – from vending machines in trams and from the driver on buses (except *4er Tickets*); but not on trains. You used to be able to get them from station ticket offices but in the last year or so more and more of these have been closed in favour of ticket vending machines. Unfortunately the machines tend to come in a bewildering number of shapes and sizes which makes it difficult to give you any firm information about how to use them. Most take coins and bank notes, a few only bank and

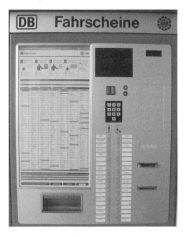

credit cards, some are run by German railways (DB), others by the VRR, some are titled 'Fahrausweise' or 'Fahrscheine' (posh German for 'tickets'), others 'Tickets', and others yet again 'Nahverkehr' ('Local transport'). Almost all of them have English language information and the best ones have a touch-screen facility. But even for a hardened traveller like myself the problems can be very frustrating. Nonetheless I'll try to give you some essential tips to help you bluff your way through like a native.

Using the ticket vending machine. The first thing you need to know is whether you want an A, B or a C zone ticket. To determine this you have to decide the furthest destination you will be travelling to that day. If you're only travelling within the boundaries of the town you start in, this will <u>always</u> be an A tariff. B tickets will take you to adjoining towns; and anything else will be a C ticket. You then press the appropriate button, A, B, or C. Crazily enough, on DB (German railways) vending machines there is no appropriate button!. Instead you have a bewildering system of digits – as you see in the photo – and a list of individual stations. But instead of getting a stomach ulcer trying to find a particular station on the machine you'd do better to establish the tariff you want in advance. Then, if you are confronted with a DB vending machine all you have to do is tap in the appropriate **four digit code number**: for an **A ticket, press in 0-0-1-1**, for a **B ticket 0012**, and for a **C ticket, 0013**. Now look in the display to confirm you've got the ticket you wanted. If not, press the C (here C = correct!) button and try again. Once you have confirmed the tariff level is right – and the following procedure now holds good for all machines – you now choose what sort of ticket you want: single journey, four journey, or day ticket. If your machine doesn't have a touch-screen facility you'll probably find two parallel lines of rectangular buttons below the display as in the photo shown here. The row on the left is for adults where you can find the zone ticket you want; the one on the right for kids, dogs, bikes and first-class supplementary tickets (the German is 'Zusatzticket') on trains. This latter is not a bad idea when you're travelling to and from the airport, especially at rush-hour times. Both rows give tickets in all categories and prices, which explains why there are so many buttons. But let's keep it simple by giving you one concrete example. If you want to buy a day ticket for one person look down the left-hand row for the word 'Tagesticket' and press the button next to it.

The price will now be shown in the display. You then insert enough coins or bank notes to cover the price shown on the display. If your bank note shoots back out again you've probably put the wrong end in first. Turn it round and try again. Now, if all goes well, the machine will give a metallic rumble as it digests your money before dropping your ticket, and any change due, into a tray at the bottom of the machine. If you only want a single-journey or a four-journey ticket the same routine applies: first the appropriate tariff, then the type of ticket. But in this case, you have to choose an adult or a children's ticket where necessary. Should you be travelling with your bike you must buy an additional ticket (*Zusatzticket*) for it. It's the same price as the 1st class supplement. And even if you have a group day ticket for up to five people you must buy one Zusatzticket per person (1st class or bike).

A word of warning, unless you are buying a 4er Ticket **don't buy a lot of single tickets in advance** as they drop out of the machine already stamped with the date and time and you have to use them immediately. This also applies to the Zusatztickets. If you buy a 4er ticket you must stamp it in a so-called "Entwerter"

(Devaluer). You do this by inserting one side of the ticket into the orange-coloured stamping machine which is generally right next to the ticket machine. There are also stamping machines inside buses and trams but none on trains. Since there are regular ticket controls and on-the-spot fines of 40 € per person for travelling without a stamped ticket it's not worth trying to travel free.

Travelling by bus or tram

Bus stops are indicated by an **H**, which is short for *Haltestelle* (Halt-place!). On the front of all buses and trams you will see the number of the route and the name of the final stop. Many of the buses have an air-suspension system which enables the

driver to lower the bus to the level of the pavement when it stops, thus making it easier for prams and wheelchairs to roll on board. Once in the bus or tram you will find a diagram of all the individual stops along the way. Better still, almost all vehicles have an illuminated sign inside which changes as you travel from stop to stop, and tells you the name of the next stop. In case you can't read or have fallen asleep this info is reinforced by a robot's voice saying something which sounds like 'Nexter Halt' (no translations needed! You're learning fast), followed by the name of the stop. This does <u>not</u> mean, however, that the bus will definitely stop there. You still have to press a button or the driver will simply drive on

("Ve have vays of making you vork!"). And one last tip: trams often dive underground near city centres, thereby turning into temporary underground trains. So if you're searching in vain for a tram stop in city centres it's often beneath your feet: look for signs with a large **U**. Any references to trams and underground trains in this book are likely to be mutually transferable.

Travelling on the local trains: U-Bahn, S-Bahn, RE and RB

First a few more words in German. (This is more than a guide-book, it's an education!) **U** is underground, **S** *'schnell'* or 'speedy' and Bahn, railway. And if you've ever wondered what **Hbf** stands for when you arrive at a station, these are the three letters in *Hauptbahnhof* (lit: main or central railway station). And once you're there **Eingang** is 'In-walk' and **Ausgang**, 'Out-walk': what you and I know as entrance and exit. Ain't it easy?

During your stay you will be hopping frequently between **S-Bahn** and **U-Bahn** trains. The **S-Bahn** will take you between the major towns, where you can go underground with the **U**. If you fly in for a holiday in the Ruhr area you will in most cases arrive at **Düsseldorf Airport**. When you arrive at terminal A-B-C look for the signs to the "sky train" shuttle service to "Düsseldorf Flughafen" station. There are lifts and escalators to the first floor platform where you

can purchase your VRR ticket for the whole journey from a ticket machine. From Düsseldorf Flughafen station there is an S-Bahn connection (line **S1 to Dortmund**) every 20 minutes or so which will take you directly into the **Hbf**s (got it?) and all other stations in Duisburg, Mülheim, Essen and Bochum before terminating in Dortmund. If you're staying in or near any of the abovementioned towns the **S1** is going to be your main means of travel, so make a note of it now. There's also a direct Regional Express (line **RE3**) train from the airport once an hour to Duisburg, Oberhausen, Gelsenkirchen, Herne and Castrop-Rauxel. On the Eastern side of the Ruhrgebiet **Dortmund** has a growing **airport**. If you arrive here there is a regular bus shuttle service into the city centre.

Like the buses the fronts of the trains display the number of the line and sometimes the final stop. To find the right platform for the S Bahn in the major stations, simply look for the green S sign. When you get to the platform an information sign hanging above will tell you which train is coming in next with a list of the major stops along the way. And if you think you may still have got on the wrong train, who cares? Holidays are about surprises. And wasn't it

Oliver Cromwell who once said 'No man goes further than he who does not know where he is going'? Enough culture. You can always check where you are by consulting the detailed route maps in every compartment.

There are two other sorts of trains on which you can use your VRR ticket. The **RE** stands for Regional Express. This travels once an hour and only stops at main stations. For this reason if you're travelling from **Hbf to Hbf** (or from **Düsseldorf Airport to a Hbf**) and your timing's good it's quicker than the S-Bahn. The same applies to train routes beginning with the letters **RB** (Regional Bahn). **VRR tickets**, however, **are not valid on Inter-City** (IC) or Euro-City (EC) trains. So unless you want to risk a hefty fine, avoid them. At this point I could start telling you about all the different varieties of bus and rail available. But since the VRR has internet information and info leaflets in English (available from their travel centres and at major stations) any of you who are really curious can catch up on current prices and all the rest of the niggling details which are mainly irrelevant to your needs as a tourist. But do forgive me if I give you a tip about one more kind of ticket which is useful if you're visiting big shows or venues. It's called the **Kombi-ticket**, an entrance ticket to the venue or event you are going to, **combi**ned with free travel by public transport in both directions from anywhere in the whole

region. The extra cost for travel is a give-away at only one or two €uros.

Special tips for wheelchair users, pram pushers, anyone else with mobility problems and all people visiting Essen and Duisburg

I thought a long time before deciding to write a 'segregated' section especially for you but it's unavoidable. I have said that a lot of the public transport system has been updated to cater for your special needs. Nonetheless from personal observation and talking to wheelchair travellers I have discovered that there can still be considerable difficulties and I want to warn you about them here. Firstly, as a general rule you'd be advised to travel only with a non-handicapped person. This will become clear as you read on. Next, buses. Despite the air-suspension systems enabling drivers to lower the bus to the level of the pavement kerb they sometimes fail to pull in close enough which means you have an awkward gap to manoeuvre. Tram stops on the other hand sometimes have platforms from which you can roll onto the tram direct. When they become U-Bahns this is always the case. In some towns like Duisburg, however, there is only one (marked) U-Bahn carriage per train suitable for entering on wheels directly. A further problem with trams is that once they get outside the centre they tend to stop in the middle of the road where there are no platforms. A good example of this is Essen where you can roll onto the tram/U-Bahn at the Hbf to get to the Zeche Zollverein, but you'll have no chance of rolling off when you get there as it stops in the middle of the road. The main line, overground Hbf in Essen is particularly bad at catering for wheelchair passengers. Here you can roll off the S-Bahn with ease but there is only a goods lift to take you down to the main concourse. This is kept locked of course, so you will have to send your companion down to the Service Centre near the main exit, and they will send someone up to the platform to unlock the lift and accompany you down. (The station is supposed to be modernised soon and I am told this problem will then no longer exist. But they've being saying that for years…) At Duisburg the problem is even crazier. Here there are wonderful lifts up to the platform, but when the train stops it is impossible to roll off or onto the train without help because of the huge difference between the level of the platform and the passenger coach. Furthermore if you want to go down into the U-Bahn or central bus station from Duisburg Hbf they can be reached, not by going down into the central concourse as I did because the signs were so badly placed, but by heading for the Eastern end of the very long platform, where there are only steps! So if you're on wheels you'll have to take a lift down to the main concourse and roll round the

front of the station. Apart from the problems mentioned, the great majority of railway stations – and I include the suburban stations here – have lifts up or down to the platforms, and getting on S and U-Bahn trains should not provide you with any difficulty. I must, however, warn you that I have observed that **RE**s and **RB**s are often very difficult for people in wheelchairs or with prams to negotiate as platform heights – as in Duisburg – are not on the same level as the coach exits.

To help you on your way round there's a **VRR area map** in the inside cover of this book.

From autumn 2008 there will be a radical change in the public transport zoning and pricing system. So I advise you to check all this on the **VRR Internet information** (also in English, French and Turkish). It has excellent advice on tickets, route planning and timetables. www.vrr.de

Travelling the region by car

Since you'll mostly be using the motorway you might find it useful to know some of the signs you're likely to come across, so that you can decipher them immediately without going into a blue panic. The first word you should memorise is *Gefahr!* which means danger. This is often accompanied by *Stau(s)*, or traffic jam(s). *Umleitung* means that the road ahead is blocked for some reason or other and the traffic is being re-directed. Just keep following the signs and in due time they should lead you back to the motorway. If, on the other hand, you want to get off it, look for **Ausfahrt** which means exit and has nothing to do with breaking wind. On other roads, unless otherwise indicated, traffic coming from the right has legal priority. The Ruhr area still has a lot of tram lines, many of which stop in the middle of the road. If a tram has stopped it is an offence to overtake it on the inside until it moves off again, as you're likely to kill any passengers who happen to be getting on or off. The Germans have just as many crazy drivers as any other country but here it's against the law to express your opinion of them by gestures such as tapping your skull or showering them with verbal abuse. So if you want to let off steam, curse in English extremely rapidly with a friendly smile on your face ending with the words "my friend". It works wonders, not only for you but sometimes also on your victim – unless he or she can understand English! In which case you're back in trouble.

There are two more points you should note. Germans have a fondness for abbreviations because so many of their words are ridiculously long. And in the Ruhr area every suburb has its own particular tribal pride. What's the connection, I hear you asking. I'll tell you. When you're looking for a particular town on a motorway sign and start seeing unheard-of destinations like 'MU-STY-RUM', 'DU-NEUMÜHL', GE-BUER', 'E-KRAY' 'BO-WERNE', 'DO-MAR-TEN' or the like, don't panic. The first two letters are the abbreviation of the name of the town you're searching for in vain, whilst the complete name you've never heard of is that of a particular suburb. Since you'll generally be looking for the middle of the town on your travels, you can figure this out from the first two letters of the town in question, followed by the word **Zentrum, Innenstadt, Stadtmitte** or simply **Mitte**. If by now you still can't decipher the letters MU, DU, GE, E, BO, and DO, let alone OB, RE, BOT and all the rest you're likely to come across, I suggest you leave your car in the garage and travel by public transport. See what I mean about the stress?

Now you know how to get around, it's time to tell you the best places to visit.

3. Run-down on the Ruhr

MY TOP TWELVE HIGHLIGHTS *(and other instant tips)*

After a couple of days looking round your immediate vicinity you'll probably be curious to visit the outstanding venues in the area. Normally travel guides provide their readers with a list of Top Ten Highlights, but who wants to be normal? I'm going to give you 20% more at no additional cost. Take them or leave them, these are my particular tips and tops. The selections I have made are all in some way unique. In addition I have judged them on the basis of how well they cater for 1) English-speaking visitors; 2) physically handicapped visitors; 3) families. To qualify for the list each must fulfil at least two of the three categories pretty well. Following that I've compiled a few quick-tip lists for particular interests, especially for those on a budget.

But first of all – here they are! <u>In geographical order</u> from west to east

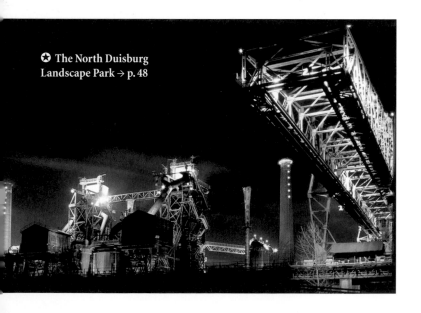

✪ The North Duisburg Landscape Park → p. 48

✪ Oberhausen
(as a day trip)
→ p. 61

✪ Villa Hügel, Essen → p. 109

✪ The Old
Synagogue,
Essen → p. 93

✪ The Tetrahedron, Bottrop → p. 73

✪ The Zollverein Pit XII,
Essen → p. 95

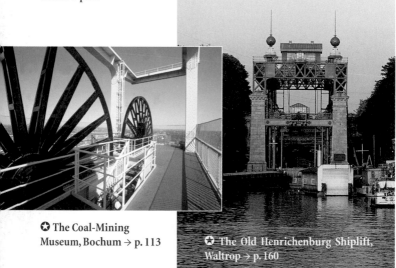

✪ The Coal-Mining
Museum, Bochum → p. 113

✪ The Old Henrichenburg Shiplift,
Waltrop → p. 160

✪ The Zollern II/IV Colliery,
Dortmund → p. 180

✪ Maximilian Park,
Hamm → p. 194

✪ DASA, Dortmund → p. 179

✪ The Westphalian Open-Air
Museum, Hagen → p. 134

I've always been told you don't get something for nothing in life. Wrong. Take a look below.

Free indoor venues
(at all times unless stated)
Bochum: Bochum Museum (first Wednesday in the month) → p. 119
Bottrop: Quadrat Museum Centre → p. 73
Dortmund: Art and Cultural History Museum (Saturdays only) → p. 176
Dortmund: Ostwall Museum (Saturdays only) → p. 176
Dortmund: Natural History Museum (Saturdays only) → p. 187
Dortmund: Steinwache → p. 177
Essen: The Old Synagogue ✪ → p. 93
Gelsenkirchen: City Museum → p. 79
Gelsenkirchen: Horst Castle → p. 83
Gelsenkirchen: Science Park → p. 87
Hagen: Karl-Ernst Osthaus Museum → p. 131
Hamm: Gustav Lübke Museum (First Sunday in the month) → p. 195
Herne: Emscher Valley Museum → p. 164
Herne: Wanne-Eickel Museum → p. 169
Marl: Glaskasten Museum → p. 157

If you want to have a budget-saving day in the fresh air I can recommend any of the following.

Free sunny day out venues
Bochum: Botanical Gardens → p. 119
Bottrop: Tetrahedron ✪ → p. 73
Dortmund: Romberg Park Botanical Gardens → p. 189
Dortmund: Hohensyburg → p. 190
Duisburg: North Duisburg Landscape Park ✪ → p. 48
Duisburg: Six Lakes → p. 48
Gelsenkirchen: Berge Castle Grounds → p. 80
Gelsenkirchen: Nordsternpark → p. 83
Haltern: Lake Haltern → p. 150
Witten: Hohenstein → p. 130
Witten: Mutten Valley → p. 127
All of the Revierparks → pp. 46, 55, 72, 89, 166, 191, 202
Any of the panorama points → p. 213

Family amusement parks
Bottrop: Schloss Beck → p. 77
Bottrop: Movie Park Germany (esp. for teenies) → p. 76
Haltern: Ketteler Hof → p. 152
But if the weather's not too good, don't forget:
Duisburg: Legoland Discovery Centre → p. 44

You know the feeling? You're on holiday and wake up in the morning to the sound of rain battering on the windows. Don't worry, the following will put paid to those rainy-day blues.

Best rainy-day holiday solutions
Bochum: Mining museum ✪ → p.
Dortmund: DASA ✪ → p. 179
Duisburg: Legoland Discovery Centre → p. 44
Essen: Phenomania → p. 102
Revierpark Baths: (→ ch. 11)

And for holiday shopping:
Bochum: Ruhrpark Shopping Centre → p. 116
Oberhausen: CentrO Shopping Centre → p. 65
Gelsenkirchen: Halfmannshof Artists' Colony (craftwork) → p. 89
Waltrop: Manufactum (quality) → p. 162

The most attractive old town centres
Hattingen → p. 124
Kettwig (Actually this is an old village, now a suburb of Essen) → p. 111
Unna → p. 199
Westerholt → p. 156

The lazy list for water-lovers

Best Boat trips
Duisburg: Harbour round-trip and others → p. 40
Mülheim: White fleet river trip → p. 58
Essen: White fleet Lake Baldeney and River Ruhr → p. 111
Dortmund: Harbour to Henrichenburg Ship Lift → p. 192
Oberhausen: "Kaisergarten" park: up or down the canal → p. 70
Waltrop: from the new Shiplift and the Shiplift museum → p. 161

These are the ones you're going to talk about over dinner when you get home.

Most architecturally unique venues
Dortmund: Zollern II/IV Colliery ✪ → p. 180
Essen: The Old Synagogue ✪ → p. 93
Essen: Zollverein Pit XII ✪ → p. 95
Essen: Villa Hügel ✪ → p. 109
Gelsenkirchen: Science Park → p. 87
Herne: The Academy Mont-Cenis → p. 166

Most outstanding art galleries

Duisburg: Küppersmühle Museum, a mini Tate Modern.

Essen: Folkwang Museum, 19th and 20th century masters.

Mülheim: Kunstmuseum in der Alten Post

Oberhausen: Ludwig Gallery, great popular exhibitions and the centre for Landmark Art in the region.

If you're looking to stay up all night having a full-blown holiday rave.

Most popular night-life areas

Bochum: Bermuda Triangle *(Bermuda-3Eck)* → p. 114

Oberhausen: the Promenade in CentrO → p. 65

The Ruhrgebiet has got some strange characters with even stranger private interests. Catch up on some of these here. You'll probably have to phone in advance to get in.

Funny peculiar

The Magnet Museum:

120 sq. metres containing everything you ever wanted to know about magnets. An authentic attraction (Sorry! I couldn't resist it) on the grounds of TriDelta in Dortmund-Aplerbeck.

Tel: 0231/4501271

The Funfair Museum:

Wooden horses, posters, organs, stands, large fluffy animals and a huge library. In Essen near the Central Station.

www.schaustellermuseum.de

The Bee Museum:

This is not a sting, honey! (It's getting worse and worse!) Live biology lessons on the living thing in Duisburg.

www.bienenmuseumduisburg.de

The Office Museum: Three floors of typewriters (remember them?), tippex, hand wound calculators, and clocking-in machines which make you thankful for the invention of the computer. This one's in Mülheim.

www.muelheim-ruhr.de/cms bueromuseum2.html

Annual recurring events

Finally a short list of **annual recurring events**

February
Bottrop Organ festival

March
Dortmund 'Femme Fatale', women's film festival (every two years).

April
Oberhausen International Short Film Festival in the old town centre. The best short films from around the world. Many young directing talents have made their debut here and gone on to become household names in film. English simultaneous translations for foreign language films. Some years in the first week in May.
www.kurzfilmtage.de
Duisburg. Rhine-Ruhr marathon.

May to July is the high season for **festivals**.

May
Klavierfestival Ruhr. Regional festival with top international pianists – **mid-May to mid-July**.
www.klavierfestival.de
Bottrop: Horse market (first Saturday of the month)
Duisburger Akzente: Concerts, films, dance and literature festival.
Recklinghausen European Festival. 1st May to mid June. International shows: many in foreign languages.

Mülheim Theatre Festival The best new <u>German language</u> plays of the year in productions from Germany, Austria and Switzerland.
Witten. Festival of modern chamber music.

June
Extraschicht: Extrashift, the long night of industrial heritage. All night celebrations in the museums and industrial heritage sites. Special bus and train services takes ticket holders between the various venues.

Festival-Theater in Recklinghausen

July
Bochum. 'Bochum Total' – the big live music street party in the Bermuda Triangle. It's held once a year on the first weekend of the region's summer holidays. So it might be in late June in some years.
Dortmund Chess Meeting. One of the strongest international tournaments in the world.

Witten/Bochum/Hattingen.
The Kemnade Lake Festival

August

Dortmund: Inner-city road cycling race.

Herne: Cranger Kirmes. 10 days of raucous raving in one of the biggest fairgrounds in the world. 4 million visitors a year!

Schwerte: World street theatre festival (the last week of the month).

Cranger Kirmes

September

In Autumn 2002 the region launched a mammoth performing arts festival called the **RuhrTriennale**. Although it's an annual festival, it's called the Triennale because the artistic director changes every three years. It generally starts towards the end of August and runs through to the first ten days of October.
www.ruhrtriennale.de

Bochum and other towns: International Puppet Theatre Festival. (FIDENA)

Bottrop Horse market (first Saturday of the month).

Essen: International Regatta on Lake Baldeney.

Lünen: the annual „Lünsche Mess" street festival (second weekend of the month).

October

MELEZ: Intercultural festival in many cities in the area.(Last week of October and first week of November)

Dortmunder Herbst: A huge exhibition with the latest trends in consumer and DIY goods.

Gelsenkirchener Organ Festival. Annually in Autumn.

Lünen: Kite festival (4th biggest in Germany).

November

Herne: The Festival of Early Music. (A gentle antidote to the August ravings?)

Dortmund: The Six Day Indoor Cycle Race (Westfalenhallen)

Lünen: Jazz festival.

Lünen: Festival of new German films.

Mülheim, Dortmund, Bochum, Essen, etc. 'Impulse' Fringe Theatre Festival.

December

Christmas Markets in most towns, especially **Duisburg, Dortmund, Essen** and **Hattingen**

Now it's time to get down to the nitty-gritty …

4. Walking on Water
DUISBURG AND MÜLHEIM

DUISBURG (pop: 498,000)

Tourist Information:
Duisburg Information,
Königstraße 86, 47051 Duisburg.
Open: Mon-Fri: 9.30-18.00,
Sat: 10–13.00. Tel: 0203/28544-0.
The Königstraße is the main shopping street and the information office is just minutes from the Hbf. (Turn right when you come out of the front entrance and follow your nose.) Here you can get some excellent maps and information on all the town's attractions, including a cyclists' map of the city. There are quick and frequent trains from Dusseldorf.
service@duisburg-information.de
English website:
www.duisburg-tourism.com/en/

Duisburg, 25 kilometres to the north of Dusseldorf, is the eleventh largest city in Germany with a population of just under 500,000. It's ranking could almost be symbolic as it's never been a top ten attraction in the eyes of either Germans or foreigners. Nonetheless it does boast the largest inland harbour in the world and its communications at the junction of the rivers Ruhr and Rhine are excellent. Like Dusseldorf, the first mention of the town was relatively early. In 883 the Vikings headed up the Rhine and captured the town of 'Oppidum Duisburch' from the Franks who had established a royal court on the site of the present-day Burgplatz. In the 10th century Duisburg's court became a royal palace, the starting point for the Hellweg east-west trading route. Commercial prospects looked good but then the Rhine silted up, Duisburg was gradually stranded and by the end of the 14th century the town's importance as a trading-centre had sunk to insignificance. One of the city's great names was the Dutchman Gerhard **Mercator**, who settled here in 1552. For the next forty years until his death in 1594 Mercator developed his revolutionary system of transposing the spherical form of the earth's surface onto a two-dimensional map, a system which has been passed down in history as the Mercator projection. A compendium of his maps was published in 1595 under the title 'Atlas'. (→ City Museum). Duisburg University was opened in 1655 in the Salvatorkirche (Church of Our Saviour). With its four faculties of theology, philosophy, law and medicine it was, until its closure in 1818, one of the most important centres of learning in Germany. In 1674 a regular merchant shipping route to Holland was established and in 1712 the first shipyard opened in the Ruhrort, one

of the two harbours which now comprise the inland port. Nonetheless, by 1800 Duisburg was still a mediaeval town with only 5000 inhabitants. Indeed it was not until 1873 that the town became an administrative centre in its own right. By now it had become a thriving trading port serving the whole of the Ruhr area and, on account of its huge grain warehouses, was known as the 'breadbasket of the Revier'. By 1905 when it finally merged with Ruhrort and Meiderich (→ Landscape Park, p. 48) the population had increased to over 100,000, huge industrial plants were dotted alongside the river and railway line, and Duisburg could boast more millionaires per head of population than any other city in Germany. The 20th century has seen an inexorable decline in traditional industrial production and, with the closure of the local steelworks in Rheinhausen, Duisburg has suffered accordingly. Today the city is undergoing a huge facelift, not least thanks to the British architect Lord Norman Foster who has been responsible for several major new projects including the ElecTronic park and the inner harbour complex. His latest project is a huge new master plan to modernise the city centre and relate it to the harbour in order to emphasise the city's historical connections to the water. And if you really want a surprise head for the south of the city. Here I discovered miles of woodland

Duisburg harbour – evening

greenery and probably the most lovely collection of lakes for miles around. (→ Six Lakes, p. 48)

The inner city

Duisburg's main shopping area is the Königstraße, over the road to the right as you leave the Hbf. It's a spacious, tree-lined boulevard for pedestrians and cyclists only, with many open-air cafés. At the centre, König-Heinrich Platz, there's a huge new building called the **city palais** which contains a slick new **gambling casino** in the shape of an ocean liner, the "Restaurant Inside" (it's actually called that!) and a concert hall for the city orchestra. On the other side of the city palais in Neck-

arstraße is the classical old **theatre and opera house,** originally built in 1910, and restored in 1950 after being badly damaged in the war. And on the shopping boulevard itself is the huge new City Forum. Just off the Königstraße near the 'Kuhtor' at Sonnenwall 8, you'll find **Caféhaus Dobbelstein.** This is not only the oldest coffee-house in the Ruhrgebiet, it claims to have the largest collection of coffee mills in the world. Just the place to take your aunty for coffee and cake.

Once you're in the middle everything is within walking distance, including the Schwanentor where you can indulge in the most popular tourist attraction in town...

✳ A cruise round the harbour.

The two hour round trip of the Duisport (as it's now called) is a must, for it gives you an excellent idea not only of the size of the harbour and the River Rhine, but a close-up view of its everyday activities. The boats are very comfortable and (on the lower deck) wheelchair accessible. You can sit inside or out as you wish, and there is on-board catering. The commentary is only in German. Notwithstanding, the boat was packed with contented foreigners the day I was on board. Queue at the boarding stage and pay on board. The boats run daily from mid-March to November unless the waters are iced up. In the season they start at 11.30, 13.30 and 15.30 from Schwanentor and 75 minutes later from the

Schifferbörse in the Ruhrort. The half tours begin only at Schwanentor and end at Ruhrort. Other boat trips include tours to Oberhausen and Essen during the summer season. www.wf-duisburg.de

Tram/U Bahn 901, alight 'Rathaus'. **Bus: 933 and 934** to 'Schwanentor'. You can walk it in no time once you're in the city centre.

Car: park anywhere near the Rathaus or Schwanentor and walk

✳ German Inland Waterways Museum *(Museum der Deutschen Binnenschifffahrt)* ERIH

This delightful museum is worth visiting in combination with the harbour trip. I broke my journey at Ruhrort, went to the museum and boarded the boat again two hours later. The individual exhibits have no information in English but the museum will provide you with an English-language route-plan giving you an overview of the basic themes. There are plenty of models large and small, fascinating pictures and photos of inland waterway life, but no hands-on activities for the kids. Before (or afterwards) you can go on board two museum ships which are tied up right next to the Ruhrort landing stage. A single ticket is valid for both ships and museum, which are separated by a fifteen-minute walk. Unfortunately the route is poorly signposted for pedestrians. So if you're coming from the Ruhrort

German Inland Waterways Museum

Duisburg inland harbour

Tram/U Bahn 901 from Hbf (direction: Marxloh), or RB 36 train from Oberhausen Hbf to "Duisburg-Ruhrort", and it's a ten minute walk. Or alight at "Duisburg-Ruhrort" and take **bus 907** directly to "Binnen-schifffahrtsmuseum".

By car: A59, exit Meiderich/ Ruhrort, or **A40, exit Duisburg Hafen/Ruhrort**. Pick up a museum brochure in the local tourist office: there's a sketch map on the back which is also useful for pedestrians. There's a **caravan park** here. Apply in the museum.

✳ **Wilhelm Lehmbruck Museum**
This lovely building is right in the middle of town in a park full of sculptures. Lehmbruck, a local man, was a well-known German sculptor and the museum is a European centre for modern sculpture. It has a first-class collection of exhibits including works by Giacometti, Tinguely, Arp, Barbara Hepworth, Brancusi, Alexander Calder, Picasso and Max Ernst as well as many younger artists whose names were unfamiliar to me. I was particularly knocked out by a large group of figures by Duane Hanson entitled 'War Group (Vietnam-Piece)'. For more on these, the paintings and graphic works, there's a very informative, free English brochure. Wheelchair visitors must get a friend to inform the person at the box office who will then put the lifts into action. The day I was there the café was closed but I found a very good bistro alternative,

keep following the river towards the Ruhrort harbour entrance and head towards the tallest factory chimney you can see – the one with the dirty-green cap. Once you've crossed a small blue arched steel bridge, you'll see a steel winding-staircase leading down to an area of grass. The museum is right next door.

Open: Tues-Sun: 10.00 – 17.00. Half price on the first Friday of the month! The ships are open from Easter to the end of October. Apostelstr. 84, 47119 Duisburg. Tel: 0203/80889-0. www.binnenschiff-fahrtsmuseum.de

Wilhelm Lehmbruck Museum

the **Café Museum**, in a corner of the park next to the Cubus-Kunsthalle.

Open: Tue-Sat: 11–17.00. Sun: 10–18.00. Friedrich-Wilhelm-Straße 40, 47049 Duisburg. Tel: 0203/2833294. www.lehmbruckmuseum.de (English pages)

Public transport: All buses and trams going into the middle of town stop here. It's quicker by foot if you arrive at the Hbf. Leave by the main exit and walk straight ahead for five minutes.

By car: Head for the town centre and park alongside the Kant Park.

If you're more interested in social history take a walk around the area near the Rathaus. This is the oldest part of the city and there's an archaeological zone which demonstrates graphically why Duisburg was so vulnerable to high water. A couple of minutes away you'll come to...

✳ **The Duisburg City Museum (Kultur-und Stadthistorisches Museum)**
🇬🇧

The museum, situated on the inner harbour bank near the Town Hall, was originally a grain warehouse. The central exhibition on the history of the city has just been completely overhauled. It takes visitors on an extremely attractive and informative tour through the city from the earliest times to the present day. Every section not only has excellent short English texts but is presented in an attractive staging which greatly enhances the whole experience. For example, the section on learning is presented in a mock library, and the section on industrialisation is displayed against a background silhouette of coal mines and steel works. There are large models showing the town at different stages in its history, and a huge model of the largest floating crane in the world in a section on

Gerhard Mercator

grain trading. Other themes deal with entertainment in the 20th century, the Nazis in Duisburg, women's domestic life, traffic, and the post-war era. On the second floor, the museum also boasts a valuable collection on the life and work of the city's best-known immigrant, the cartographer, Gerhard Mercator, including original globes.

Open: Tue-Sun: 10–17.00. (Fridays till 14.00. Sundays till 18.00). Johannes-Corputius-Platz 1, 47049 Duisburg. Tel: 0203/2832640. ksm@stadt-duisburg.de. www.stadtmuseum-duisburg.de

Public Transport: Tram/U Bahn 901 from Hbf, alight Rathaus.

By car: Park anywhere near the Rathaus or Schwanentor and walk.

If you are looking for a quick meal after your museum visit, you're only a short walk away from the oldest house in the city. The **Dreigiebelhaus** (anno 1536) in Nonnengasse 8 offers a good selection of food and drink and you can sit out in the beer garden in summer. Lunch-time and evening only.

Alternatively, why not take a ten minute stroll along the canal bank through the old town park to the prize-winning **inner harbour** (ERIH) which has been extensively re-designed to make it an attractive leisure area. This contains a large number of restaurants and cafés. Before you reach the Old Town Park

The Marina

(Altstadtpark) you'll come to a new hanging bridge over...

✳ The Marina

This was opened in 2001 and currently has permanent and overnight mooring facilities for 127 boats between 6 and 20 metres long. The whole complex is being built up over the next two or three years and will include a further hundred mooring sites, shops with yachting accessories, flats, offices and a leisure centre. Phone: 0203/3055–0. www.innenhafen-duisburg.de

The Old Town Park contains a Memorial Garden next to the Jewish Cultural Centre. Here the Israeli artist Dani Karavan has integrated the old town walls into his landscape architecture, leaving the outlines and the outside facades of the warehouses and their stairways as they were before they were destroyed. Keep walking along the river to the next bridge, and once you have crossed the road you'll find yourself looking at a row of old warehouses known as the "Speichermeile", behind which are little Dutch-style "grachten" canals with trendy new housing. There are restaurants and cafés on both sides of the harbour basin. At Philosophenweg 19, you'll find the **Hafenforum**, designed by Lord Norman Foster, which will give you some idea about the changing face of Duisburg. Right next door is the **Legoland Discovery Centre,** that offers an interactive Lego playworld complete with 4-D cinema, Philosophenweg 23-25, 47051 Duisburg. The **Atlantis Children's Museum** used to be sited here, but is currently looking for another site in the city. Check it out online to see if they've had any luck. If so, it's a great place to take the kids.

The best place to park for the inner harbour area is in Stresemannstraße which has over 450 parking lots.

If you walk right to the end of Philosophenweg, just before you get to the motorway bridge you'll find a new museum of contemporary art called the

∗ **Küppersmühle Museum**
 (Museum Küppersmühle Sammlung Grothe)

If you've experienced Tate Modern in London then you'll have an idea of what this is like – on a smaller scale. The museum was opened in April 1999 in a huge red-brick building built between 1908 and 1916, which served as a corn silo until the 1970s. It has been impressively converted into a wonderful airy museum with an exhibition area comprising around 5,000 square metres, which houses a huge collection of works belonging to a local man, Hans Grothe. The works by the 30 or more artists featured here include some extraordinary paintings by Georg Baselitz, Joseph Beuys, Rebecca Horn, Jörg Immendorf, Anselm Kiefer, Markus Lüpertz, Sigmar Polke and Gerhard Richter. As a bonus, there's a stylish restaurant/café in the building.

Open: Wednesdays: 14– 18.00 Thursday, Saturday and Sunday: 11– 18.00. Fridays by telephone arrangement only. Students under 18 free on production of student ID.

Philosophenweg 55, 47051 Duisburg. Tel: 0203/301948-11. www.museum-kueppersmuehle.de (English pages)

Public Transport: Tram/U-Bahn 901 to Rathaus and a ten minute walk along the inner harbour. Bus 932 from Hbf to Küppersmühle.

By car: Motorway A59, exit Duisburg-Duissen. If you're driving north-south: when you exit the motorway, take the first right into Kardinal-Gahlen-Straße and Philosophenweg is the fifth street on the right. If you're driving up the motorway from the south: turn left into Oranienstraße, then left into Falkstraße and this will lead you into Kardinal-Gahlenstraße etc etc. There's a small car park near the museum

Duisburg night-life

Duisburg is not renowned for its night life but there are one of two 'scene' cafés to the west of the Düsseldorfer Straße opposite the Wilhelm Lehmbruck Museum. **Café G,** on Krummacherstraße 14, is a dimly-lit, popular student haunt: and just round the corner at Dellplatz there are three bars right next to each other. **Webster**'s brewery house is the most conventional, has a roomy, bright German atmosphere and a beer garden in the summer. **Café Movies** is situated inside the **filmforum**, the city's art movie house, which shows occasional original sound-track films. And, probably best of all, there's **Hundertmeister**, an extremely attractive, spacious café which is part of an arts centre offering parties, discos, concerts and theatre (Goldstr. 15).

A short walk away at Kasinostr. 5 you'll find **Desperados**, a very popular Mexican-style cocktail bar. Nearer the centre, in the pedestrian precinct at Düsseldorfer Straße 21, I recommend a visit to the extraordinary **Brauhaus Schacht 4/8.** It's named after a Thyssen coal mine of the same name and housed in the building of the former Reichsbank. Even if you don't eat here it's worth looking inside for the décor and architecture, not to speak of the mining and brewing relics. They even brew their own beer! **Café Credo**, right next door, is a more intimate and elegant bistro/bar. But if you're feeling hopelessly home-sick, head straight for a great little Irish pub called **The Pogs** in Untermauerstraße, right next to Kuhtor. Here you can put the world to rights over a pint of Kilkenny's, as well as enjoying the home-cooked Guinness stew and bread. The night I was there a folk singer was snarling out Bob Dylan. Great stuff!

Many of the good **restaurants** in Duisburg are outside the city centre. **Dettmann's** (Kalkweg 26. Tel: 725790) specialises in high-class regional cooking. Kalkweg, in the suburb of Wedau, is the main avenue leading down to the Six Lakes. I'm told that **Gasthof Brendel** (Kaiserstr. 81, Tel: 02065/47016) in the suburb of Rheinhausen is also a fine place to eat. Still in Rheinhausen on the borders of Uerdingen, you can try excellent, traditional Ruhrgebiet fare in a lovely atmosphere at **Mühlenberger Hof.** (Hohenbudbergerstr. 88. Tel: 41565). **Schumachers** is also somewhat out of town in idyllic surroundings in the suburb of Friemersheim. But the food is supposed to be well worth the journey. Friemersheimer Str. 23, Tel: 02065/49738. www.restaurant-schumachers.de. And if you really want to find a highly praised gourmet gem tucked away in the middle of a wood, try **Im Eichwäldchen** at Im Eichwäldchen 15c, 47259 Duisburg, Tel: 0203/787346. www.im-eichwaeldchen.de

Apart from these, the place to go is the inner harbour where a whole new series of bars and restaurants is springing up around the marina. Most spectacular amongst these is the **Diebels** beer garden on a floating pontoon adjoining the brewery of the same name. Philosophenweg has a number of new places to eat and drink. Right next door you'll find the **Faktorei** (number 21), a symbiosis of bistro, café and restaurant (Tel: 3468379). Alternatively you can eat Mexican and sip cocktails at **Bolero** (number 31). If you prefer an elegant espresso bar with Italian and Spanish cooking try **Café Lounge Eivissa**, which faces onto Philosophenweg 31-33 rather than the harbour. And at the top end of the road (number 49) the **Küppersmühle** café and restaurant offers a select gastronomic experience in appropriately elegant surroundings. It's attached to the museum of the same name: the café/bar is open all day but the restaurant only in the evening (Tel: 2983690). Committed vegetarians

head for **Café Pic** (Am Dyck 69. Tel: 495149) in the suburb of Wehofen, near Revierpark Mattlerbusch, right on the border of Dinslaken. To go that far you have to be committed but the food is supposed to be first-rate! I passed it one afternoon when it was closed, gazed at the mouth-watering menu which includes ecologically-grown wines, and swore to myself to return some day.

There are three main discos in the city centre. **Remind** – formerly the Globe Club – is tucked away at Unterstraße 61 in the heart of the red light district near the canal: hard techno music, occasional live bands and more than a touch of the drop-out scene. The town's traditional favourite is **Old Daddy** (do they mean me?) in a cellar at Steinsche Gasse 48. If you're looking for an evening in an original venue, you must visit the so-called "event castle" **Pulp,** (open Thursday-Sunday) which offers a lot of other events in addition to the discotheque through the night on Thur/Fri/Sat. The most convenient way to get there is to take the local train from the Hbf (7 minutes) and alight at Duisburg-Hochfeld Süd Bf. Believe it or not, I actually went to a philosophical discussion here one evening! www.pulp-duisburg.de.

But you can't leave Duisburg without looking around outside the centre. Just five minutes away from the Hbf is...

✳ Duisburg Zoo
    ♿ ♿ ☺

This is one of the largest and most popular zoos in the region with everything from Koala bears to camels. It's main attraction is the large dolphin house which offers shows three times a day (extra price) at 11.30, 14.30 and 16.30. There's also a cuddly corner where the kids can stroke and pat the animals (but not the tigers). I was most surprised by the Chinese Garden – a present from Duisburg's twin town – which offered some peace from the hum of the nearby motorway.

Open: 9.00-17.30 (Winter: 9.00-16.00). Mülheimer Str. 273, 47058 Duisburg. Tel: 0203/3055-90. www.zoo-duisburg.de

Tram/U-Bahn 901 from Hbf (direction Mülheim) **to Zoo** (every 10 mins).

By car: Motorways **A3 or A40** to junction **AB-Kreuz Duisburg-Kaiserberg**. The zoo is practically next door.

There are three more open-air attractions which you must not miss. To the south is an absolute mecca for open-air fans...

Duisburg Zoo

The Six Lakes

* **The Six Lakes**
(Sechs-Seen-Platte)

I'd read about this in publicity leaflets and it sounded too good to be true. But no! This is a glorious stretch of wooded parkland around six lakes, with over 17 kilometres of paths and cycle trails, an open-air swimming bath, boat-hire facilities and places to picnic, angle, sail, wind-surf or run your model boat. The tourist office has an excellent map showing all the paths and attractions, with a street map overview of how to get there. You can reach it by...

Public transport: from the centre of Duisburg by taking the **944 bus** (every 20 mins) **to** the terminus at **Wolfsee.** It's a bit of a ride round the houses but the journey itself will give you a good idea of the many facets of the city. Alternatively you can take the **S1** directly to **Duisburg Schlenk** (on the way to Düsseldorf) and **then** change onto the **944**.

By car: Motorway **A59** to Düsseldorf, **exit Duisburg-Buchholz**.

As an absolute contrast in parkland leisure and one of my top twelve highlights in the region you must visit the

* **North Duisburg Landscape** ⊔
Park *(Landschaftspark
Duisburg-Nord)*
✪ ♿ ☺

Anybody who's been here will assure you that this is more than just another landscaped park on a disused industrial site. It's a 200 hectare area on a former ironworks site belonging to Thyssen. 37 million tons of iron were manufactured in the life-time of the works which went into production in 1903. On the same site to the west there had been a coal mine. The original pit had been sunk in 1899 but the most important shaft (no 8) was opened in 1926. The site was badly damaged by air raids in 1944 and production only resumed in 1947, continuing until 1959 when the pit became the first major victim of the coal crisis. The nearby coking plant managed to soldier on until 1977 when the coke oven and cable railway were torn down. The ironworks were highly productive, turning out almost a million tons of pig iron alone in 1974. Ten years later Blast Furnace 5, as it was known, was modernised at a cost of millions, only to be dealt a death-blow in 1985 by an EC quota restricting steel production. The fires which had been roaring 24 hours a day, every day of the year, lighting up the night sky for the majority of the century were finally extinguished and Duisburg was sitting on a ruin. What was to be

North Duisburg Landscape, light show – designed by the British artist Jonathan Park

done? Raze it all to the ground and wipe away the filth and industrial failure from human memory. Or restore it in some way as a tribute to the industry and its workers who had contributed so much to the city. Duisburg opted for the latter: the site should be kept alive and given a new use, the original structures and elements sensitively restored and their aesthetic and ecological features promoted. The project took ten years (1989-99) to complete and the end result is a fascinating mixture of industrial heritage and leisure park, which at weekends is lit up at nights by a spectacular light show – designed by the British artist Jonathan Park – a sight unrivalled anywhere else in Europe. Since I was so impressed by the place – indeed my whole family had a great time – I'm now going to describe the site in more detail to help you find your way around.

Day or night you can climb the steps of 'Blast Furnace 5', look inside the workings on the way, and enjoy an incredible panorama from the 70 meter high platform at the top. The old central power station had a dual function. It used to supply the furnace with oxygen and the factory and workers' settlements with electricity. Now it is a multi-functional hall for exhibitions, outside broadcasts and concerts. Right next door in the former distribution station you'll find the **visitor centre**, a snack bar/restaurant and beer garden. The Steam Blast House, responsible for the combustion process once blasted the furnaces with 3 million cubic metres of 'furnace wind' per day. Yes, per day! It's now known as the 'basilica'. Diagonally opposite you'll find the foundry belonging to blast furnace no. 1. Until 1982 this was where molten iron used to pour down into gullies. Now it's used as an open-air cinema in summer with seats for 1,100 filmgoers. Right opposite is the old gasometer which has now been turned into an **indoor diving centre** (see separate box). Walk across the so-called "piazza metallica" and round the corner you'll find an area of bunkers which have been converted into **free-climbing ranges**. In the area in front of the bunkers the water which had been used to clean the blast furnace gas used to be clarified. Now the broad area is used for open-air festivals and concerts. Running parallel to this is the clarified water canal. There's plenty of fun for the children just behind the canal on the sinter grounds where there are three playgrounds – one of them a water playground – gardens and a wind tower. Next to it is the so-called Nest and Egg square where many varieties of birds have found a new home. The old raised railway line from the bunkers to the coke plant via the blast furnace has largely been taken apart and replaced by cycle tracks and footpaths overlooking a landscape full of plants and wild life.

Hence, the 'wilds'. This jungle-like basin was originally garden-land, but it was cut off from its immediate neighbourhood by the construction of the nearby motorways. You can walk right round it and view the site from all sides at different levels. The park is criss-crossed with many cycle trails, one of which – the green trail – follows the route of the old goods line between Duisburg Ruhrort harbour and Oberhausen. Don't groan because you've not brought your bike. Hire one in the visitor centre and try it yourself. On the north-east side of the park there's a "journey through industrial nature". This is a gallery of items taking walkers on a journey back through time where they can find out more about how the landscape here has changed over the last few centuries. From here you can see the new "Emscher Sports Hall" which has been built on the old ferromanganese storage site. And finally, in complete contrast, directly adjoining the industrial site is the Ingenhammshof, six hectares of meadows and farmland dating back to 1644. It

North Duisburg Landscape, free-climbing ranges

North Duisburg Landscape Park
The underwater-diving gasometer (Tauchgasometer)

Here I had a so-called "try-a-dive" session, and I can tell you it's something you won't forget in a long time. Of course if you're an experienced diver you can dive there on your own providing you present an open-water diving certificate (SSI, Padi, or CMAS) and a doctor's certification of health at the box office. But since most of you, like me, won't ever have attempted such a thing I'll tell you what to do. "Try-a-dive" – the Germans call it "Schnuppertauchen" which really means "get a whiff of diving" – can only be undertaken on a one-to-one basis with an experienced instructor, so it's advisable to ring up beforehand and book a set time. You'll need to take along a bathing costume and towel; the rest of the equipment you can hire on the spot. After you've paid you'll be given an entrance card as proof of payment for when you enter the gasometer. Your instructor will then fit you out with all the right equipment and give you some basic instruction on hand

signals, breathing techniques and how to clear your ears of pressure – this last is very important – which you can practice before going underwater. There's a changing-room with lockers where you can change into your diving clothes. After this you wheel your equipment (it's heavy!) over to the gasometer where you put it in a lift at the bottom. You then have to walk up the gasometer stairs to the top where you'll be met by someone who will check your entrance card and bring your equipment up on the lift. Your instructor will then load you down with weights and breathing apparatus and flippers, by which time you'll be feeling like an overweight frog. All you've got to do now (ha! ha!) is stagger backwards over to the steps leading into the water. Try going forwards, as I did, and you're likely to stumble head-over-heels over your flippers. Luckily the steps have a rail leading down to a platform which is about waist high. This is where I knelt down in the water, said my last prayers, spat in my mask and washed it out before ducking beneath the surface to take my first breaths underwater. And then it was time to launch off. Holding tightly onto my instructor's shoulders I gradually descended onto further platforms, clearing my ears as I went. The sound of your own breathing is just like it is in the movies – loud and bubbly. I have to say that my instructor who spoke a little English was very good indeed in that he made me feel very secure. All the same it was clear that from now on all decisions concerning my own well-being were my responsibility. In other words it was up to me to indicate when I was willing and ready to try something or not. The two most important things I learnt were watching for and respecting the signals from my instructor and weighing this up against my inner voice and what it was telling me. Like the sauna experience I describe in chapter 12, the main thing is not to rush. And you know what? Gradually I lost all sense of time, stopped wondering about breathing, worrying about drowning and began to enjoy the experience of looking outwards. Right at the bottom there's a wrecked car and various other objects to explore. When we finally came up I was amazed to learn we had been around half an hour in the water. All I can say is – if you're at all curious, give it a try. It'll be one of the highlights of your holiday. The current price for try-a-dive is 26 € with a further 16 € for hire of all the equipment. They're closed on Tuesdays.

used to supply food to the steel-works but is now a general recreation area for the neighbourhood and an ecological centre for school parties. The farm site also has a small café and beer garden.

Entrance to the park is **free**. There's a café/restaurant called "Hauptschalthaus" in the visitor centre with an adjoining beer garden where you can sit and gaze at the light-show at night. It's open from 11–24.00 every day. Tel: 0203/41799180. www.hauptschalthaus.de. If you understand German you can go on a guided tour (also by night). In the summer there are live rock concerts, occasional theatre shows and an open-air cinema. For up-to-date information go to the **vis-**

If you want to stay on the Landscape Park overnight or longer there's a new on-site **Youth Hostel** (♿ ☺) here. I had a look round the rooms (for two, four or six persons, all with showers) and they're well up to hotel standard. The prices are very reasonable. Anyone can stay there but if you're not a member of the International Youth Hostels Association it'll cost you about 3 € a night more. For bookings: 0203/417900. Jugendherberge Duisburg-Nord, Lösorterstraße, 133, 47137 Duisburg. www.djh.de/jugendherbergen/duisburg-nord

itor centre in the former central distribution station. Here you can get a map of the site filled with information (in German) on all the different features to be found there, in particular the many types of industrial vegetation, enquire about guided tours and hire bikes. It's open from Monday to Friday from 10–16.00. On Friday evenings from 18-21.00. Saturdays, Sundays and public holidays from 10-21.00. weekends and public holidays 13-21.00. Tel: 0203/42919-42. www.landschaftspark.de. The visitor centre also houses the offices of **Tour de Ruhr.** This isn't where I work when I'm writing en français. It offers practically every tourist service you can imagine – ready-made or according to your wishes – including day tours round the region in English, French, Dutch and Spanish.
Tel: 0203/42919-19. info@tour-de-ruhr.de. www.tour-de-ruhr.de

Tram/U-Bahn 903 from **Duisburg Hbf** in the direction of Dinslaken Hbf, **to Landschafts-park.** (every 10 mins, weekdays, journey time 20 mins). **Bus 909 to "Hüttenwerk".** I cheated and went by...

Car: Motorway **A42, exit Du-Neumühl**, turn right into the main road and drive straight on until you see a sign to the park pointing right, by which time you should have spotted the place.

And last not least there's a fascinating panorama point to the north-west of the city called:

Alsum Hill *(Alsumer Berg)*

Drive out on the A42 towards Kamp-Lintfort and take the exit at Duisburg-Beeck. As you drive down the slip road don't turn right into the Kaiser-Wilhelm Straße but keep to the left. Here there is a set of traffic lights with two lanes: keep in the right hand lane. Then drive on beneath (and parallel to) the motorway, and take the first right into Alsumer Straße. By now you'll be wondering why any tourist guidebook in the world should have brought you to the end of the world because you'll be heading into the heart of industrial filth and noise. Keep going past the gigantic complex of Thyssen steel works – Duisburg is still the largest producer of steel in Europe – and the road will eventually start to lead uphill. Almost at the top of the hill there's a brown road-sign pointing left to a car park at "Alsumer Berg". Leave your car there, walk up the path and you'll be met with a view of the Rhine rolling steadily downwards the Dutch coast, lapping its lazy waves against the grassy banks. Some people are taking their dogs for a walk, others are cycling, still more are flying kites. A herd of sheep is grazing peacefully. By this time you'll have walked half-way round the hill and you still can't find the way up. Don't worry. Keep walking to the end of the path when you'll be about as far from your car as possible. Here at last you'll find the entrance to the path leading upwards. At the top of the hill you'll be rewarded with as contradictory a view as you're likely to see anywhere in the world, one which symbolises the bipolar nature of the area: industry and rural idyll side by side. The panorama to the east will confirm every prejudice you ever had of the noisy, stinking, industrial Ruhrgebiet (just multiply it by fifty to get an idea of what the area must really have been like a century ago); whilst the view to the west reveals not only the mighty river but a vast area of fields and meadows as far as the eye can see. Alsum Hill was built from the rubble left by the allied bombings in the war – there's a cross at the northern edge to commemorate this – and industrial waste but nature has now completely greened it over. At both ends there appear to be steps leading down to the bottom again and you think you've finally found the short-cut back to your car. Don't be fooled as I was. They both end in the midst of nowhere and you'll have to climb back to the top again and walk down properly with everybody else. Clearly construction work was started and then stopped again for lack of funds, or due to the realisation of the sheer expense involved in keeping nature's growth at bay.

Duisburg was a delight but now I'm exhausted. If you are too, take a trip north-east to the borders of Oberhausen and visit the **Revierpark Mattlerbusch** which has pony stables, an elegant farmhouse restaurant with beer garden, the **Brauhaus Mattlerhof**, and best of all...

The Lower Rhine Thermal Baths

✳ The Lower Rhine Thermal Baths *(Niederrhein-Therme)* ♿ ♿ ☺

The thermal baths were recently tested by an independent consumers' organisation and came out third best in the whole of the country. They are part of a luxurious swimming-pool complex which includes mineral water baths, 14 (!) different saunas, a Caribbean wave-bath, whirlpools, outside gardens, a Roman pool with mock Italian sun terraces and sandy beach, restaurant, snack bar and health drinks bar. I went there on a perfect late-August day, soaked away my aches and pains, stretched out on a deck-chair in peaceful garden surroundings and dreamt I was somewhere in the Mediterranean. 'O Sole Mio!'

Open: Daily: 8.30-23.00. Prices are dependent on the length of your stay – 2 hours, 4 hours or a day ticket – and whether you want to use the sauna area. Arrive before midday and you get four hours for the price of two. Sauna/mineral section not open for children under 4. Children under 6 have free admission provided they are accompanied by an adult. Wehofer Straße 42, 47169 Duisburg. Tel: 0203/9958412. www.niederrhein-therme.de

Bus: 905 to Niederrhein-Therme. This is so far out of town it's easier to come...

By car: Motorways **A3, exit OB-Holten,** or **A59, exit DU-Fahrn** and follow the signs. Plenty of free parking. For the baths park in areas P2 or P3.

Southeast of Duisburg, linked directly by tram 901 and the S1 railway is

MÜLHEIM an der Ruhr
(pop: 174,000)

Tourist Information:
Schloßstraße 11,
45468 Mülheim an der Ruhr,
Tel: 0208/9609612,
www.muelheim-ruhr.de

Mülheim was once the largest town in the area and the major loading and unloading centre for coal which was shipped along the River Ruhr. As mining moved northwards it gradually lost its strategic importance as an industrial centre although August Thyssen built a huge steel mill here. Now it's a peaceful little town with a large area of parkland along the Ruhr, centred around Broich Castle. In the adjacent park you can visit the Camera Obscura.

Aquarius Water-Museum

The town has a well-known theatre company and also sponsors an annual new play festival in May to decide the German dramatist of the year. Horse-racing fans can try their luck at the Raffelberg race course. But Mülheim is most likely to appeal to open-air enthusiasts because of its attractive walks and bicycle trails. (You can hire bikes at the Hbf and at Styrum station). I took a sunny 45-minute stroll along a nature trail to the...

* **Aquarius Water Museum** 🏛
  (Aquarius Wassermuseum)
  ERIH

This imposing structure served as a water-tower (capacity: half a million gallons) for private and industrial water-supplies until 1982. Instead of demolishing it the local water company has turned it into a prize-winning, multimedia museum with lots of hands-on activities for visitors of all ages. There's a great view of the town and river from the glass gallery at the top. Having said this because there are no English texts, this is **only recommended if you can understand German**. If you're hungry take your pick from the restaurant and beer garden in Styrum Castle or "Zum alten Bahnhof" at Hauskampstr.14.

Open: Tue-Sun: 10–18.00. Adults 3,00 €. Children 2.00 €. Family Ticket: 8.50 €. Burgstraße 70, 45476 Mülheim. Tel: 0208/4433-390.
aquarius@rww.de
www.aquarius-wassermuseum.de

Public transport: S-Bahn S1 or S3 to Mülheim-Styrum. Follow the signs outside the station. It's a ten minute walk. **Bus 122** from Mülheim or Oberhausen to "Mulheim-Styrum Bahnhof".

By car: See map on info brochure or website/"Öffnungszeiten und Eintrittspreisen". If lost, head for the suburb of Styrum and look for the "Routeindustriekultur" signs.

Back in the centre of town I walked along the river bank to the water station (*Wasserbahnhof*). But before I took a pleasure boat I dropped into the...

✳ **Ruhr Nature House**
(Haus Ruhr Natur)
♿ ☺ 🇬🇧

This is a small and beautiful museum with lots of interactive fun and information on the geology, biology and hydrology of the Ruhr valley. To make it even better they have an English language information leaflet which helps you to get the most out of it.

Open: Tue-Sun: 10-18.00. Adults: 2 €. Children: 1.50 €. Family ticket: 5.50 €. Combined ticket with Aquarius Water Museum: 4 € / 3 € / 11.50 €. Alte Schleuse 3, 45468 Mülheim. Tel: 0208/4433-380.
www.haus-ruhrnatur.de

The Ruhr looking towards Mülheim

Public Transport: Tram: 110, alight Wilhelmstraße. Bus: 151 to Wilhelmstraße, or 132, 133, 752 to Kasenberg. If in doubt, practically everything goes to 'Stadtmitte'. From there it's a ten minute walk.

Car: Try and get into the "Innenstadt" Then keep an eye out for signs saying 'Wasserbahnhof/Weiße Flotte'. Parking fees at the Wasserbahnhof car park.

If you're looking for refreshments here, **Franky's im Wasserbahnhof** has everything from fast food to a beer garden via cocktail lounge and restaurant. Here you can while away the time whilst waiting for the next boat. From the Wasserbahnhof I took a peaceful trip down the Ruhr valley to Essen, ending up in the extraordinary suburb of Kettwig. (More in chapter 6).

Boat trips: May-October, single or round trip, hourly or two hourly at the top of the hour depending on the weather.

Tel: and Fax: 0208/451-2507

✳ The Art Museum in the Old Post-Office *(Kunstmuseum in der Alten Post)*

Some small towns have provincial art museums, others are lucky. This is one of the latter. It's in a beautifully restored old red-brick post office building near the station. But what makes it so remarkable is its collection of expressionist art, most of which once belonged to a local Nobel prize winner, Dr Karl Ziegler and his wife. Amongst the truly first-class works on show in the Ziegler Collection are paintings by Erich Heckel, Max Beckmann, Karl Schmidt-Rottluff, Auguste Macke, Franz Marc and Emil Nolde. Not to speak of the odd Picasso, Jawlensky, Kandinsky and Ernst Ludwig Kirchner. The museum also has regular temporary exhibitions of contemporary artists and a collection of graphic works by the Berlin artist Heinrich Zille. The day I was there the whole of the ground floor was devoted to works by some of the school children in the town. I was so knocked out by three of the paintings I wanted to buy them straight away. Lucky Mülheim. If you're hungry afterwards, adjoining the museum is the Palette bistro which is open every day from 9.00 onwards. I had an excellent bowl of home-made soup and a baguette over lunchtime.

Open: Tue-Fri: 11-17. Thurs: 11-21.00. Sun: 10-17.00. Adults: 3 €, reductions 1.50 €. Free admission on Wednesdays between 14.00 and 17.00, 45468 Mülheim a.d. Ruhr.

Tel: 0208/ 4554138.

www.muelheim-ruhr.de/museum

The Art Museum in the Old Post-Office

Public Transport: everything which goes to the Hbf. The museum is five minutes away, just off the main shopping street.

Night life in Mülheim

Mülheim doesn't exactly buzz at night. The main venue for parties, discos, cabaret and live music is the **Ringlokschuppen** next to Schloss Broich in the park. On the plus side the town does have a fair number of **above-average restaurants**. If you're after a satisfying evening meal in pleasant surroundings, I've heard good reports about **Dalaman**. Bachstraße 8 in the town centre (Turkish. Tel: 380200), **Da Enzo**, Kölnerstraße 170 in the suburb of Saarn (Italian. Tel: 4669813) **Mölleckens Altes Zollhaus** Duisburgerstr. 228, (new German regional. Tel: 50349), **Alte Schule,** Kölnerstr.68 in the suburb of Saarn (German, French, Fish. Tel: 483300), and **Fata Morgana**, Mühlenberg 12 opposite Schloß Broich (Egyptian. Tel: 4376261).

✳ **Leather and Tanning Museum**
Leather workers have existed in Mülheim since 1639 and, at their height, did a lot of trade with the coal and shipping industry. This small new museum will give you some insights into what it was all about.

Open: Wed-Sun: 14–18. Adults: 2 €. Children 1 €. Düsseldorfer Straße 269. Tel: 0208/4554101. www.leder-und-gerbermuseum.de

Public Transport: from Hbf. Bus 132 or 133 (platform 3), alight Mülheim/Lindgens. From there it's a two minute walk.

One last word of warning: Mülheim is a motorist's nightmare. The road system seems to have been designed by some lunatic planner who's main aim is to keep you from reaching the town centre. So just as you think you're there, you are forced onto a spaghetti network of endless by-passes with signs every fifty yards or so listing twenty different destinations ('Is mine somewhere there?! Help! Too late!') ordering you to zigzag from left to right, up hill and down, across six lanes, dodging between other equally lost drivers caught up in the same ordeal. To be fair the system probably looked fool-proof on paper. But as with most German theories it's a disaster in practice. (What a disgustingly racist comment! Unfortunately it's true). By contrast the town has excellent public transport connections to the other major cities in the area. In particular it is very conveniently linked to Oberhausen by tramline 112. This departs at ten minute intervals during the week (15 at weekends) and will take you directly to most of the attractions listed in Oberhausen. Since that's in the next chapter let's go there, shall we?

5. Past toils, present fun, future visions
OBERHAUSEN, BOTTROP, GELSENKIRCHEN

✪ OBERHAUSEN (pop: 220,000)

Tourist Information:
Verkehrsverein Oberhausen,
Willy-Brandt-Platz, 2, 46045 Oberhausen (opposite the Hbf).
Tel: 0208/824-570. Information in
English, French and Dutch.
tourist-info@oberhausen.de
www.oberhausen.de
(English pages) or
www.oberhausen-tourismus.de
(English pages)

Present-day Oberhausen is a microcosm of almost all the characteristics of the Ruhr area, good, bad, old and new. This is why **I am recommending the whole town** rather than any individual venue **as one of my Top Twelve highlights** for a day out. Oberhausen was once a huge industrial centre, based on zinc and ore, and the scars of its history are still evident. The town – it was little more than a village at the time – was the site of the first iron foundry in the region (→ St Antony Hütte) in 1758. Fifty years later three iron works merged to become the industrial concern 'Gütehoffnungshütte' or 'Good Hope Mill'. In 1808 work was started on the construction of Oberhausen Mansion and in 1846 the oldest workers' housing estate in the area was built in Eisenheim (for both → below). The following year saw the opening of the railway station and in 1854 the first mine in the town was sunk. Nonetheless Oberhausen was only granted <u>rural</u> parish status in 1862, its civic status following in 1874. In 1929 it amalgamated with the adjoining towns of Sterkrade and Osterfeld with a consequent boost in population. Today the town has a lot of unemployment and is not particularly wealthy. Nonetheless in the past few years it has made remarkable, if not to say, revolutionary efforts to meet the demands of the 21st century. In the last few years its commercial life has been re-located around one of the largest shopping centres in Europe, known as the CentrO (based on a similar shopping complex outside Sheffield, England) which is served by a splendid fast-track public transport system. As a result Oberhausen has become a shopping mecca for the whole region. This has not only affected shopping patterns in neighbouring towns, it has also caused a marked deterioration in the old town centre. Alongside this radical economic upheaval, the town has also been responsible for introducing major cultural and leisure attractions which reflect the area and its history in a fascinating manner. However you arrive in town you should make your starting point the Hbf. – free car-parking at the rear – and continue from there by public

transport as this is part of the experience. That said, those who prefer exercise can hire a bike at the station. Since you'll never be able to visit everything I mention in a single day, I shall leave you to pick and choose from the attractions according to your particular interests. They can all be easily and quickly reached – indeed the town as a whole is excellently sign-posted for pedestrians and cars – but since the Rhineland Industrial Museum is right behind the Hbf it's the ideal venue to start or end your day.

∗ **Rhineland Industrial Museum** *(Rheinisches Industriemuseum/ RIM)* ⃛ 🏴 🏴
    ♿ ♿   French, Catalan, Dutch
ERIH

Opened in 1997 and built on the site of the former Altenberg zinc factory, the museum gives a rich insight into the history of heavy industry in the region. More than 1,500 exhibits – including ingot moulds, mill rollers, steam engines, a locomotive and an almost 10 metre-high steam hammer – arranged under specific themes, together with a brand-new exhibition on municipal provision of gas, water and electricity make this a must for visitors to the town. This is the HQ of RIM which has 5 other on-site museums in the Rhineland area – ask for the foreign language info brochures. There's a very attractive, detailed English-language brochure on the exhibition here (0,50 €)

and the main themes in the exhibition are also sub-titled in English. If you want to know even more as you go around, they'll lend you a folder in English or French giving full translations of all the main texts. (5.00 € returnable deposit). One last plus which could be copied by many other institutions in the area: there's a railway timetable opposite the box office to enable you to plan your return journey in peace. So if you've time on your hands, you can relax over a snack in the museum café or get yourself some souvenirs from

Rhineland Industrial Museum

their excellent shop in the knowledge that you're only two minutes away from your train.

Open: Tue-Sun: 10-17.00. Adults: 4 €. Concessions: 3 €. Family ticket 8 €. Ticket valid for St. Antony Ironworks (see below). Hansastr. 20, 46049 Oberhausen. Tel: 0208/8579-281. You can save money by purchasing a combined ticket for the Rhine-

land Industrial Museum and the Gasometer (7 €).
www.rim.lvr.de

Public Transport couldn't be easier because the museum is directly opposite the west (back) entrance to **Oberhausen Hbf.** Look for the signs above the stairs at the platform exits.

Car: Head for **Oberhausen Hbf.** Behind the station there is plenty of free parking space.

If you want to save your RIM visit till the end, start your day at the front of the Hbf, arm yourself with any information you want from the Tourist office opposite, and head for the specially-built bus/tram stop on Bahnsteig (= *Platform*) 1, which provides you with a ninety-second shuttle service to the 'Neue Mitte' (*New Centre*) station. To the right as you exit is the **CentrO** shopping centre. But if you go left and up past the Oberhausen Arena you'll come to ...

✳ **The Gasometer** 🖳
 ♿ ERIH

That's what it is and that's what it isn't! The 'Big Tin' is 117 metres high with a diameter of 67 metres and can rightly claim to be the most unique museum building in the country. Built in 1929 to store blast-furnace gas from the nearby steelworks it was shut down in 1988 and scheduled for demolition at a cost of one million €. The story goes that the

head of the International Building Exhibition (IBA: a huge area renewal project) promptly offered to take it over and keep it open for the same amount of money. A deal was made, and in 1994 the gasometer threw open its doors as a venue for exhibitions, trade fairs and entertainment. An astounding exhibition on television a few years back attracted over half a million visitors, and in 1999 the Gasometer played host to a 26 metre high installation of 13,000 coloured oil barrels by Christo and Jeanne-Claude (they of the Reichstag-wrapping). In 2000 there was an exhibition on 100 years of German football and in 2001, on „Blue Gold" (water). Once inside you can go to the top in a glass lift which slides terrifyingly up the inside wall. From the roof, there are wonderful views of the neighbouring towns and surrounding countryside.

Open: Tue–Sun: 10.00–18.00. Adults: 6 €. Concessions: 4 €. Family ticket (2 adults and up to 5 children): 14 €. Am Grafenbusch 90. 46047 Oberhausen. Tel: 0208/8503733. (German info only) www.gasometer.de (English pages). Here's a nice tip: you can save money by purchasing a combined ticket for the Gasometer and the Ludwig Gallery (7.50 €), or the Gasometer and the Rhineland

Industrial Museum (7 €) in all three venues.

Car: Motorway **A42, exit OB-Zentrum.** If you haven't spotted the Gasometer by now, consult an optician.

Back at the Neue Mitte station you can visit...

∗ **The CentrO**

No matter what you feel about unbridled consumerism this has to be experienced. If you're not interested in shopping make for the long water-lined boulevard outside which is full of cafés and restaurants of every description. On the other side of the water there's a fairground cum adventure park where for a few €uros you can park the kids and enjoy the day at your own pace. I headed for the Guinness Island Irish Pub, now renamed "An Crannog", a huge building near the adventure park, where I spent rather longer than I intended in the company of a cool Guinness, the Irish barman and a South African businessman who was trying to convince me of the delights of a strange drink called 'Cherry Beer'. I can tell you, it doesn't mix with Guinness. The shops are open until 20.00, bars and restaurants much later.

Public transport: From Oberhausen Hbf bus station platform 1,

Night-life in Oberhausen

is very much centred on the CentrO promenade. In the summer the water-lined promenade is awash with coloured parasols and guests can sit outside and while away the evening over drinks or a meal. Most of the fast food chains are inside the shopping centre and therefore closed after 20.00. But on the promenade itself there is a myriad of bars and restaurants – everything from American to Japanese, Chinese and Italian – so it's really a case of whatever takes your fancy. A lot of food lovers make for an Indonesian restaurant called the **Bali Rendezvous,** part of which has an aquarium built into the floor. I tried it one Sunday lunchtime and it was packed to the hilt. My saté dish was pretty run-of-the-mill but my wife had a delicious grilled duck. The prices are amazingly inexpensive (Tel: 800270). At no. 71 you'll find **Efendy**, a new Turkish restaurant which in 2002 won a prize as the best new restaurant in Germany. (Tel: 8284575). Many of the bars have canned music but the Gaelic house **An Crannog** in particular also has regular live artists. The night I was there I heard a good Irish folk singer. If you want to sample the local beers, right next door is the **Brauhaus Zeche Jacobi**, a huge beer house with an open-air terrace, I was also taken by **Victors Grand Café**, a

French bistro with a bit of style. The promenade has a large cinema complex, the **Village Cinemas,** at one end. At the other it's rounded off by **Viva,** a disco which was packed with teenies when I arrived. (I was told the clientele gets older as the night gets longer). As I came out I was swept away by the crowds pouring out of the nearby **König-Pilsener-Arena** from a show by Sting. This is a mega venue with a capacity of over 12,000. Apart from major pop concerts it presents large touring shows and sporting events: www.koenig-pilsener-arena.de.

Just a short walk away from the Centro, off the Essener Straße, is a small road called Im Lipperfeld. Go right to the end and you'll arrive at the **Turbinenhalle,** the biggest disco in town (Thurs-Sat only), which has five dancing areas covering techno, black, 80s, hip-hop, soul, charts, Gothic and/or Alternative, whatever that might be. This was the place where I discovered I'm getting old. I couldn't tell the difference! As a complete contrast, on the very corner of Essener Straße/Im Lipperfeld you'll find one of the most highly regarded restaurants in town, **Hackbarth's**, which has the added advantage of a pleasant beer garden in summer. (Closed Sundays, booking essential: Tel: 22188 or online at www.hackbarths.de). I've eaten well in high-class surroundings at the **Schloss Gastronomie im Kaisergarten** right next to the Ludwig Gallery. (Tel: 290220). This also has a room for cheaper snacks and lunches, as well as a large beer garden.

Back in town, the alternative scene meets at the **Altenberg Centre** behind RIM at the Hbf. They've a very pleasant bistro bar which is open from 18.00, regular programmes of live music, jazz, cabaret, comedy and of course discos. In the old town centre the two scene cafés are **Transatlantik** and **Café Lux** near the **Lichtburg cinema**, home of the International Short Film Festival.

For my money the most atmospheric pub in the old town is **Gdanska**, a great Polish pub/restaurant that has excellent live jazz shows every Thursday night. The food is great too. Altmarkt 3. Tel: 620 1375. www.gdanska.de.

In the last few years, the **Oberhausen Theatre** has been consistently voted by critics as the best in the region (Ebertstr. 82. Tel: 85780. www.theater-oberhausen. de). In the same square you'll find a variety venue called **Ebertbad** (www.ebertbad.de). And right next door there's an above average Italian bistro/restaurant called **Gallo**, which has a pleasant outside terrace (Ebertplatz 4. Tel: 26656).

take bus CE90, 91, 92 and 96 or tram 112 to "Neue Mitte".

By car: There is plenty of free parking space, open 24 hours a day. If **A42, exit OB-Osterfeld/Neue Mitte**. If you come after 20.00 and find yourself in one of the parking lots behind the main shopping centre, you can walk through to the promenade via the main entrance to the shopping centre. The route, which is open all day and night, is very well lit. www.centro.de

Sea Life

* **Sea Life**

This is the largest underwater zoo in the whole of Germany. Visitors go on a tour through a series of different areas including a harbour, a mountain landscape, a stalactite cave, a fjord, an Atlantic deep sea tunnel with fish swimming above and around you, and finally a huge deep-sea grotto containing every size and variety of fish imaginable. There's also a cinema where you can gaze down the throats of the fish, and a

Greenpeace area where you can sign up to protect the whales and save our seas. It's on the northern edge of CentrO right next to the new Oberhausen marina on the canal. www.sealife.de

Open: Daily from 10.00-20.00. Final admittance 18.00.

By car: Motorway A42, exit Neue Mitte and follow the signs. Free parking.

Public Transport: As for CentrO and walk through (10 mins): or, in the school holidays and at weekends, take bus 989 and 939 direct to "Aquarium/ Marina" (ca. 18 mins).

Now you should return to the Neue Mitte station (Bahnsteig 1). You can then go from the future to the past in two short stops by continuing your journey towards:

✱ the Eisenheim Settlement in the suburb of Osterfeld

I got out of my tram at an ultra-modern station to find myself looking down onto a peaceful idyll of workers' cottages from the turn of the last century. The town authorities originally wanted to demolish this working-class settlement (the very first in the area) but eventually gave up in the face of heavy protests from the residents who demanded their homes be renovated rather than replaced by high-rise tower blocks. I wandered through the streets past geranium-bedecked houses, had a chat with a coal miner of Bosnian origin who was

mending his bike, saw a couple of Turkish girls giggling in a doorway and an old man sunning himself on a bench next to a couple of garden gnomes and a curled-up cat. It's that sort of feel-at-home place. From Easter Sunday to the end of October on Sundays (10-17.00) you can visit the Old Wash house (10a Berliner Str.) where RIM houses an exhibition on the settlement and its history.

Public transport: Tram 112 or **buses CE90 and CE96** from the Hbf **to Eisenheim**.

By car: A516, exit Eisenheim, head for Stadtmitte, and follow the signs.

If you still haven't had your fill of industrial history, a little further to the north in the peaceful suburb of Osterfeld you can visit the cradle of the German industrial revolution...

The Eisenheim Settlement

The St. Antony Iron Works 1835

The St. Antony Iron Works

Here on 18th October 1758 a nine metre high blast furnace was put into operation as the first iron-ore processing site in the region. The original factory pond still exists. Apart from that the only remaining vestige of the works is the half-timbered office building and foundry manager's house at Antoniestr. 32-34 where RIM now houses a rich archive of photos and documents on industrial industry. Visit by appointment: RIM telephone as above. Your entry ticket for RIM also entitles you to visit here.

Bus 958 from Hbf. (Bus Bahnsteig 'C') to St. Antony Hütte, or **CE92** to Klosterhardter Straße.

Car: Motorway **A516** direction Arnheim, **exit Sterkrade**.

Back in town – if you've got time – head diagonally right when you come out of the Hbf and take a look at the old centre (Alte Mitte) to see the downside effects of CentrO. There are some pleasant cafés around the Lichtburg cinema, the home of the International Short Film Festival (see night-life box).

There are two other major attractions you should not miss whilst you're in town. One of them contains one of the most interesting and dynamic art galleries in the region.

✳ The Ludwig Gallery, Oberhausen Mansion *(Ludwig Galerie, Schloß Oberhausen)* ♿ ♿ ⌗

The mansion – built for a local Count at the start of the 19th century – has been thoroughly overhauled and turned into a luxurious art museum. The atmosphere in the Ludwig Gallery can rival that in any large capital, and its temporary exhibitions devoted to popular themes are able to draw on a rich private collection as well as outside works. Everything I've seen to date – including exhibitions on Harry Potter, Playboy cartoons, contemporary US American art, China and Henri Cartier-Bresson – has been first-class. In the foyer there's a well-stocked bookshop and a visitor centre providing information on all the region's highlights, in particular the region's landmark art, which is another recurring exhibition theme. There are occasional Sunday morning open-air concerts in the summer.

The Ludwig Gallery, Oberhausen Mansion

Open: Tue-Sun: 11-18.00. Gallery admission: 6.50 €. Concessions: 3.50 €. Family ticket: 10.50 €. Free guided tour of the exhibitions: Sundays 11.30 and 15.00 (German only). If you're intending to visit the Gasometer, save money and buy a Combiticket for 7.50 €. Konrad-Adenauer-Allee 46, 46042 Oberhausen.
Tel: 0208/4124928.
www.ludwiggalerie.de

One wing of the castle, the **Gedenkhalle**, has been dedicated as a memorial to the victims of fascism in Oberhausen. (Open: Tue-Sun. 10-18.00. Entrance free).

Public transport: Bus 122 (every 20 mins) from Hbf, bus platform C to Schloss Oberhausen. An alternative start to the day is to travel here from the Hbf first and then go...

By foot to the Gasometer which is only a short walk away. It's well signposted. From there on you can walk into the CentrO and continue as you wish.

Car: Motorway **A42, exit Oberhausen/Zentrum**. Head for the centre. It's about 200 metres on the right.

Afterwards you can visit the adjoining restaurant – for more see 'nightlife' – or its beer garden, before taking a stroll along the Rhine-Herne canal or a walk through the castle gardens (Kaisergarten). Here there's a **small zoo**, a so-called skate board **'open airea'** and a boarding stage for **boat trips** along the canal to Henrichenburg or westwards to Duisburg. Even better news if you're **travelling with a mobile home;** the Kaisergarten can offer 60 overnight parking facilities with all mod cons – an excellent and attractive base for touring the region. 5 € per vehicle per night. If it's full try Vonderort below.

Just to the North-East of CentrO you can find outdoor peace and refuge at:

✳ **Haus Ripshorst**
This is a must for nature-lovers, botanists, biologists, ramblers and cyclists. It's the main information centre for the Industrial Nature Trail through the Ruhrgebiet and is at the centre of some fascinating park and woodland. I went out here one September morning, sniffed around their herb garden and then

went inside to look around the information centre where there's plenty of inter-active computer-on information on how the area has been cleaned up and landscaped (unfortunately it's all in German). After that I hired one of their 'Revierrad' bikes (→ p. 207 for more) and, with some helpful advice from the man behind the desk, set off to explore the immediate neighbourhood. Within three minutes I had crossed the border into the suburb of Frintrop in Essen and was cycling amidst butterflies through a fascinating natural jungle of strange plants and trees which have grown

Haus Ripshorst

up on the site of the "Sammelbahnhof Frintrop", formerly one of the largest shunting yards on the Cologne to Minden railway. I then pedalled round the forty hectare site of Haus Ripshorst itself through the many different thematic woodlands. I was told there are over 6,000 trees here mirroring the history of trees over the last 60,000,000 years, but you'll have to take this on trust as I had no time to count them myself. There were plenty of new modern wooden information boards along the way. Finally I crossed the Rhine-Herne canal over a very elegant bridge, took a few pictures of the water traffic sliding below me with the Gasometer in the background and headed over the parallel Emscher river towards a late gothic 16th century fortress called **Burg Vondern**. The building looks great from the outside but it seems only to be accessible on Thursdays between 18 and 19.00, or during the occasional classical concert for which I saw a poster on one of the gates. You can also hire the place for private parties!

Haus Ripshorst, open: Tuesdays to Sundays. 10-18.00. (Nov. to Feb. 10-17.00) Ripshorster Str. 306, 46177 Oberhausen. Tel: 0208/8833483

Public transport: Bus 958 (direction Bottrop Spechtstraße) or **978** (direction Tackenberg) from the Hbf will take you to **"Werkstraße"** (west park entrance). Alternatively bus **957** to **Eisenbahnbrücke** (south park entrance) From here it's a 10-15 minute walk through the woods or along the canal bank to the House

Car: A42, exit OB-Osterfeld/ Neue Mitte and head for the CentrO. Immediately after you cross the Rhine-Herne canal turn left into Ripshorster Straße and carry on for about a kilometre. It's up a road on the left.

Now we're on the north-east side of town, let's go right to the edge and visit the...

✳ **Revierpark Vonderort**
  (→ ch. 11)
  ♿ ♿

The park is divided by a tree-lined road connecting Oberhausen with Bottrop. On the one side is a leisure centre where you can pick up a map of the park. Here you'll find a restaurant, mini-golf, open-air chess, children's paddling pool, boating lake and a toboggan run when the place is snowbound. On the other side are tennis courts, a football ground, ice-skating hall (Oct-March) and a light, airy mineral bath, sauna cum open-air swimming pool, the so-called **Solbad,** which is...

Open. Mon-Sat: 8-23.00. Sundays: 8.00-21.00. The Solbad itself is a mineral bath. If you just want to swim here and in the heated outside bath, 2 hrs will cost you 5 €; 4 hrs, 6 € and a day ticket 7 €. Incl. sauna: 9, 10, and 13 € respectively. If you're going to use the sauna you'll need two 1 € coins – one for the main locker, another for the sauna. Both returnable. Leave before 14.00 and you only pay the 2 hour tariff.

Bottroper Straße 322, 46117 Oberhausen. Tel: 0208/9996830
www.revierpark.com

Bus: **SB 91** between Oberhausen Hbf "1" and Bottrop central bus station, **alight Revierpark Vonderort**

By car: Motorway **A42** to **exit Essen/Bottrop Zentrum**, head for Bottrop and look out for the sign pointing left after about a kilometre. Or **exit Oberhausen Osterfeld/ Neue Mitte** and head for Osterfeld.

There's an overnight **parking** lot **for mobile homes** in the Koppenburgstraße on the Oberhausen side of the Revierpark. It's free, has a toilet but no water supplies.

As I came back to my car I noticed I was standing next to a large so-called 'Health Park' exactly over the town border in Bottrop. The nicely-laid out trails lead you to all sorts of peculiar fitness stations, best of all, a café adjoining a hospital. (Does this park make you fit or ruin your health for good?). The worst thing about the park is definitely the title, which doesn't exactly hold out the promise of unadulterated pleasure. Very typisch deutsch, jawohl! Anyway now we're in….

BOTTROP
(pop: 120,000)

Tourist Information:
Stadtinformationsbüro,
Osterfelderstr. 13,
46236 Bottrop.
Tel: 02041/766950.
www.bottrop.de (English pages)

Bottrop lies to the north-east of Oberhausen. For most of its existence it was a quiet rural community but between 1863, when 'Prosper I' colliery was put into operation, and 1914 the population exploded from 4,000 to 68,000. During this period it came to be known as the largest village in Prussia. In 1976 the town was fused with its northern neighbour, Kirchhellen, and can boast of being one of the greenest in the region. Indeed the Kirchhelle Heath (Kirchhelle Heide), with over 100 kilometres of signed footpaths and cycling tracks, is a popular haunt for fitness and fresh-air fans.

The centre has a pleasant old town hall and a little further to the north, in the town park, you'll find the **Quadrat Museum Centre**. The building contains three main sections. The first, the Josef-Albers Museum, exhibits the work of Bottrop's most famous international artist. Albers was a student and teacher at the Bauhaus before emigrating to work in the USA. He experimented with squares and rectangles and the effect of adjacent colours on the viewer's perception. On the other side of the building is a museum of pre- and local history which contains some gigantic authentic skeletons of mammoths and rhinoceroses. The third gallery is used for visiting exhibitions. I was lucky enough to see a fascinating series of photographs by a Swedish photographer on divided Berlin. Further into the park is a large children's playground. From here it's a hundred metres to **Overbeckshof** where you can sit out on the terrace and enjoy a meal or some light refreshments.

Open: Tue-Sun: 10-18.00 **Admission free.** In Stadtgarten 20, 46236 Bottrop. Tel: 02041/29716. www.quadrat-bottrop.de

Bus: line 267 (direction Richard-Wagner-Schule) from Central Bus Station, alight "Quadrat". SB 16 (Dorsten), alight "Im Stadtgarten".

Bottrop might be a small town, but, like its British twin-town Blackpool, it has some mighty large holiday attractions. Don't on any account miss...

✳ **The Tetrahedron** *(Tetraeder)*
✪ ☺

This is one of the high points of the region in all senses of the word for it can be seen from miles around. It's a huge, skeletal, steel pyramid (sorry, tetrahedron! – if you know what that means. I don't.) constructed on a equally high, disused mining tip,

The Tetrahedron

now landscaped, on the edge of town just off the A42 motorway. Lit up at night it glows in the sky like an object from outer space. But don't just gape at it, climb it (no admission) and feel the viewing platform shaking in the wind under your feet as you try to enjoy the view. Take the kids and hold on tight! You won't for-

get this in a hurry. Not, I'm afraid, for the physically handicapped.

Bus: 266 from Bottrop Hbf in the direction of Boy, **alight Bernhard-Poether-Weg.**

By car: The way to the Tetrahedron from the motorway is shamefully badly signposted but basically you should follow the signs to the Alpine Centre which is a little to the south. To be sure, I'm going to try to give you exact details. There are two possible exits from the **A42** motorway depending on which direction you're coming from.

1) From the west, exit Bottrop-Süd/Bottrop and head for the centre. When you're almost there (it's about 1.5 kilometres), you'll see a sign pointing right to Bot-Welheim. Turn right here into Prosperstraße and continue for

about 2 km to Ostring. Here turn left and immediately first right into Beck-straße where you can park. If you miss the Prosperstraße, carry on to-wards the centre until you see a large sign pointing right to Gelsenkirchen. This is the Horsterstraße. Continue straight along here for three kilome-tres or so. The Tetrahedron is on your right and at the very last moment there's a small sign telling you to turn right at some traffic lights.

2) From the east, exit Autobahn Kreuz Essen Nord, head up the B224 towards Bottrop-Boy and follow the signs to the Alpine Centre. Go past it until you come to Ostring. Turn right and immediately right again into Beckstraße.

If you're interested in seeing how a local workers' settlement has been given a new lease of life take a look at the Welheim settlement next door.

✳ The Alpine Centre at the Tetrahedron *(Alpincenter)*

Here's some good news for winter-sports fans! Right below the Tetrahe-dron is the largest indoor ski piste in Europe where you can go skiing and snowboarding all the year round. Skiing in the Bottrop Alps! No, I haven't gone off my head. The Alpine Centre claims to be the longest in-door ski slope in the world and who am I to say they're wrong? The piste is 640 metres long and 30 metres

The Alpine Centre at the Tetrahedron

wide on a surface of 40 centimetres of genuine man-made snow. Those who want to get 'piste' in a completely different fashion can do so in one of the four genuine imitation Tyrolean mountain huts at the top of the slope. Outside the beer garden there is a highwire climbing garden where you can risk your neck at a height of almost ten metres, so don't drink too much in advance.

Open. Daily: 9-24.00. Day ticket: Adults: 35 € (Mon-Fri) and 45 € (Sat-Sun). There are a range of cheaper ticket offers, including family tickets. See their website and click on 'Skihalle'. Once there you can hire all the equipment you need including shoes and sticks. Prosperstraße 299-301, 46238 Bottrop. Tel: 02041/7095-0. www.alpincenter.com

Bus: Lines 262 and 263, alight "Alpincenter". Have you ever tried carrying ski equipment in a bus?

By car: A 42 motorway, exit Bottrop-Boy and follow the signs. Up in Kirchhellen you'll find...

✳ **Movie Park Germany**
  ♿ ☺☺ 🇬🇧 🇬🇧

If pre-packed fantasy is your idea of paradise this huge film-set world with fair-ground rides, live shows and exhibitions based on Hollywood themes is the place for you. It's divided into several main areas: Hollywood Street set, Wonderland Studios, NICKLAND, Streets of New York, Santa Monica Pier and the Old West, all with plenty of exciting rides,

rollercoasters and stunt shows. Movie Park is a whole day experience and you'll be paying accordingly. Two pieces of advice: get there early to avoid long queues at the best rides. And – especially if you're with kids – take along some drinks and snacks. There are over 20 different cafés, restaurants and bars but refreshments are – for me at least – a bit over-priced.

Open: Mid-March through mid November, 10.00–18.00, 19.00 or 21.00 (Check for exact dates and times. It's also closed on some Mondays early and late in the season). Day ticket: Adults (i.e. 12 years old upwards!) 30 €. Children (4-11 incl.), 26.00 €. Under 4, free. You can also get in free on a Sunday if you are over 55! But you must take an ID to prove it. Warner-Allee 1, 46244 Bottrop-Kirchhellen. Tel: 02045/8990. www.movieparkgermany.de (English pages)

Public transport:
The VRR have a **Kombi-ticket** (→ p. 25) for Movie World. This costs only 2.50 € more than the individual admission price and can be purchased at all VRR Sales Points. The ticket will work out cheaper than a VRR day ticket and separate admission. It has the additional advantage that you won't have to queue at the box-office when you get there.

Train: RB43 from Dortmund, Castrop-Rauxel Süd, (Tariff C) Herne and Wanne-Eickel (B) in the direction of Dorsten. **RB44** from Oberhausen Hbf (B) to Dorsten. **RE14** from Essen (B). All trains from Dorsten (A). Alight at **Bottrop-Feldhausen** station. It's an eight minute walk through the woods and across the car park. Check when your train returns, since some only run once an hour.

By car: A 31 to exit 39 Bottrop-Kirchhellen Nord. Parking fee 5 €.

Movie Park Germany isn't the only fun in Bottrop. If your kids are a bit younger they'd probably prefer...

✳ Schloss Beck Leisure Park
♿ ☺

This ideal mixture of playground and fairground fun set in the grounds of an 18th century country house had my kids squealing with joy. There's a roller-coaster, which even I dared to try, a water slide, a

Schloss Beck Leisure Park

big wheel, water-crash boats, a very long six-lane mat-slide, pony rides and go-carts (these last two at extra cost) as well as various other indescribable rides which I'd never seen before in my life. If things get too hectic you can take a paddle boat onto the lake or stroll along a nature trail. And for the very young there's every sort of swing, roundabout and trampoline you can imagine, as well as a rocking-horse railway. Don't miss the inside of the house itself where there's more of interest for the kids. The grounds are ideal for picnics. There's also a café, snack-bars and a beer garden, all at reasonable prices. There are new loos with a nappy-changing room and a wheelchair lavatory. Where is it? Almost opposite Movie Park Germany. There must be something in the air in Bottrop.

Open: Mid March – mid October (not every day from September onwards). 9.00-18.00. Rides from 10.00. Adults: 9 €. Children and senior citizens: 8 €. Freizeitpark Schloß Beck, Am Dornbusch 39, 46244 Bottrop-Kirchhellen. Tel: 02045/5134. www.schloss-beck.de

Train: same as for Movie Park Germany, but head right when you leave the station.

Car: Take the **A 31 to exit 40 Kirchhellen**. If there are jams, leave at exit 41 and head for Kirchhellen. Car park: 5 € (4 € returned when you leave on production of entrance ticket).

GELSENKIRCHEN
(pop: 280,000)

Tourist Information:
Stadtmarketing Gesellschaft mbH,
Bahnhofsvorplatz 1,
45879 Gelsenkirchen.
Tel: 0209/95197-20.
www.gelsenkirchen.de
(English pages)

The Stadtmarketing Gesellschaft has a list of hotels, general information and special information on all the latest events If you can read German ask for their excellent booklet on Gelsenkirchen for tourists entitled "Besondere weGE" This gives you all the basic information on the town and takes you along eight different theme routes.

If you're touring by caravan there's a **caravan park** with all camping facilities right next to the new Arena AufSchalke.
Mobil-Camp Gelsenkirchen, Adenauerallee 100, 45891 Gelsenkirchen. Exit Autobahn A2 'Gelsenkirchen-Buer', turn right at the first roundabout and then first right into Adenauerallee.

Gelsenkirchen was first mentioned in the 11th century. Sited in the middle of a marshy plain it boasted more horses than people for the next seven hundred years. Indeed, as late as 1839 it was still a hamlet of 96 houses with a total population of 624. Just 90 years later the combined effects of coal, steel, glass, chemicals and the railways had exploded the population to over 206,000 with a density of 5,600 people per square kilometre. The Irish entrepreneur William Mulvany was responsible for much of this expansion, thanks to his Hibernia Pit which went into operation in 1856 with a revolutionary system of tubbings to prevent the intrusion of water. Miners were brought in from Newcastle, County Durham and Ireland to take up the best jobs. Indeed in 1859 two thirds of all the hewers were British, and for a time Hibernia was the most productive pit in the region. Mulvany housed his British 'guest workers' in a specially-built settlement called the Balaclava 'colony' which also catered for fellow countrymen working in nearby Herne. The 'colony' was largely isolated from the rest of the growing village but Mulvany made sure that the children got some English language schooling and hired two priests to care for the souls of his Anglican workers. (A German priest had to look after the Catholics!). Round the turn of the century workers from Poland and the eastern areas of Germany began to flood into the town, setting up a large Polish-speaking community with its own churches, societies and banks. This accounts for the many Polish family names still to be found in the area. By 1910 Gelsenkirchen had become one of the most important coal producing towns in Europe and was known as the "Town of a Thousand Fires". Its economic importance was all too well-known to the Allies in the Second World War and large parts of the town were left in ruins as a result of bombing raids. Despite this Gelsenkirchen began to grow again, this time with the help of textiles and clothing factories. In 1959, the year in which the new music theatre was built, the population had reached a peak of almost 400,000. The town may have suffered more than any other in the region from the brutal effects of 19th century industrialisation and the coal and steel crises since the 1960s, but in the past few years it has made admirable efforts to make itself an attractive place for townsfolk and visitors alike, and now large parts of it are extraordinarily clean and green. Indeed energy production has now moved into the 21st century and the city is well on the way to becoming Germany's solar power capital. For more, see below…

Despite its present-day population of only 280,000 Gelsenkirchen seems to straggle interminably across the region and consist solely of suburbs. This can be explained by the fact that it is bisected by two motorways and is an administrative conglomeration of three separate communities; Buer in the North, the old town of Gelsenkirchen in the south (joined symbolically in the middle by the suburb of Schalke, the original home of the legendary working-class football team → ch. 11), and Horst in the west. Correspondingly I shall start in the north and deal with it in three parts.

Gelsenkirchen-Buer

✳ **Lüttinghof Moated Castle**
  (Wasserburg Haus Lüttinghof)
The 14th century castle, at the northernmost part of the town, was originally built by the Archbishop of Cologne to protect his territory and is an ideal place for a country ramble or bike ride. The building itself cannot be visited but it does house a café and restaurant.

Car: Drive northwards out of Buer on the Polsumerstraße for about five kilometres until you get to the crossroads at a little village called Polsum, turn left into Scholvener Straße and carry straight on. Immediately after the road crosses the A52 motorway there's a signpost on the left-hand side to Burg Lüttinghof. Follow the road to the car park next to the castle. If you prefer to walk to the castle I noticed a signed path leading off the Polsumerstraße on the left as I drove northwards.

✳ **City Museum**
  (Städtisches Museum)
  ♿ ♿

This attractive airy museum not only contains a fine collection of modern art (Magritte, Max Ernst,

Laszlo Moholy-Nagy, Max Lieber-
mann and Emil Nolde etc.), the basement area has a most remarkable exhibition of international kinetic art,
including a beautiful illuminated
spinning globe by the British artist,

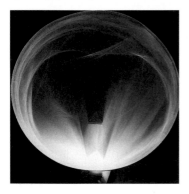

City Museum

Peter Sedgley. Here you can interact
with a lot of the exhibits by banging,
(schlagen) sliding *(schieben)* or
pushing *(drucken)* them where indicated: look for the green hand and
one of the above words. Afterwards I
enjoyed a midday snack on the terrace of the museum café. For those
who prefer to eat elsewhere there's an
ice-cream parlour almost directly
opposite. And about a 100 meters
further along the road there's a lovely
old half-timbered restaurant with a
beer garden. And lastly, a couple of
tips! If you've still got a bit of time,
the centre of Buer is worth a short
stroll. Head down the pedestrian
shopping precinct towards the St Ur-

banus church, which was topped by
a British bomb during the Second
World War. Here there are a couple of
pleasant old cafés where you can also
sit outside. Since the museum is just
up the road from Schloss Berge, you
can visit the two in a single day.
Open: Tue-Sunday: 11-18.00.
Admission free! Horster Straße 5-7.
45897 Gelsenkirchen.
Tel: 0209/169 4361.
Bus: to Buer Rathaus, cross the
road past the VRR sales office and
the museum is about 200 metres
down the Horster Straße. There are
17 different buses and trams to Buer
Rathaus. For five of them see info
under Berge Castle, Alfred Schmidt
paintings and Horst Castle.
Car: Motorways **A2 exit Ge-Buer**
or **A52 exit Ge-Buer West**.

✳ **Berge Castle and Gardens**
   (Schloss Berge)
If you're looking for peace and calm
in rich parkland surroundings on a
hot day this can scarcely be bettered.
The original castle dates back to the
fourteenth century and the grounds
contain a French rococo garden, an
English-style park, a fragrant herb
garden, large adjoining woodlands
and a lake (across the Adenauerallee,
where your bus stops). The castle has
its own café/restaurant from whose
terrace you can gaze over the gardens and imagine you're somewhere
near the Loire. If the kids get restless
take them over the road to the park
by the lake. Up in the woods you'll

Berge Castle

find three playgrounds for them to run around in. And you can row off any surplus energy by hiring a boat at the snack-bar by the lake, which also provides a wide variety of cheap food and refreshments to eat outside. Adenauer-Allee 103, 45894 Gelsenkirchen. www.schloss-berge.de

Public Transport: Tram **302** or Bus **380 from GE-Hbf** (direction Buer-Rathaus) to **Berger See**. The tram is quicker (17 mins) but the bus (30 mins) stops much nearer the castle. If you're travelling the other way **from Buer-Rathaus** it's literally two stops with either.

Car: Motorways **A2 exit Ge-Buer**, turn right at the roundabout and then first left into Adenaueralle. Or **A52 exit Ge-Buer West** and drive into the middle of Buer.

If you now travel south towards the Altstadt, shortly after you pass the A2 motorway you'll find Gelsenkirchen's proudest new monument, the

✳ **"Arena Auf Schalke".**

This is the most modern football stadium in Germany and home of Schalke 04. The stadium can be turned into an enclosed arena in only 30 minutes and has a roll-in-roll-out pitch, making it ideal for mega pop and opera events and tv shows, not forgetting the World Cup

"Arena Auf Schalke"

matches in 2006. The club do guided tours of the stadium so I thought I'd give it a try. The **70-minute tour,** starting at the Schalke Museum, was fascinating as it took in all areas of the arena inside and out, including the VIP's restaurant and seating area, the stadium chapel, press conference room and changing rooms. Afterwards you can look round the football museum which has films of some of the legendary matches. N.B. All tours must be booked in advance: telephone: 0209/3892900 (Tuesdays to Fridays, 12.00 and 16.00. Saturdays and Sundays: 11.00 and 15.00. Not on match days). A tour costs 9 € per head. www.arena-auf-schalke.de (English pages)

Bus: 380 and **381** to **Sportparadies.**

Car: Motorway **A2 exit Ge-Buer**. Then left round the roundabout. At the next traffic lights turn left onto the Kurt-Schumacher Straße, heading for the town centre. After going over the motorway take the first turn-off right. For the tours, park at car park P1.

✳ Schüngelberg Housing settlement and panorama point

The Schüngelberg housing settlement was built to house miners and their families – Germans and Turkish guest workers – working in the nearby Hugo Pit which has now ceased production. It's a great example of a self-enclosed intact settlement which has been modernised and partly rebuilt without being ruined. To get there turn off the Horster-straße into Schüngelbergstraße, take the first right hand street and park. You will now be at the old gateway to the settlement in Gertrudstraße, the starting-point of a well signed circular trail. The trail which takes around forty minutes will lead you around some fascinatingly different streets to the top of the Schüngelberg panorama point containing two huge cast-iron spotlights that light up the night above the nearby motorway. From here you can gaze across to north towards the smoking chimneys of the Scholven Power Plant or south-east to the massive Schalke Arena.

Bus: 301 to Hugostraße.

Gelsenkirchen-Horst

✳ Horst Castle *(Schloss Horst)*
This is the most important renaissance castle in north-west Germany.

Horst Castle

After many years neglect it was restored and re-opened in 1999. The building, which you can wander around at will, now houses local government offices, a registry office and a restaurant in the cellars (not just for newly-weds). The original courtyard walls have been protected under a huge glass hall which is used for jazz, chamber concerts and readings. The castle museum is still being built but it's open (free) on Sunday afternoons from 13.00–17.00. Turfstraße 21, 45899 Gelsenkirchen. www.schloss-horst.de

Open: Mon-Fri: 8.30-16.00. Saturday closed. Sun: 14-17.00

Public transport: **Bus** routes same as for Nordstern park plus 111, 253, 257, 259, 260, 301, 396. to 'Schloss Horst'. The last two go to and from Buer Rathaus. **U-Bahn/Tram: U17 from Essen Hbf** to 'Schloss Horst'.

Car: A42, exit Gelsenkirchen-Heßler and head for Horst. It's just after the race-course.

✳ **Nordstern Park** 🏛
♿ ☺ ERIH
This former coal mine site was cleaned up and redesigned to present the National Garden Show in 1997 and now it's an attractive place for a stroll and a snack. Look out for the children's play areas, art installations and, in summer, for shows and pop concerts in the open-air amphitheatre on the canal bank. **Admission free**. www.nordsternpark.de

Nordstern Park

Just inside the main entrance you'll find **Deutschland Express,** one of the world's largest model railway layouts with 200 trains running over viaducts, round mountains, past fairgrounds and city centres. Your kids'll love this.

Open Thurs: 10-19.30. Fri-Sunday: 10-18.30. Daily during local school hols. Adults: 5 €. Children 6-14: 4 €. Family ticket: 13 €.
Am Bugapark 1c, 45899 Gelsenkirchen. Tel: 0209/5083660.
www.der-deutschlandexpress.de
(Rail fans → p. 127)

Bus: CE56 and **383** to **Nordsternpark.**

Car: As for Horst Castle. The Nordsternpark is sign-posted.

Gelsenkirchen Altstadt (old town), east and south

This is where the **Hbf** is. If you emerge on the north side of the station, you'll find yourself in a pedestrian precinct leading to the Neumarkt where there are some pleasant cafés. A little further on you'll come to the **Hans-Sachs House**, once the architectural pride of the city. On the northern boundaries of the *Altstadt* is the **Musiktheater** (Tel: 4097220), a revolutionary piece of architecture in its time, which can claim to be one of the liveliest opera and dance houses in the area. Some of the interior decorations were done by Jean Tinguely and Yves Klein. Have a look in the U-Bahn here; it's adorned with some very good opera scenes.

Even better, travel a few stops further along on **line 301**, get out at 'Bergwerk Consolidation' station (the site of a disused pit) and take a look at:

✳ **The Alfred Schmidt paintings** which are extraordinary pictorial tributes to coal-miners. **The U-Bahn/tram line 301** connects Gelsenkirchen *Hbf* with Rathaus Buer and also goes to the...

✳ **Ruhr Zoo – "Zoom"**
The zoo has just been extensively modernised into three main "adventure worlds": Africa, Asia and America. It boasts a fine collection of antelopes, giraffes, zebras, ostriches, hippos, rhinos, chimpanzees, wild cats and the largest land predator on earth, the Kodiak bear, not forgetting penguins, pelicans and seals, all in quasi-natural surroundings. There's a good children's playground opposite one of the refreshment areas.

Open: 9-18.00 (Nov – End Feb: 17.00). Admission: 12 €. Kids: (4-12) 8 €. Family ticket (1 adult, 2 kids) 24 €. (2 adults, 2 kids) 34 €. Bleckstr. 47, 45889 Gelsenkirchen. Tel: 0209/95450 www.zoom-erlebniswelt.de
(English pages)

Public Transport: Tram 301 from Gelsenkirchen Central Station and Buer Town Hall, alight "ZOOM Erlebniswelt". Rail: RB43, alight "Gelsenkirchen Zoo".

Car: A42 exit **GE-Bismarck** and follow the signs. From the Altstadt, take the B227 northwards.

Ruhr Zoo – "Zoom"

Night-life in Gelsenkirchen

Gourmets and night-life fans in Gelsenkirchen tend to head for Bochum and Essen. But don't give up straightaway. If you want to dance and eat, **Kronskis** in the Stringemarkt in Buer is the trendy place to be. It's also a favourite place for breakfasts. The posh place to eat in town is **Schloss Berge**. The castle restaurant could scarcely be bettered for atmosphere and surroundings, and the food matches the standard well. (Adenauerallee 103. Tel: 17740 www.schloss-berge.de). At a more casual end of the scale, you can find a good down-to-earth Spanish restaurant in the Altstadt at Ruhrstraße 3. At the **Café Madrid** I treated myself to an evening of well-cooked tapas, washed down with a tasty glass of Rioja. The place is open until one in the morning. I'm told the Musiktheater crowd slum it here late nights. Fifty metres further east at Wanner Straße 1 you'll find a cosy pub/restaurant called **Consilium**. They not only serve Irish beer: as far as I know this is the only vegetarian restaurant in town. (www.consilium-gelsenkirchen.de). Gelsenkirchen also boasts the best Indian restaurant in the whole region. I tried it myself and can confirm that the food is not only excellent but reasonably priced. You can find **Shere Punjab** tucked away in **Elisabethstr. 7.** (Tel: 206763. www.sherepunjab.de) Up in Buer I discovered a great Chinese restaurant called **Szechuan** at Königswiese 2 (Tel: 32971). I was lucky enough to be accompanied by two of my Chinese readers, Yue and Yong-Mae, who persuaded the owner to cook for us in the Chinese manner, rather than the European. It was fantastic. And just five minutes away by car in Buer, there is an excellent Italian hotel/restaurant at Schlesischer Ring 3 called **La Scala,** with a vinotek in the basement for wine-lovers. Booking essential for an evening table (www.hotel-lascala.de. Tel: 30741). Back to basics: if you're looking for a good beer house you should try the **Hibernia Brauhaus** right opposite the Central Railway Station. Here you can try their own brews including a drop of Mulvany's special. If you don't know who Mulvany is, you haven't been reading this book.

Back at the **Hbf**. if you now go south towards the working-class suburb of Ückendorf, you'll come across evidence of the 21st century in the shape of...

✳ The Science Park
(Wissenschaftspark)
☺☺ 🇬🇧

This centre of innovation, open to the general public, is a metaphor for the structural transformation of the region. The breathtaking building is bounded on one side by a 300 metre glass wall looking out over a lake. It houses future-oriented companies, and is also used for staging exhibitions, occasional concerts, congresses etc. On the roof you can view one of the largest solar installations in the world. Inside the building there is a free exhibition called "solar expo". This presents the most spectacular projects of the region in the field of new and renewable energy technologies in two languages (English and German) on large displays, complemented by a comprehensive set of brochures. This is well worth a visit if you are at all interested in renewable energy.

Open: Weekdays: 8-19.00. Suns: 8-18.00. Munscheidstr.14. 45886 Gelsenkirchen. Tel: 0209/1670. www.wipage.de (English pages). For the exhibition, click on "Ruhr Energy" and then the visitor centre, and you can then opt for the English pages.

Public Transport: Bus 385 to **Wissenschaftspark,** or **389** from Hbf in the direction of Bochum-Höntrop, **to Rheinelbestraße. Tram/U-Bahn 302** from Ge-Buer via Ge-Hbf, direction Bochum Hbf, **to Wissenschaftspark**

Car: It's minutes away from Ge-Hbf to the south.

The Science Park

In complete contrast, just five minutes away to the east is **Flöz Dickebank**, an old working-class housing estate which has been recently returned to its pristine 19th century condition. The oldest houses are in Virchowstrass 30-56 and 31-59.

If you now fancy a country walk with a difference, go southwards (i.e. away from the town centre) through the grounds of the Wissenschaftspark. In no time at all you will reach a small road called Virchowstraße. Here there are signs to a car park directly over the road for the Industrial Heritage Trail. The car park marks the starting point of a great walk through the so-called **Sculpture Wood** (*Skulpturenwald*). Here natural life has taken its revenge on a disused industrial site and at times you might feel as if you are walking through a jungle – were it not for some unconventional pieces of sculpture hidden in and around the paths. The climax of the walk is an

Stairway to Heaven

amazing stone construction on the top of a peak called the **Stairway to Heaven** (*Himmelstreppe*) by the landscape artist Hermann Prigann. The first time I took this walk I missed it completely because I had no idea where it was and, despite its height, it was blocked by a high circle of trees. So don't give up, but keep walking to the very south of the wood, and then head upwards through the trees where it will suddenly appear in all its magnificent beauty. You can climb right to the top and get a fantastic view of Gelsenkirchen (look out for the white-roofed new football arena, 'Auf-Schalke') and Essen (including the mighty Zollverein Pit and Coking Plant), all the way to Dortmund in

Sculpture Wood

the East and the Tetraeder in Bottrop to the North-west.

If you want to climb the Stairway to Heaven without walking through the sculpture wood, drive southwards from the Wissenschaftspark down the Rheinelbestraße which leads into the Leithestraße. At the bottom of the Leithestraße on the left-hand side, after the turning to Halfmannsweg which leads to the Halfmannshof Artists Colony, you'll come across a huge blue-green beach ball perched on a stand on the left-hand side. Actually it's a gas-holder, but a beach ball sounds more interesting. Park the car here. There's a path leading straight into the wood and although you still can't see the 'Staircase' it's actually very near. Take the very first path diagonally uphill and after a couple of minutes you'll be gaping at the sight ahead of you. By the way, who said Gelsenkirchen wasn't green?

And now if you're at all interested in good arts and crafts or want to buy a great souvenir, you mustn't miss:

✳ The Artists colony in Halfmanns hof *(Künsterlersiedlung Halfmannshof)*

One of the oldest artists' colonies in Germany, Halfmannshof provides a peaceful oasis for ten different artists, including a painter, potter, bookbinder, sculptor, goldsmith etc. Here you can see an exhibition of their works and, in the week, also visit the workshops where the artists have works for sale. Afterwards take a stroll round the Rheinelbe Park, which used to be the site of one of the largest coal-mines in the region. www.kuenstlersiedlung.de (English pages)

Bus: 389 from Hbf in the direction of Bochum-Höntrop, **to Halfmannsweg**.

Car: As above, or from the other way: **A40, exit Gelsenkirchen (B227).**

And now it's time to relax:

✳ Revierpark Nienhausen

The all-round family park with minigolf, children's playground, snack bars, and a leisure centre is situated to the south-west of the town on the border with Essen. For swimmers and sauna addicts the compact **Activarium** (♿☺) is open from 9-22.00 (Sundays 20.00). Nudist bathing, Sats. 19-22.00. Adults: Two hrs: 9 €, Four hrs: 11 €. Day ticket: 13.50 €. Children up to 10 yrs (only when accompanied by adults): 2.80 €, 11-15 yrs: 6.50 €. Arrive on Monday to Saturday before 13.00 and you pay 9 € for 4 hours. Feldmarkstr 201, 45883 Gelsenkirchen.
Tel: 0209/941310.
www.revierpark-nienhausen.de

Tram/U-Bahn: 107 between Ge Hbf and Essen Hbf, **to Revierpark**

By car: see map on their brochure.

6. The Powers of Heaven and Earth
ESSEN (pop: 590,000)

Tourist Information:
Essen Marketing GmbH,
Am Hauptbahnhof 2,
45127 Essen.
Tel: 0201/19433.
touristikzentrale@essen.de.
www.essen.de (English pages)

The city of Essen holds a central position in the region, not only geographically but spiritually and economically. Not least because of this reason it was selected – on behalf of the region as a whole – to be the **Cultural Capital of Europe** in 2010; or to give it its official title **RUHR.2010**.

Essen has been a centre of power from the earliest times, when Christian missionaries built an abbey near the River Ruhr in the suburb of Werden towards the end of the 8th century. Further inland a convent was set up by a family named Asnidi, (the root of the present city name) around which the town began to grow. The Münster church as it is known, is located in the heart of the present-day city centre. Women's power came early to the city for the Münster was ruled by Abbesses who, in the 10th and 11th century, helped the town to its first period of economic and cultural flowering. As time went by the pious ladies seem to have confused religious faith with political power and claimed total control over the town. The citizens were understandably none too happy about this and around the end of the 14th century tried to free themselves of their religious yoke. The Abbesses were having none of this, however, and by the time of the Reformation the dispute had escalated to a major conflict. Indeed things deteriorated to such an extent that in 1581 the Women in Black called in Spanish soldiers to keep control of the townsfolk. Thus the town was drawn into the long war between Spain and the Netherlands and suffered several foreign occupations which left it plundered and poverty-stricken when the conflict came to an end in 1648. The quarrel between the predominantly Protestant town council and the Abbesses continued unabated accompanied by century-long legal wrangling to try to define the status of the town. By the end of the 18th century the Abbesses had even taken steps to hold on to their power by moving into iron-ore production. In 1803 (the year in which the first steam engine for use in coal mines was built) the citizens of the town finally managed to break free. Almost immediately they became the subject of a territorial dispute between the State of Prussia and Napoleon which practically reduced the town to bankruptcy. Only a few decades were to pass before they came under the paternalistic control of another, and very earthly, power.

The name most people associate with Essen is Alfred Krupp, 'the cannon king', who at the age of 14 took over an almost bankrupt foundry from his father and, over the course of the next sixty years, turned it into

Alfred Krupp

one of the largest steel empires in the world. He was the man who revolutionised railway transport with the invention of the seamless iron tyre (1852) and when he died in 1887 his firm employed no less than one third of the 60,000 people living in the city. Although the first council elections had been held in 1846 an effective urban infrastructure scarcely existed. In 1850 there was only one postman in the city, whose population was under 10,000 (Manchester had 300,000). Indeed Essen had to

Margarethenhöhe

wait until 1862 for the first railway line to be built through the centre. To all intents and purposes Alfred Krupp ruled the town. With patriarchal benevolence he introduced a sickness insurance scheme for his workers, built them housing settlements with bakeries, grocery stores, washrooms, beerhouses and gardens, and even a hospital and school. After Krupp's death, the firm and the city continued to grow. By 1913 the city's population exceeded 300,000 and the firm possessed no less than 7,000 dwellings exclusively for its workforce. (The most attractive of the settlements, the **Margarethenhöhe,** a small garden-city was set up by Krupp's widow and is well worth visiting). But in the eyes of the outside world Krupp was a byword for German militarism and Essen its capital. As a result, in 1945 the townsfolk experienced some of the worst bombing raids in the country which left over 60% of the city in ruins. Since the war the city has grown

again and diversified. Coal and steel might have declined but Essen is still a powerful economic centre, the headquarters of eleven of the top one hundred German companies mainly in the fields of energy, engineering, environmental technology, chemical and service industries.

Down-town Essen

Essen city centre is a compact area, the majority of which is pedestrianised. The main thoroughfare, the Kettwiger Straße which runs from the Hbf northwards is now a spacious boulevard with a wide variety of different shops, including Baedeker's a large traditional bookstore with a downstairs café and a good

First pick up a map of the town in the **Information office** opposite the Hbf. This provides a detailed plan of the city centre, an excellent overview of the whole city (invaluable for motorists) and a short run-down of all the highlights in English, Dutch or French. Anyone based in the city should also get a copy of the English brochure: 'Essen Active – Leisure Time' which gives comprehensive information and details of almost everything you can do in the city. Handicapped visitors can get a booklet and city centre map showing special parking lots and loos.

selection of foreign-language books (including this one I hope). Half way down on the right you'll find Essen's Catholic Cathedral which is known as the **Minster** (Münsterkirche). The original convent was founded here in 852 and there's a list of all the Abbesses along one of the walls. The Gothic church itself was built be-

The Minster

tween 1275 and 1307 and is a serene refuge from the bustle outside. It contains the Golden Madonna, the oldest fully sculpted figure of the Virgin Mother in Western Europe, and a seven-armed candelabra, likewise the oldest extant example of its kind. To one side is a Treasury with a valuable collection of church art, and on the other, a tranquil cloistered garden. If you proceed a little

further down the Kettwiger Straße you'll come to Woolworths. Wow! Since I didn't visit the place I'm not in a position to judge its value as a tourist attraction. But if you turn right here into a small street named 'Zwölfling' and walk down to the bottom you'll find yourself staring across a barbaric inner ring-road at what I think is the most remarkable religious building in the whole of the Ruhrgebiet. **The Old Synagogue,** which I have selected as **one of my Top Twelve Highlights,** was consecrated in 1913. At the time it was the largest synagogue north of the Alps. On the 9th November 1938 it was brutally damaged in the Nazi pogrom but much of the building survived. In 1959 the city bought up the charred remains, tore out the heart of the building and re-opened it as an exhibition centre for industrial design (agh, the sensitivity!). The fickle finger of fate stepped in with another fire in 1979, after which it was decided to re-construct the character and contours of the old interior and reopen it as a religious memorial site and documentation centre. Standing on the central floor of the building I was filled with mixed feelings of wonder, sadness at its history and joy for its defiant survival. Here you can walk about at leisure and view the permanent exhibition on 'Milestones in Jewish Life. From Emancipation to the Present Day' focusing on perspectives of Jewish action, thinking and feeling.

In the gallery there is a further exhibition on 'Persecution and Resistance in Essen from 1933-1945'. Don't miss it: especially if (like me) you're not Jewish.

Back in the centre the huge new consumer attraction is the luxurious shopping mall at Limbeckerplatz. It contains more than 700 shopping outlets, boutiques and cafés. There are also a number of attractive cafés around Kennedy Platz. Almost next door is the city's main theatre, the Grillo Theatre, which leads in turn to a stylish shopping arcade called the Theater Passage. This used to be the home of the **German Poster Museum**, that can boast of a huge archive of 340,000 posters from all over the world. At the moment the

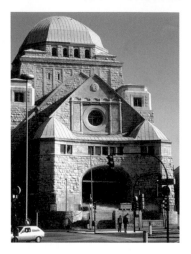

The Old Synagogue

museum is closed and will be integrated into the brand new Folkwang Museum building when it opens in 2010.

Now you deserve a rest. Back on the Kettwiger Straße don't miss the best Italian ice-cream in the region. Toscani de Lorenzo's can be found at either end of the street. I sat outside in the sun and drooled over a tall glass of blueberries with lemon and vanilla ice-cream topped with cream, followed by a coffee whose aroma whisked me back to the streets of Florence.

The Old Synagogue

Essen: North

As you might expect Essen has probably a greater number of tourist attractions than anywhere else in the

City Centre Addresses:

The Minster *(Münsterkirche)*
⚲

Open: (The Treasury) Tue-Sat. except during services.: Tue-Sat: 10-17.00, Sundays 11.30-17.00. Treasury: Adults 3 €, children 2 €. Family ticket: 6 €. Burgplatz 2, 45127 Essen. Tel: 0201/2204206. www.domschatz-essen.de

The Old Synagogue *(Alte Synagogue)*
⚲ ⚲ 🏴󠁧󠁢󠁥󠁮󠁧󠁿 🏴󠁧󠁢󠁥󠁮󠁧󠁿

Open: Tue-Sun: 10-18.00. **Admission free**. Steeler Straße 29, 45127 Essen. Tel: 0201/8845-218. Fax: -225. (→ Dorsten p. and Dortmund p.). The nearest U-Bahn is 'Porscheplatz'. www.alte-synagoge.essen.de

The German Poster Museum *(Deutsches Plakatmuseum)*
⚲ ⚲

The museum is closed at the moment and will reopen in 2010 in the new Folkwang Museum building. If you want to keep up with the latest information, visit www.museum-folkwang.de and click on "Deutsches Plakatmuseum".

✳ **The Zollverein Pit XII** ⊔
(Zeche Zollverein XII)
✪ ⚲ (Outside site) 🏴󠁧󠁢󠁥󠁮󠁧󠁿 🏴󠁧󠁢󠁥󠁮󠁧󠁿 ERIH
First things first before I go into details: the Zollverein Pit XII and the neighbouring Zollverein Coking Plant were inscribed as a **UNESCO "World Heritage Site"** in 2001. When you read on you'll get an idea why. Zollverein XII was the largest coal mine ever to be built in Europe. As the name implies it was the 12th shaft in the Zollverein pit, which had

The Zollverein Pit XII

begun production in 1847 right next to the first railway line in the region. Shaft 12 was opened in 1932, to feed the insatiable energy requirements of the German 'United Steelworks', the second largest steel company in the world after the U.S. United Steel. The Bauhaus architects Fritz Schupp

area. To the North in the working-class area of the city you'll find what many regard as the number one tourist attraction in the region.

Essen night-life

Unlike the Bermuda Triangle in Bochum, there is no single concentrated night-life centre in Essen. The city centre tends to quiet down in the evenings although there are a few pleasant cafés in and around the **Grillo theatre** and **Kennedy Platz.** Here the **Café Bar Europahaus** has a pleasant open air terrace and the food is good. In the same building you'll find **Stratmanns** cabaret theatre which presents some of the best artists around including the legendary Dr. Stratmann himself. If you're going to the cinema, there are a number of places to eat and drink around the **Cinemaxx** complex and the **Colosseum** musical theatre (U-Bahn: Berlinerplatz).

Most of the best bars and restaurants are to be found south of the centre in and around the Rüttenscheidstraße. **Crosskultur's** (corner Wittering/Brigittastr. 2. Tel: 780504) is a super place to spend an evening: good atmosphere, lively bar, easy listening jazzy music; and good food upstairs. Further down the road at Brigittastraße 22 you'll find **Le Chat Noir,** where you can taste the night away on a large selection of wines from France, Italy and Spain accompanied by soups, salads, salami, olives and the like, all at reasonable prices. In complete contrast, if you're

looking for a typical German pub, **Ampütte** (Rüttenscheider Str. 42) has a legendary history going back to 1901. But the real scene begins south of U-Bahn Martinstraße. Here you can find some lively music bars and good restaurants. **Eulenspiegel** is directly at the back of the square in Wehmerkamp. And a few minutes further on, there are more bars in and around Girardet house which houses the **Satiricon** theatre, a good place for music, jazz and cabaret. There's even the occasional English group. Whilst we're talking about the arts, one of the leading alternative arts centres in the city is **Grend.** Set up in 1996 in an old schoolhouse in the suburb of Steele, it offers artists space for theatre shows (it's the base for the Ruhrgebiet's own Theater Freudenhaus), concerts and poetry raps, and also functions as a young people's centre. As well as its own restaurant and bar, **El Patio**, it even offers overnight accommodation. Westfalenstr. 311, 45276 Essen. www.grend.de

If dancing's more to your taste try one of the following five. In the northern suburb of Altenessen on the site of an old coal-mine there's the legendary **Zeche Carl** (Wilhelm-Nieswandt-Allee 100). This is not only a community centre, it's a great venue for parties, discos, live music and cabaret. And in the summer there's a beer garden. Way out west, inside the station building at S-Bahn Essen-West, I discovered **Café Cuba,** a Caribbean no-frill dive which took me back to my days in Brixton. Black-and-white-unite-late-night-and-the-reggae's-out-asight, man! And planets apart, the ultimate meeting place for the sleek and the slick, the designer disco par excellence: **Delta Musikpark** on the site of one of Krupp's old factories in Frohnhauser Straße 75. The interiors of the old buildings have been ripped out and re-designed into a huge complex of different music areas, inside and out. On Fridays and Saturdays it's head down and rave through the night. Krupp would have a heart attack. The **Temple Bar** at Salzmarkt 1, in the city centre, is a good place for partying. It opens at 12 noon, but I guess the action doesn't begin till sometime later. A lot of students swear by the disco in the **Hotel Shanghai** at

Steeler Straße 33. There are, of course, plenty more discos in town and I'm sure genuine fans can find them on their own.

Mega pop concerts are generally held in the **Grugahalle.** For variety theatre, try the aptly named **GOP Varieté** (Tel: 2479393) in Rottstraße. 30. For musicals the best address is the **Colosseum** at Berlinerplatz. (Tel: 01805-4444) where you can catch up with the latest international hits – in German. The theatre used to be one of Alfred Krupp's works halls and it has been beautifully and lovingly redesigned. If you're not going to a show take a look inside the huge foyer or have a drink in the bar. There's also a restaurant for pre-show eating. Lastly, if you're looking for a cinema where you can see original sound-track English-language films, head for number 73 Julienstraße where you'll find the **Galerie Cinema**. Go early. It's only got 45 seats.

and Martin Kremmer intended it to be a symbolic expression of modern power. As they put it: 'We ought to acknowledge that gigantic industrial buildings are no longer a blot on the urban landscape but a symbol of work, city monuments, for local citizens to show to outsiders alongside other public buildings, and with as much pride.' All the buildings in the

pit were intended to harmonise with each other and even the perspectives from one to another were worked out in minute detail. Bestraddling the whole site is a huge four-wheeled pit-head tower leading symmetrically to the ground on both sides. And when you look from the main courtyard below towards the Boiler House (which houses the present-day De-

The Zollverein Pit XII

sign Centre), the tops of the lamp-posts along the way lead your eyes down exactly to the top level of the Boiler House doorway. How was this achieved? They had lamp posts specially built to different sizes. If you look down the line of lamp posts now this does not appear to be the case. Unfortunately some of them were replaced a few years ago by a firm which assumed they were all the same size!

Within three years of opening, the yield of coal from this one shaft alone was a mind-boggling 12,000 tons per day, four times the average for any pit in the region. This was achieved through an extraordinary level of mechanisation. Loading the coal-tubs into the 620 metre deep shaft, hauling them up and tipping them out took a mere 83 seconds. 15,000 tubs per day were emptied in the tipping house which was controlled by a single man. Only where the coal was hand-sorted could you see any other miners in the building. In-

deed, the 500-700 miners working underground travelled up and down from other shafts nearby. The pit was closed down in December 1986 and is now under a preservation order. The site is open to individuals at any time but you can't go inside the main production buildings without a guide. The two hour guided tour is of course given in German but they can do them in English and French on request. So if there's a few of you together ring the visitor centre and ask. If this proves impossible to arrange, simply buy their very informative English guidebook and take it with you on the tour. You shouldn't miss this because what there is to see is awesome in its dark magnificence and once you're inside the building there are also large notices with excellent English explanations. Wear a good pair of shoes and leave your best white trousers at home! Oh! And when you finish your tour, ask your guide to show you the one – small – building the architects forgot to include in their original plans and which had to be thrown up at the last moment. (Have a guess!).

You pay for your tour in the Ruhr Visitor Centre which can be reached by the highest outdoor moving staircase in Germany, a 58 metre gangway leading to the Ruhr Visitor Centre, on the 24 metre level of the coal washing plant. where you can also get comprehensive information on the Industrial Heritage Trail as a whole. Your tour begins below, directly in front of the shaft house and pithead tower (1), in the so-called Courtyard of Honour, one side of which borders on the Electricity Distribution Station (2). The courtyard name sounds a bit pompous but it was deliberately chosen to impress contemporary visitors just as ancient castle courtyards had impressed their visitors centuries before. The workshop buildings (5) and (6) house temporary art exhibitions. The road between them leading from the Courtyard of Honour takes you directly to the **Reddot Design Museum** in the Boiler House. (7). This was redesigned by Lord Norman Foster and is well worth a separate visit as it houses state-of-the art exhibitions of prize-winning objects from all areas of industry and communication. In front of the Boiler House on either side are the High-Capacity Compressor House (8) and the Turbo-Compressor House (9), which is now an elegant café/restaurant called the **Casino**

(Tel: 830240). This is the only place you can get refreshments on the site but if your budget's a bit tight there's an unpretentious pub/restaurant on the left as you come out of the main gate. Beyond the Casino you can see two cooling towers (15 and 21). Going back the other way, on the far side of the High-Capacity Compressor House next to the railway sidings is another workshop building (10) which houses a variety of small

Plan of Zollverein Pit XII

firms. And further beyond the car park is the Boiler-Ash Bunker (13). Your tour through the inside of the building begins with a trip round the Coal-Sorting House (12). Here the coal-tubs were brought to the surface and emptied of their contents which were then sorted on conveyor belts by hand. Very small pieces of coal were sieved out and conveyed further upwards into the

Washing Plant (14) where they were separated from stones in a process similar to gold-washing and sorted out into different qualities. About 90% of production was processed into coking coal and you can visit the bunker (16) from which it was sent by train to plants both near and far. The highest-point of the tour is a trip onto the roof from where you can see forever on a clear day. (There has to be a song there somewhere).

The Ruhr Visitor Centre also contains a huge souvenir and bookstore, as well as a snack bar. In autumn 2009 it will also be the cash desk for a visit to the new **Ruhr Museum**, housed on an area of 4,800 square metres in the coal washing plant, and dedicated to the history of the region before and after the Industrial Revolution. Regular work-in-progress tours are available, and there are occasional temporary exhibitions. Simply ask at the Visitor Centre.

The escalator to the Visitor Centre

Steam railway lovers should enquire in the Visitor Centre about trips along the old industrial plant routes from the **Zollverein Railway Station.** These mostly take place on Saturdays and Sundays during the season. Info and booking at Tour de Ruhr in the North Duisburg Landscape Park: 0203/4291919. (→ p. 48)

In the evening there are regular music concerts – everything from John Cage to Irish Folk, Alfred Brendel and Jan Garbarek – festivities, theatre and dance shows on the site.

Visitor Centre Open: Summer 10 –19.00. The site is free but guided tours cost 6 € per head (kids 3 €). Times vary according to seasonal demand but in the summer they usually start at 14.00 on Mondays to Fridays: 14.00; Sat/Sun and public holidays, 11.00, 14.00, 15.00 and 16.00. To be sure, ring in advance and ask. Gelsenkirchener Straße 181, 45309 Essen. Tel: 0201/3020133. Groups (max. 20 persons, 70 €) must book tours in advance. Why am I telling you this? Their internet address has English language information so you can get all the latest news, times and prices under: www.zollverein.de

Tram/U-Bahn: 107 between Essen and Gelsenkirchen Hbfs, **alight 'Zollverein'.**

Car: Motorway **A40, exit Essen-Frillendorf** or **A42 exit Essen-Katernberg/Gelsenkirchen-Heßler** and follow the signs. Free parking.

✳ **Reddot** Design Museum
&

Open: Tue-Thurs: 11–18.00. Fri-Sun: 11-20.00. Adults: 6 €. Concessions: 3 €. Under 12s free. Tel: 0201/301040. Fax: 3010444. www.red-dot.de

Don't leave here yet! Just a five minute walk away on the same site is the gigantic...

✳ **Zollverein Coking Plant**
    (Kokerei Zollverein)

This was built between 1957 and 61, and designed by one of the Zollverein architects, Fritz Schupp. At its height in the 1970s it was one of the largest coking plants in the world with an output of 5000 tons of coke per day. The sudden crisis in the steel industry meant a quick death to the plant which ceased production in 1993. Two years later it was taken over by

the Foundation for the Preservation of Industrial Monuments and Historical Culture and integrated into the Emscher Park International Building Exhibition (IBA), a ten-year programme of urban and ecological regeneration in the region around the River Emscher. The long-term plan is to turn the site into a huge centre for European design. The central plant has presented one or two magnificent exhibitions, most notably 'Sun, Moon and Stars' in 1999/2000 which drew hundreds of thousands of visitors from all over the country. But whether there's a current exhibition running or not, a tour round this plant is an adventure with some magnificent, vertiginous perspectives, both above and below ground At times it's like being inside huge man-made caves with bunkers falling away into the centre of the earth. At the time of writing guided tours are on Thursdays at 20.00, Saturdays at 14.00 and 16.00. Sundays and holidays: 11.00, 14.00 and 16.00. Meet at the entrance 'am Wiegeturm' in Arendahls Wiese. Further within the complex in the former salt warehouse there is a new permanent exhibition by the Russian artists

Ilya and Emilia Kabakov called the **Palace of Projects.** Visitors walk through a huge snail-like installation which is packed with crazy visionary ideas. Wed-Sun.: 12.00–20.00. Entrance 4 €/reductions 3 €, under 14s free.

More English information under www.the-palace-of-projects.net. For events in the Coking Plant, ring 0201/8309090; fax: 8309020. www.kokereizollverein.de.

Last minute news for top-fit industrial heritage freaks: on Saturdays and Sunday at 13.30 there's a combined four hour guided tour of both Zollverein Pit and Coking Plant with a coffee break in the Coking Plant café. Price 9 €. Survivors should plan a warm bath and an early night's sleep afterwards. If you're planning to stay overnight nearby, **Zollverein Touristik** will fix you up with B & B and any further catering information you require. Tel: 0201/8605940.

Still in the north you'll find

✳ Phenomania
(Phänomania Erfahrungsfeld)
☺

Yet another sensational experience in Essen, but this time we're talking literally. Phenomania offers visitors of all ages a plethora of opportunities to test their senses in a series of hands-on games and challenges. It is located in a very attractively renovated engine house of a former coal pit. There are around 60 various testing stations on the way including the bare-foot blind trail over various surfaces; balancing; smell and touch tests; prisms, mirrors and optical illusions; sound experiments; and making visual patterns from musical vibrations. (This last particularly fascinated my children). Instructions on what to do are only in German, but you shouldn't have any problem working it out for yourself. If so, copy the rest of the visitors, or ask someone in charge and they'll willingly show you. There's a good whole-food cafeteria with vegetarian dishes, and if the kids get restless while you're eating they can go and play in the playground outside.

Open: Mon-Fri: 9-18.00. Saturday and Sundays: 10-18.00. Children 3-6: 3 €; 7-18: 5 €. Students: 6 €. Adults: 7 €. Families get a 15% reduction on the total cost. Am Handwerkerpark 8-10, 45309 Essen. Tel: 0201/301030.
www.erfahrungsfeld.de

Schurenbach mining tip

Public transport: Tram 107 from **Hbf** in the direction of Katernberg. Change at "Abzweig Katernberg" onto **bus 348** in the direction of Gelsenkirchen **and alight at "Huestraße".**
Car: Head for Zollverein and follow the signs to "Handwerkerpark".

Right on the northern edge of the city, towering atop the **Schurenbach mining tip** (Halde Schurenbach) is the mighty 15 metre high steel **Slab for the Ruhrgebiet** by the American artist Richard Serra. From the motorway it doesn't seem very imposing but don't be fooled by distant impressions. To experience it close-up, head north from the city centre up the Altenessener Straße or the Emscher Straße towards Karnap, and under the A42 motorway. Or, from outside Essen, leave the A42 at Essen-Altenessen. Turn right and

drive straight on for about a kilometre. Then right again into Nordsternstraße and park on the road by some factories. From there you can climb up to and wonder at the monument which seems to be sinking at an angle into the bowels of the earth like a gravestone to an industrial past. I went there alone on a wild and windy morning with the sunlight shooting in and out of the scudding clouds and racing shadows across the earth beneath. One tiny man stranded on a bleak-black moonscape with a gigantic iron slab beneath the indifferent universe. Not pretty, but pretty impressive.

Tucked away in the suburb of Borbeck between Oberhausen and Mülheim you can find **Borbeck Mansion** (Schloss Borbeck), an elegant moated building which used to be the residence of the Abbesses who ruled the city. The mansion itself cannot be visited unless you want to eat in the restaurant or get married there: it houses

Borbeck Mansion

a registry office. But on a fine day you can enjoy a pleasant stroll through the 42 hectares of adjoining parkland. Just five minutes drive away you can enjoy more bleary beery pleasures at the **Borbecker Dampfbierbrauerei.** (Tel: 0201/630070. www.dampfe.de. English pages). The brewery is open every day from 11.00. There are also occasional music events.

Essen: South

As in other Ruhr cities the southern suburbs of Essen tend to be occupied by the middle and upper classes. Accordingly the more traditional art and music venues can be found here. Just a kilometre south of the city centre you'll come to:

✳ The Folkwang Museum
    ㅎ ㅎ

This Folkwang Museum has the largest and most comprehensive collection of modern art in the region, and also stages major shows like the William Turner Exhibition in 2001 which attracted over a quarter of a million visitors. A new extension was added in the 1990s to house the many masterpieces of painting, graphic art and sculpture from the 19ᵗʰ century to the present day.

Nonetheless the building has proved to be inadequate to deal with the collection and on 13ᵗʰ March 2007 a design for a spanking new building by the British architect David Chipperfield was selected as the winning

Folkwang-Museum – Van Gogh

entry in an international competition. Construction work has now begun on the building which should be completed in late 2009, in time for the start of the RUHR.2010 capital of culture festivities.
www.museum-folkwang.de

Open: Tue-Sun: 10-18.00. Fri: - 21.00. Tel: 0201/8845314. Adults: 5 €, concessions: 3.50 €. Family ticket 10.50 €. (→ Hagen p. 131)

Public Transport: Tram/U-Bahn 101 and **107** from **Hbf** towards Bredeney, or **U11** (Messe/Gruga). Alight **Rüttenscheider Stern**. From here it's a badly signed ten minute walk. Or **U-Bahn 17** and get off at **Gemarkenplatz**. From there it's a five minute walk.

Car: Motorway A40 exit Essen-Zentrum. Take the B224 (Bismarck Straße) southwards from the centre, and turn right into Kahrstraße, and right again into Goethestraße. It's about a two minute drive from the motorway.

The Ruhrland Museum used to be housed in the same building as the Folkwang Museum, but moved out in summer 2007. It is due to open once again in late 2008 in a completely new environment. For more, see Zollverein Pit XII above. www.ruhrlandmuseum.de

The southern inner city area also contains two magnificent music venues.

✳ The Aalto Opera House

The Aalto opera house is not only the home of an opera company, a ballet company and the Essen Philharmonic Orchestra, it is also one of the most remarkable pieces of architecture in the Ruhrgebiet. It was designed by the Finnish master, Alvar Aalto who, along with the likes of Gropius, Mies van der Rohe and Le Corbusier, was one of the most prominent architects of the 20th century. Aalto presented his first plans for the opera house as early as 1959, but it took almost 30 years before the building was finally completed. By this time Aalto (1898–1976) had already been dead for 12 years.

The outside form of the building is reminiscent of the flowing contours of the Finnish landscape; and the gently curving, asymmetric auditorium (capacity 1125) is based on the Greek theatre in Delphi.

The Aalto opera house

Eating out in Essen

Before I wrote this book I had always assumed 'Essen' derived its name from the German for eating. It's not the case but it could be. For many regard the city as having the widest range of good restaurants in the region. I can only give a small selection here, so if you want comprehensive information you'll have to ask your friends or look in the city's web pages. If you want to blow your holiday budget in a single night on an unforgettable meal, the **Résidence** in Kettwig (Auf der Forst 1. Tel: 02054/95590. Closed Sundays and Mondays. www.hotel-residence.de), is one of the most exclusive and very best restaurants in the country. It's attached to a small hotel of the same name. For those who prefer to feast and sleep rather than drive they have a very reasonable overnight package deal which I can highly recommend. My wife and I revelled in a exquisite seven-course dinner after which we just about had the energy to climb the stairs and fall into a very comfortable bed. A must for gourmets. As an alternative in Kettwig, try **Schloß Hugenpoet** (August-Thyssen-Str. 51. 02054/12040). The renaissance moated castle is not only a hotel, it has two restaurants. You can either eat in the aristocratic surrounding of **Nesselrode** or feed off the atmosphere in the much less expensive old coach house, **Huguenpötchen in der Remise.** Staying in Kettwig, **Ange d'Or Junior** (Ruhrtalstr.326. Tel: 02054/2307) enjoys a huge reputation, not only for its food, but also it's luxurious atmosphere. **Der Bonner Hof** (Kringsgat 14. Tel: 02054/5386. closed Tuesdays) has a delightful Spanish atmosphere to match the mouth-watering dishes. They offer a particularly inexpensive midday menu.

The chic place to go in the north of the city is the **Casino** (→ Zollverein Pit XII), where you can watch the local businessmen chatting up their secretaries. As with the bars there is a knot of fine restaurants in and around Rüttenscheid. Rüttenscheiderstraße, in particular, has a whole line of eating places. **Lorenz** (Rüttenscheiderstraße 187, Tel: 79946) is a typically cool and hypermodern mixture of bistro, restaurant and bar. If you're simply looking for a tasty snack, the place to go is **Mama's** (Rüttenscheiderstr. 183). Here you can take your pick of freshly prepared Italian salads, panini, antipasti and the like. **Raum Eins** (Rüttenscheiderstr. 154. Tel: 455 3747) is a huge favourite, not only amongst trade fair visitors. It combines a cool intimate atmosphere with outstanding food at reasonable prices. **Miga-Sushi** (Rüttenscheiderstr. 54. Tel: 792811) is generally rated as the best sushi bar in town. The food is supposed to be exceptionally mouth-watering in **La Bonne Auberge** (Witteringstr. 92. Tel: 783999). **Zodiac** in the same street at number 43, is generally agreed to be the best vegetarian restaurant in town (Tel: 771212). Two highly-praised Italians are **Oase** (Friederikenstr. 45-7. Tel: 770791) and, further southeast in Rellinghausen, **La Grappa** (Rellinghauserstr. 4. Tel: 231766), which is practically an institution. It claims to have over around 3,000 different wines so don't just ask for 'red'. Not far away, housed in an old nunnery, you'll find **Altes Stifthaus**, (Stiftsplatz 1, Tel: 472736). Here you can eat and drink in the richly decorated banqueting hall or, when the weather's good, outside in the inner courtyard. **Restaurant M** is a stylish new restaurant in the Margarethenhöhe settlement. (Steile Str. 46. Tel: 43860) It's open from 12-23.00 and also does coffee and cake: the ideal place to head for after a stroll through the settlement. (Tel: 43860). Over to the west in deepest workers' country the **Kölner Hof** (Duisburgerstr. 20/corner of Kölner Str. Tel: 763430) enjoys an excellent reputation. The latest shooting star on the gastronomic scene is also in the west of the city. **Gummersbach** (Fürstenbergstr. 2. in the suburb of Borbeck. Tel: 676764. Closed Tuesdays) combines outstanding food with incredibly reasonable prices. Many apologies to any good restaurants I've left out. For more bar/restaurants see the night-life box.

For years the Aalto Opera house has been widely regarded as one of the very best in the whole of the German-speaking world. Its artistic director, Stefan Soltesz, was appointed in 1997 and since then the theatre has gone from strength to strength. If you are at all interested in music theatre this is a "must". The most convenient way to purchase tickets is via the internet: www.aalto-theater.de

Public transport: The opera house is very easy to reach, since it is only a few minutes away by foot from the Central Railway Station. Exit at the back of the station. If this is too much for you, you can always take a bus or underground train and alight at the stations "Philharmonie/Saalbau" or "Aalto-Theater". Your concert ticket will give you the right to use the public transport system free of charge in both directions.

By car: No matter which motorway you arrive by – A40, exit Essen-Zentrum; A42, exit Kreuz Essen-

The Philharmonic Hall

Nord; A52, exit Essen-Rüttenscheid – follow the signs to "Essen-Zentrum" and "Philharmonie". There are parking lots directly in front of the Philharmonic Hall and in two other underground car parks.

✳ The Philharmonic Hall

The Philharmonic Hall, traditionally known as the "Saalbau", lies almost opposite the Aalto Opera house. The building has a long tradition dating back to 1864. It has been the scene of several historic concerts including the first performance of Mahler's Sixth Symphony directed by the composer himself, in 1906. The original Jugendstil building was destroyed in July 1943, when the majority of the city centre was wiped out by Allied bombers. It was replaced by an unadorned building between 1949 and 1954, and completely renovated in 2003-4. The new concert venue contains two auditoria. The Alfried-Krupp Saal (capacity 1,906) is a handsome concert hall with excellent acoustics and sightlines. The smaller RWE Pavilion, a square room between two staircases, is the only part of the building which has been completely added during renovation work. It is not only used for concerts, but also for conferences, congresses and festivities. There are several other large rooms within the building, spacious foyer areas, a CD and merchandising shop called "Rondo", and a fine gourmet restaurant, "Wallberg", that is open all day from 11.30 to late at night. (Tel: 8122 8610) www.philharmonie-essen.de

How to get there
As Opera House above.

✳ Gruga Park botanical gardens and Gruga Halls

♿ ♿ (both venues)

This is one of the largest inner city parks in Germany, created for the <u>Gr</u>eat <u>RU</u>hr <u>GA</u>rden show (gorrit?) in 1929. Apart from the many attractive theme gardens, there are playgrounds and pony rides for the kids, a music pavilion and four restaurant/cafés. The Gruga Halls at the entrance to the park contain a huge array of facilities variously used for congresses, trade fairs and large-scale concerts.

Open: all the year round from 9.00 till dusk. Adults: 3.50 €. Children 6 to 14 years of age: 1 €. Children 6-14: 1 €. Students: 1.50 €. Family ticket: (two adults) 6 € (one adult) 4 €.

Public transport: U11 from **Hbf to Messe Ost/Gruga.**

By car: Take the B224 out of town going south. Or motorway **A52, exit Essen/Rüttenscheid.**
www.gruga.de

Gruga Park botanical gardens

Villa Hügel

✳ Villa Hügel 🔲

❂ ERIH

The Buckingham Palace of the Ruhr, this is the house that Alf built: Alfred Krupp that is. In 1864 he bought a country estate on a bare hillside above Lake Baldeney and had it extensively rebuilt and extended. Not content with the result he gradually withdrew from the everyday running of the firm in order to devote his energies to building a completely new residence with an English park. Krupp had fixed ideas on how the place should look: cosy, domestic and stringent, yet magnificent enough to receive Kings and Kaisers alike. And that was just the first problem. He forbade the use of wood because it was a fire risk, demanded rooms be built on differing levels and the place equipped with up-to-date heating and ventilation: but no electric lighting. Given such a pig's breakfast of demands and Krupp's insistence on meddling in every last detail, conflict was inevitable. During construction, responsibility for the project was passed from one desperate architect to the next and the result, as might be imagined, was a technical disaster. The main house was a draughty refrigerator and the ventilation, far from removing undesirable smells, pumped them in. After Alfred's death the house suffered a wave of alterations and bombastic extensions which swelled it to a total of 269 rooms. Four generations of the Krupp family lived here from 1873 to 1945. From 1953 onwards it was used for cultural and representative purposes, and in 1981 was taken over by a cultural foundation to house international exhibitions, for chamber concerts and receptions. Given Alfred's phobia against fire, (this from a man who made his millions out of furnaces!) it is interesting to note the amount of wood which his successors used in re-furbishing the interior. This is especially true of the main staircase, which replaced the original iron one and is carved in a Moorish style mock wickerwork pattern. The Garden Hall next to the library on the lower floor has a major collection of Gobelin tapestries.

One of Alfred Krupp's major tenets was that the fruits of hard work should be used for the common good, and this philosophy still makes itself felt in the form of the Krupp Foundation. In the so-called 'Kleines Haus' (Small House) of the villa you can see an exhibition on the work of the Foundation, and upstairs there's a very informative exhibition on the history of the firm from its lengthy early struggles, through the boom years to the present day. Such a pity there are no English texts, and no special fittings in the lavatories for handicapped visitors (although the lavatory in the main house looked large enough to accommodate a wheelchair, and there are lifts in both houses). Perhaps the Foundation could invest a few Euros in this direction.

The grounds of the house are well worth walking around and good for a picnic. The Villa also plays host to occasional high-class **chamber concerts** and **art exhibitions** for which there are special prices.

Open: Tue-Sun: 10-18.00. House and grounds: Adults: 1 €. Children under 14 and OAPs free. Hügel 1, 45133 Essen. www.villahuegel.de. English pages.

Public transport: S-Bahn **S6** from Hbf **to 'Hügel'.** Wheelchair travellers avoid! There are only steps at this station.

Car: Autobahn **A52, exit Essen-Rüttenscheid,** then B224 in the direction of Solingen, and left at the first major crossroads at the top of the long hill. Drive right down to the gate where you pay. Parking inside the grounds is included in the entrance price.

Lake Baldeney *(Baldeneysee)*

Not content with his villa Krupp created a huge English-style park in the grounds above Lake Baldeney for which he had hundreds of full-size trees uprooted and imported from the

Lake Baldeney

neighbouring countryside on specially built wagons! (He wanted to enjoy the finished park before he died). The gardens in the front of the house lead down to the riverside which was excavated at this point in the 1930s to create the present-day lake. Walk down from the S-Bahnhof 'Hügel' and you come to the 'Hügel' boarding stage from which you can take a boat trip and weave your way beneath the wooded hillsides on a two-hour round trip between yachts and seagulls and past water-side restaurants. There are also shorter single stretch journeys but these cost more than a round trip where you are not allowed to break your journey. If you're looking for a rowing-boat forget it. You'll have to go to Werden for this. And should you want a cruise down river, walk down the lakeside from Hügel to where the lake narrows and in five minutes you'll reach the next landing stage at

Wehr (the dam). From Wehr Unterwasser (Lower water) you can travel to Werden or all the way to Kettwig (round trip one hour). **Werden** is an old hilly suburb, originally the site of a Benedictine monastery. Around 1750 this was rebuilt in the baroque style and now houses the Folkwang Academy of Music and Drama. **Kettwig** has to be seen to be believed as it gives the lie to all the clichéd images of the Ruhr. I came here by boat from Mülheim and found myself amongst narrow streets full of half-timbered houses. Following a steep winding alley I climbed up past a wine bar and an old church and emerged into a sun-filled street, full of ice-cream parlours, restaurants and Italian delicatessens. If I had a spare million this might be the place to settle down.

Boat trips

Apart from those mentioned above, water-freaks can enjoy a 7-hour Ruhr valley round-trip all the way from Kupferdreh on the Eastern edge of Lake Baldeney to Mülheim and back, including a one hour stop-over in Mülheim. For details ask at the city information office. There is a timetable but it is so complicated as to be practically indecipherable. (I'm working on it). Basically the boats run daily from May to October – out of season in good weather, not at all if it's pouring with rain all day. Pay on board. No problem for wheelchairs. You can roll on board and they'll help you up the stairs if you want to go on the upper deck.

7. How green is my valley
BOCHUM, WITTEN, HATTINGEN, HERDECKE, WETTER HAGEN

BOCHUM (pop: 397,000)

Tourist Information:
Bochum Tourismus and Ticketshop,
Huestraße 9,
44787 Bochum.
Hotline: 01805 260234.
www.bochum-tourismus.de
(English pages)

Bochum is the northernmost town in a group of towns which have joined forces to form a new tourist region under the name of the Middle Ruhr Valley. Bochum itself can be traced back to an early Royal Court on the Hellweg, Cofbuockheim, which was surrounded by a series of farmhouses. In 1321 the folk were granted the right of self-administration, but it was another two hundred years before they managed to erect their first town hall (1526). Despite the fact that coal-mining was first mentioned here in the 16th century, Bochum's economy remained primarily agrarian up to the mid-1850s. In 1799 the first steam engine (imported from England) had been tried out here; and a century later coal-mining became the most important industry in the town, which at one point boasted over fifty shafts producing about 12% of the total regional output. Steel also made its mark here, thanks to the Bochum Steel-Casting Company which developed a new and highly successful method of casting. This was used for manufacturing sophisticated locomotives and turbines, as well as church bells. The company, later taken over by Krupp, was even responsible for making the bell in the World Peace Church in Hiroshima in 1952. Now there is little industry left in the town, which is dominated by the Opel car works. Indeed one of the largest employers is the Ruhr University, the first university in the area (1965), which is situated on hills to the south of the town.

The town centre, within a triangle of major thoroughfares just north of the Hbf, is a busy pedestrian precinct with many cafés and restaurants. But if you're looking for a night on the sticks head for a pedestrian precinct in the Kortumstraße between the Hbf and the civic theatre (Schauspielhaus), nicknamed the 'Bermuda Triangle' (see the info box). Here you can easily disappear in one of the many different bars, restaurants and take-aways. The Bermuda Triangle is reputed to have the liveliest night-life in the region.

On the north-east side of the Hbf in the area of the municipal park you will find a bundle of tourist attractions.

✳ The German Mining Museum (*Deutsches Bergbau-Museum*)
❂ ♿ ☺ 🇬🇧 ERIH

This museum – the largest of its kind in the world – attracts over 400,000 visitors a year. It offers a comprehensive survey of mining from antiquity to the present-day, with exhibits and models on every possible technical theme, not forgetting social, economic and cultural aspects. Ask for an English language ground plan so that you can sort your way through the different areas. The high point – or should I say low point? – is a visit down a specially constructed coal-mine where some of the exhibits have an English-language commentary. (Because of its authenticity this is only partly possible for wheelchair visitors). There's plenty for the kids to look at in the

German Mining Museum

113

Bochum night-life

Bochum University is the largest in the area which means the bars in the 'Bermuda Triangle' are packed with students and buzzing with music. Indeed night-life here is so lively it draws in young people from all the neighbouring towns. The 'Triangle' is centred round the U-Bahn station 'Engelbertbrunnen' but you can reach it easily by foot from the Hbf. Most of the bars stay open till 2.00 in the morning and all night at the weekends, and drink prices are pretty much the same wherever you go. In the summer the action moves out onto the street. The best way to find a bar which suits your taste is simply to open the door and walk around. If you like it stay, if not walk out. It's that free-and-easy. That said here's a small selection for starters. **Brinkhoffs No1**. Brüderstr. 13: Raunchy music. Décor a bit like an anarchic English pub. Go through to the back and you'll find yourself in a completely different summer-garden atmosphere. At **Goldenes Horn** Kortumstr.20 you can get a good doner kebab and/or chips. But no visit to the Ruhrgebiet would be complete without a visit to the **Dönninghaus** take-away, slap bang in the middle of the action. Dönninghaus 'bangers' are modestly claimed to be the best in the universe. So if you want the working-class equivalent of a five star gastronomic experience ask for a 'bratwurst mit pommes rot/weiss' and you'll get a fried sausage with chips smothered in mayonnaise <u>and</u> ketchup. To complete the action squeeze yourself a long worm of mustard ('senf') over the lot and wash it down with a good beer. After that you can revert to your usual smooth, trendy self with a visit to **Café Sachs** in Viktoriastr. 45. This is packed with students chatting away to a background of cool music. Clearly the place to be. Next door on the corner of Kerkwege you'll find the **Intershop** which is, if anything, even cooler and spaced out. Opposite that, **Extrablatt** with newspapers and loud music. Further down Viktoriastraße at number 73 is the legendary **Tucholsky.** There's no music here which means you can discuss the state of the world in peace over a drink, or take your pick from a good selection of newspapers. At the back there's a café/restaurant/tapas bar. The bar is open from breakfast-time through to 3 a.m. Further south, towards the Schauspielhaus and over the road is the **Riff** discotheque. And below that at Clemenstraße 8, the extremely popular and highly idiosyncratic

Freibad, a sensuously velvet cocktail house with fifties décor, including old cinema seats, kidney-shaped tables and a separate billiard room. Hot and cold snacks are also available. The Schauspielhaus itself has a pleasant bar/bistro in the "Kammerspiele" but it's only a few steps over the road to an extremely friendly, informal bar called **Orlando** at Alte Hattinger-

straße 31. The two most elegant bars, however, are to be found right on the north-east edge of the Triangle over the Südring in Luisenstraße. Right on the corner you'll find **Café Zentral** which has an urbane Berlin-type atmosphere; and a few steps further up on the right there's a highly trendy cocktail bar and restaurant called **The**

Living Room (Luisenstraße 9-13. Tel: 9535685). Just a few minutes away from the Bermuda Triangle, directly behind the Hbf (where there's a weekend market) is Ferdinandstraße. At number 44 you'll find **Café Ferdinand** (open from 9 a.m. to 3 the following morning). Good snacks and a laid-back atmosphere. **Café Madrid**, Nordring 57, not far from the Mining Muscum, is a unpretentiously pleasant place to spend an evening over tapas and Spanish wine. And lastly, opposite the Planetarium U-Bahn station near the municipal park, **Café Treibsand**.

The **Gastronomie Am Stadtpark** (next to the zoo) is rated as one of the best restaurants in town and enjoys an excellent reputation for high-class regional specialities but I've yet to try it myself (Tel: 507090. www.stadtpark-gastronomie.de). On the other side of the park right opposite the Museum Bochum and only a few hundred metres behind the Mining Museum you'll find the **Park-Schlösschen** (Bergstraße 65. Tel: 581840). This is an extraordinarily pleasant place for a drink or a meal. It's quite small and tends to fill up quickly so book in advance. The outside terrace is open during the summer season. **Stammhaus Fiege** (Bongardstr. 23, city centre. Tel: 12643) in the birthplace of the town's most famous brewer, has a lot of fans – and brewing relics. Moving outside the centre: in the suburb of Harpen near the Ruhr Park shopping centre, I've eaten very well in elegant surroundings at **Brinkhoff's Stammhaus,** Harpener Hellweg 157. (Tel: 233549. Closed Tuesdays). To the south-east of town, not far from the University, on Lake Ümminger there's a good restaurant and beer garden called **Suntums Hof** (Ümmingerweg 11. Tel: 9270884). In good weather you can eat outside. And to the south-west in the suburb of Weitmar, you can try the relaxed atmosphere of the **Forsthaus** (Blankensteinstr. 147. Tel: 471137).

Bochum seems to be packed with **discos**. The **Prater** (Dorstener Straße 425, in the suburb of Hamme) has eight different areas on 5,000 square metres, four dance floors with different sorts of music, live bands, a piano bar and a restaurant and is open from 20.00 till 5 a.m. The action really starts around midnight when the place seems to contain half the population of the area. Or you can try the equally huge and popular mainstream **Tarm Centre** (Rombacherhütte 6-10 in the suburb of Weitmar). This one's got lots of lasers and a garden pool. Back in the middle, the **Planet** (Kortumstr. 135) was recently voted number 2 in the

region by readers of the time-out magazine Prinz. Still in the centre, fans of the 60s and cellar discos head for **Robespierre** (Bongardtstr. 27a). And if you're not happy with any of these you can try the **Zeche** (Prinz-Regent-Str. 50-60), also in the suburb of Weitmar. The alternative scene goes east to Bochum Langendreer. Get off at the S Bahn here – <u>not</u> Langendreer-West! – and under the railway bridge in Wallbaumweg you'll find the imaginatively named **Bahnhof Langendreer.** The bar/restaurant – informal atmosphere, nice prices, good food, incl. vegetarian dishes – is open all week, there's a good art cinema and at weekends discos, parties and live music.

If you want to see an English-language film in the original soundtrack the **UCI cinema** complex in the Ruhr Park shopping centre always has at least one film in its programme.

Bochum has no opera house but the **Schauspielhaus** has enjoyed a reputation as a leading theatre for many years. The **Bochum Symphony Orchestra** give regular concerts here. Lovers of chamber music should enquire about concerts in the **Thürmer-Saal** (Friederikastr. 4. Tel: 3339033), a fine new hall which plays a central role in the annual regional piano festival. → p. 35

museum but not much hands-on activity. Afterwards you can travel up to the viewing platform in the pithead tower and enjoy a marvellous view over the city. Because it was built in the 1930s the facade of the building has lots of Nazi-type features including a pompous stairway to the entrance. Since this is under a preservation order it can't be adapted for wheelchair visitors, who should therefore come with a friend. Inform the person at the box office and they will let you in through the courtyard next to the restaurant at the side. Once inside, there are lifts to all floors.

Open: Tue-Fri: 8.30-17.00. Sat, Sun and Public Holidays: 10-17.00. Adults: 6 €. Concessions: 3 €. Family ticket: 14 €. All incl. pithead tower. Am Bergbaumuseum 28, 44791 Bochum. Tel: 0234/5877-0. www.bergbaumuseum.de

Tram/U-Bahn: U35 (to and from Herne) from **Bochum Hbf** to **'Deutsches Bergbau-Museum'**.

Municipal Park

By car: A40, exit Bochum-Zentrum and head for the town centre. It's on the left a couple of kilometres down the Herner Straße.

If you now want to blow the coal-dust out of your brains, when you leave the museum turn into the road 'Am Bergbaumuseum' and within a couple of minutes you'll come to...

✳ **The Municipal Park** *(Stadtpark)*
This is one of the oldest in the region (1875) and was designed in the style of an English garden. Apart from the park itself there are three venues of interest in the immediate vicinity. The first is the **Zoo** on the northeast side of the park, which contains bears, snakes, owls, eagles, an aquarium house with sharks, a cuddly corner and a large pool with seals and the like (feeding time a favourite). Afterwards you can wander up to the north side of the park. Here, above the lake, there's a large playing area where the kids can exhaust themselves whilst you sit around in the sun. The park is also ideal for an evening stroll. On the southern side you'll find the **Zeiss Planetarium** which is housed in an appropriately astronomical dome perched on a hillock and boasts one of the most modern projectors of its kind in the world, a Zeiss Universarium Model IX. Most of the shows have German commentaries but I have been assured that at least one show in the repertoire consists solely of music

Municipal Park Addresses

Zoo *(Tierpark)*
♿ ♿ ☺

Open: 9-16.30 (-18.00 April-Sept.). Adults: 5 €, Children 3-16, 2 €. School and other students with identity card) 4 €. Klinikstraße 49, 44791 Bochum. Tel: 0234/95029-0. www.tierpark-bochum.de

Public transport: Bus: 354 from **Hbf** to '**Tierpark**'. **U-Bahn 308** from **Hbf**, alight '**Planetarium**' (direction Bochum Gerthe/Schürbankstraße) and 10 min. walk.

Car: A40 motorway, **exit Bochum Ruhrstadion** and follow the signs.

Zeiss Planetarium
Adults: 5.50 €. Students, children and handicapped visitors: 3 €. Family ticket. 11 €. There are shows in the afternoon and evening but not every day so get a brochure or

Zeiss Planetarium

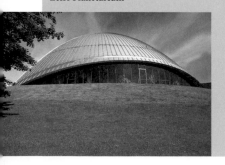

ring for bookings and information. I advise you to book in advance as the place was packed the night I was there. Castroper Str. 67. Tel: for bookings: 0234/516060 (Mon-Fri: 8.30–15.00). www.planetarium-bochum.de

Tram/U-Bahn: 308 from **Hbf** to **Planetarium,** direction Bochum Gerthe/Schürbankstraße (one stop). Both Hbf and Planetarium have lifts so this stretch is OK for wheelchairs. When you get outside at the Planetarium stop, ignore the road signs to the Planetarium. Instead, go down the Castroper Straße (the main road). There's a ramped pathway here which gets you to the entrance quicker. Handicapped people must get their friends to inform the box office as they can only get in by a special ramp at the side. There's space for wheelchairs but no special handicapped loo!

Car: From the centre of Bochum follow the signs to the football stadium or Starlight-Halle. Before you get to either, look out for the Planetarium on your left as you climb the Castroper Straße. Or **A40 exit Bochum Ruhrstadion**; straight on to the first main road (Castroper Str.), turn right towards the centre and follow the signs. It's approx. 500 metres.

Museum Bochum
Open: Tue-Sun: 10-17.00. Wed: 10-20.00. Sun: 11-18.00
Admission: 3 €, concessions 1.50 €. Family ticket: 6 €. Children under 14 and schoolchildren free. **Free** for everyone on the **first Wednesday in the month**. Kortumstraße. 147. Tel: 0234/5160030. www.museum-bochum.de.

Buses: 336, 353, 354 from **Hbf** to **Kunstmuseum.** (approx. 10 mins)
Car: There are so many different routes, the best thing is to get a map of Bochum from the town info office. When all else fails, get to the park side of the Planetarium then follow the road downhill to the corner.

and star-gazing. I saw a Pink Floyd show and was – how can I put it? – spaced out. Practically next to the Planetarium you will find the splendid new **Jewish synagogue.** Down the road on the south-west corner of the park you'll come to the **Museum Bochum** which has a good collection of modern art (including works by Graham Sutherland, Andy Warhol and Francis Bacon) and regular temporary exhibitions.

BOCHUM SOUTH

There are a number of interesting places to visit in other parts of the town. Four of them, in the south, I would particularly recommend.

✳ The Botanical Gardens
(Botanischer Garten)
I love it here. Especially in Spring when the flowers are in blossom. It's high up behind the University to the south of Bochum, overlooking the Kemnade lake. Don't miss the tropi-

cal hot-houses; even better the Chinese house garden with its small pavilions, snaking paths and tranquil ponds. Pure peace.
www.boga.ruhr-uni-bochum.de
Open: April to end Sept: 9-18.00. October through March: 9–16.00.

The Chinese house garden

Admission free.

Public transport: Tram/U-bahn U35 from Hbf to **Ruhr-Universität** and walk through. Unless you're sure of a quick connection onto bus 339 <u>don't</u> alight at Markstraße. It only goes once an hour. If you're coming from Witten the 339 is your bus so time it right!

Car: Head for the **Ruhr Universität** from where the Botanical Gardens are signed. Drive through the campus and there's a free car park near the entrance. If you're coming from anywhere east of Bochum, take the **A43** motorway and **exit Bochum-Querenburg.**

✳ Kemnade Leisure Park (*Freizeitzentrum Kemnade*) ♿

This park and lake on the borders of Bochum, Witten and Hattingen is one of my favourite haunts at all times of the year. Here you can hire

Lake Kemnade

bikes, roller-blades, sailing, rowing and paddle boats, play tennis and mini-golf, take a pleasure boat trip or simply stroll along the water banks, with the Botanical gardens and the university buildings dotted along the horizon on the hills above you. There's a café, picnic and children's play areas: and if you want a swim or a sauna try the **Heveney Leisure Bath** (→ Witten p. 129 and ch. 11). At the south-west edge of the lake you'll find **Haus Herbede** (→ Witten p. 129) www.fzkemnade.de

✳ Stiepel village church

This one was recommended to me by Axel Hillebrand and I can tell you it's a gem. The original tiny church was built around 1000 A.D., completely re-built two centuries later, and once again in the sixteenth century when its tower was heightened. Inside it's beautifully cool and peaceful. Here there are some remarkable old frescos on the walls, including paintings of the Garden of Eden and one of St. George and the Dragon. If the church is locked you can get a key from the nearby office, but I recommend either visiting it for a church service or attending one of the occasional classical concerts held there. There are a few cosy village bars and restaurants very nearby and you can always stroll down the hill to the banks of the Ruhr afterwards if you're feeling fit enough.

Address: Brockhauserstraße. Suburb of Stiepel.

Stiepel village church

✳ The Railway Museum Dahlhausen *(Eisenbahnmuseum Bochum-Dahlhausen)* ☺ ERIH

This is the largest private railway museum in Germany and a mecca for steam locomotive fans of all ages. You can go round the engine shed, climb aboard many of the over 100 engines and passenger wagons, or operate a hand-lever trolley. There are old signalling systems, a ticket office, a working turn-table and lots more – everything authentic and lovingly restored by a team of unpaid enthusiasts. There are special children's days in the summer hols, and every 3rd Sunday of the month you can actually travel on a steam engine. There's a café and souvenir shop on the site. In addition the same

people run a Museum Train – authentic old steam engine and carriages – between Hattingen and Wengern, near Wetter, on the first Sunday of the month between April and October. Nostalgia, nostalgia! (→ ch. 8)

Open: Tuesday to Friday, Sundays and public holidays: 10-17.00. Closed mid-November to end of February. Adults: 5.50 €. Children (6-14): 2.50 €. Family ticket 13 €. Dr. C-Otto-Straße 191, 44879 Bochum. Tel: 0234/492516 (Tuesday to Friday) More information on exact times and special events incl. the Museum Train down the Ruhr valley at www.eisenbahnmuseum-bochum.de

Public transport: From within Bochum: **Tram/U Bahn 318** from **Bochum Hbf to** terminus at **S-Bahn Bochum-Dahlhausen**. From Oberhausen, Mülheim, Essen and Hattingen the **S-Bahn 3** will take you directly **to Bochum-Dahlhausen**. It's about a 15 minute walk from there to

The Railway Museum

The Hall of the Century

the museum, but on Sundays and public hols there's a shuttle service with the so-called 'Pig's Snout', a weird-looking rail bus dating back to 1936.

Car: A40 to exit 29 **Bochum-Wattenscheid-West.** Head for Hattingen (Berlinerstr, then Zeppelindamm). After approx. 3 km. just before a pedestrian bridge you'll see the first sign to the museum. Turn right into the Varenholzstraße. This changes its name to the Höntroper Straße after 1.5 km, but just follow your nose and further museum signs round and down and you'll arrive at the car park. It's free. **Within Bochum**: Take the Hattingerstraße to Bochum-Linden. Turn right into the Dr. C-Otto-Straße and stay on it for 2.5 km.

BOCHUM WEST

A little to the west of the town centre you'll find...

✳ **The Hall of the Century** 🔲
(Jahrhunderthalle) ERIH
Built in 1902 for the World Exhibition in Düsseldorf, this monumental building was originally a gas blower and dynamo station. From 1933 until its closure in 1968 it was used as a compressed air station. Since 1990 it has been revived as a major venue for large-scale music and theatrical events. In 2003 it was fully renovated and refurbished as an international concert hall and made the **headquarters of the RUHRtriennale** performing arts festival. It's directly adjacent to a hiking and bike trail,

and a park is being planned nearby.

Open: It's only open for events, concerts or theatre shows. Gahlenschestraße 100, 44809 Bochum.

Tram 302 or **310** from Hbf to Bochum-Wattenscheid, **alight Jacob-Mayer-Straße.** From here it's a five minute walk through the Westpark. (Steps!).

Car: Motorway **A 40 exit Bochum Stahlhausen** and head southwards. It's signed.

Up in the north-west fans of industrial heritage and their children will find

✳ The Hannover II/V Industrial Museum (WIM) ☺

This museum on the site of the old Hannover colliery has a fantastic new open-air **life-size coal mine** with galleries and shafts etc. **where your children can play** at being miners below and above ground. Don't worry about them getting as black as soot: in this case the 'coal' is sand. And whilst they're mining away to their heart's delight you can visit the Malakov Tower and see a huge steam winding engine. The museum is still being completed.

Open: May-October, Saturdays: 14–18.00 and Sundays: 11-18.00. Günnigfelder Straße, 44793 Bochum. Tel: 0234/6100874, www.zeche-hannover.de

Bus: 368 between Bochum Hbf and Wanne-Eickel Hbf **to Hannoverstraße**. Then take the path via Hüllerbachstraße to the site (around 300 metres). Or bus **390** between Herne Hbf and Wattenscheid Hbf, **alight Röhlinghauserstraße**. Then head up the Günnigfelderstraße for around 400 metres.

By car: Take the A40 motorway and exit at Bochum/Hamme. Go north up the B226 (Dorstenerstraße) towards Herne and turn left into Riemker Str. (the turning is opposite the Hannibal shopping centre). Drive straight on, into and along the Edmund-Weber Straße until you come to Hordeler Straße. Then take a left and this will lead you into the Günnigfelder Straße where you can congratulate yourself and me for getting you there without getting lost.

The Hannover II/V Industrial Museum

HATTINGEN (pop: 60,000)

Tourist Information:
Haldenplatz 3,
45525 Hattingen
(next to the Bügeleisenhaus).
Tel: 02324/951395.
info@hattingen-marketing.de.
Before you explore the town, pick
up a copy of the city-centre map
'Hattingen hat's' with an English
translation. www.hattingen.de

Hattingen was first mentioned in
990 and was a major cloth-trading
centre in the 16th century. For my
money this is **the most attractive
historical town centre in the region** and is well worth a half-day
walking tour. The cobbled streets are
full of beautifully restored half-timbered houses; many of which are

Hattingen historical town centre

now bars, cafés and restaurants. The
Renaissance town hall dates back to
1576. It is now a municipal art gallery and presents occasional chamber concerts. Ore mining began in
the town around 1850 and from that
time on Hattingen began to grow
rapidly. For the next hundred years
the main industries were steel and
coal but these have now died out
completely. The history of the town
is reflected by three completely con-
trasting attractions, all quite near to
each other to the north of the town.

✳ **Hattingen Town Museum**
  (Hattingen Stadtmuseum)
This is a new museum which spans
the history of the town from the
Neolithic age – you know the hunt-
ers and fishers' bit! – through to the
end of the twentieth century. Additional areas have clocks, flags, coins,
furniture, and a huge rope-making
machine. Evidently there used to be
a rope-making factory very near. At
the moment there are only German
texts.
  Open: Tues to Sunday: 11-18.00,
except Thursdays: 15-20.00. Adults:
2 €. Children: 1 €. Family ticket: 5 €.
www.stadtmuseum.hattingen.de/
home.htm
  Public transport: S-Bahn: S3
from Oberhausen via Essen to Hattingen-Mitte (terminus). From there
take **bus CE31** from **to 'Burg
Blankenstein'.** This bus also goes
here from Bochum Hbf. Or **Bus
SB38** from Hattingen Mitte or from

Witten to "Katholisches Kranken-haus" (very close).

Car: Motorway **A43, exit Witten-Herbede/Hattingen** and head for the Hattingen. Before you get into town you'll climb a long wooded hill. The museum is at the top on the right. It's very difficult to find any-where to park directly next to the museum so I recommend you park in the "Burg Blankenstein" parking lot and walk. It's no distance.

By now you should have noticed a large ruin almost next door:

✻ The Blankenstein Fortress (*Burg Blankenstein*)

…was originally erected in 1226 and towers high over the River Ruhr. It was further extended in the 14th and 15th centuries, badly damaged dur-ing the 30 years war and restored in the 1860s. From the walls there are great views over the surrounding countryside from a beer garden and the restaurant of the same name.

The Ruhr at Blankenstein

The Henrichshütte Steelworks Museum

✻ The Henrichshütte Steelworks Museum (*Industriemuseum Henrichshütte WIM*) 📖 ♿ 🇬🇧 🇬🇧 ERIH

The museum was opened in Autumn 2000 and is still in the process of com-pletion. Nonetheless it's the only mu-seum in the region to date which has signs and captions in German <u>and English</u> throughout the site. After a small introductory exhibition in the room adjoining the box office area you can see an 18 min. film on the works in German or English. Then you go outside onto the old site and can follow any and all of the three trails to blast furnace No. 3. The red 'Trail of Iron' tells you about the peo-ple who worked on the site and the

Eating out in Hattingen:

The old town centre is an incredibly popular place to eat, particularly in the summer when you can sit outside. There are so many places to eat that I can only give you a selection. Two good Italian restaurants are the **Ristorante Altstadt Treppchen** (Steinhagen 4, Tel: 52823) and **Basilea** which offers Apulian specialities near the old Town Hall (Untermarkt 10, Tel: 513211). If you're looking for a pancake treat, don't miss the **Pfannkuchenhaus**, a delightful old half-timbered house dating back to the 16th century. Here you've got a choice of over 50 stomach-filling pancake variations (Johannisstr. 8. Tel: 28150). There are two restaurants right next to Blankenstein Castle. You can eat French style in a suitably chivalrous atmosphere in **Burg Blankenstein** (Burgstr. 1, Tel: 33231) or go Italian at **La Romantica** (Burgstr. 2, Tel: 31812). The Steelworks Museum – see below – has a breathtaking new restaurant called **Henrichs.** And not far from here there's the **Landhaus Grum** (Ruhrdeich 6-8), a particularly pleasant restaurant with a large beer garden directly on the banks of the River Ruhr.

material they worked with. This will lead you across ore and coke bunkers to the furnace, then back down to the foundry hall where slag and iron where tapped off. The 'Green Trail' is identical with the red trail for much of the way but then branches off to show you all the exotic specimens of nature which have flourished since the works were closed down. So if botany's your thing grab your magnifying glass, net and notebook and start searching down trees of heaven (stowaways from China!), wild marjoram, stinking cranesbill, kestrels, butterflies and the like. On Ratty's trail (identical with the red trail) children can sniff out the secrets of iron, especially in the sampling house where there are several experiments to try out. The highlight of course, is climbing to the top of the blast furnace from where you can enjoy a great view over the surrounding countryside. Get the English language leaflet at the box office as it has an excellent sketch of the three trails. More sections of the museum will be opening over the next few years including a playground and picnic area. And in the middle of the Blast Furnace hall there's a wonderful new restaurant called **Henrichs** which sells very reasonably priced good food in its three areas, the bistro, restaurant and lounge, not to speak of the beer garden "Gleis 1" which is open in summer.

Open: Tue-Sun. 10-18.00. Fridays 10-21.30. Adults: 1.60 €. Children (6-17), students: 1.10 €. Werksstraße 25,

45527 Hattingen. Tel: 02324/9247-0. www.henrichshuette.de.

Public transport: S-Bahn: S3 from Oberhausen via Essen to Hattingen-Mitte (terminus). From there take **bus**: 335, 358, SB37 or CE31 (the last two also depart from Bochum Hbf) to 'Henrichshütte' resp. 'Industriemuseum'.

Car: Motorway A43, exit Witten-Herbede/Hattingen and follow the 'Route der Industriekultur' signs. Watch out for the right turn shortly when you come down the hill after passing Blankenstein.

A little to the north of the Steelworks Museum you come to the terminus of...

∗ **The Museum Train** *(Museumszug)* (→ Railway Museum, Bochum, p. 121) www.ruhrtalbahn.de

The Nightingale Mine

WITTEN (pop: 103,000)

Tourist Information:
Verkehrsverein Witten,
Service Centre,
Ruhrstraße 43,
58452 Witten.
(English info leaflet).
Tel: 02032/19433.
Fax: 02032/12236.
www.witten.de

Witten lies on the banks of the Ruhr just south of Bochum. The town was originally full of half-timbered houses but suffered badly during the Second World War when allied bombs put paid to 80% of the town centre. This area is the cradle of the mining industry in the region. There's a legend that a shepherd was watching his flocks by night (NO, not that legend!) when he noticed that the stones of his camp fire were glowing very brightly, decided to take a closer look and guess what he found? Folkum-hokum or not, there are plenty of signs of early open-cast mining along...

∗ **The Mutten Valley and the Nightingale Mine Museum** *(Zeche Nachtigall WIM)* 🔲 ERIH

The Mutten valley on the southern banks of the Ruhr is a peaceful wooded area which is highly popular amongst ramblers and cyclists (get a brochure/map 'Bergbaurundweg

Muttental' from the tourist info office). The Nightingale Mine at the start of a 9 kilometre long trail was first mentioned in 1714. The museum opened in May 2003 and focuses on the early years of mining in the area as exemplified by the turbulent history of the mine. In the engine house there is an audio-visual show taking visitors back on a journey through time to the Ruhr valley. The former workshop building has an exhibition on the "cradle of mining" in the area. You can walk along a mock-up mining gallery with helmet and lamp to a genuine coal seam. And there's even a full-scale model of an old Ruhr barge dating back to 1840. After it was closed down the mine was taken over by a brick-making firm. Under the roof of the old brick furnace you can learn how clay was mined and turned into brick, and find out about the life and work of the brickworkers. There are hands-on exhibits for the kids who are helped by Oli the frog. More exhibitions are planned for the future. Further along the valley the trail leads through a wood where you can visit an old miners' prayer house (Bethaus) containing an exhibition of historical photos, tools and models. From there you can continue along one of the most beautiful valleys in the region containing a wealth of evidence (shaft entrances etc) of early mining operations. Back on the river bank you can walk to the ruins of Hardenstein Castle from where you can take a boat trip or catch the Museum Train which

runs between Hattingen and Wetter during the summer (→ Railway Museum, Bochum, p. 121) The Verkehrsverein (address above) does guided tours of the Mutten valley, which is a starting point for the theme trail 'Early Industrialisation'. A valley railway is being planned.
www.muttenthalbahn.de

Nightingale Mine Open: Tue-Sun: 10.00-18.00. Nachtigallstraße 35, 58452 Witten. Tel: 02302/936640. Adults: 2.40 €. Children 1.50 €. Family: 5.80 €. Gallery tour: 1 € (50 cents). www.zeche-nachtigall.de

Bethaus: April to end of October: Tue-Fri: 10-12.00 and 14-16.00 (exc. Thursday afternoon). Sat: 10-12.00. Sun: 11-18.00. November to March: Sat 14-16.00 Sun: 11-16.00.

Public Transport: To Witten Hbf., then ca 20 mins walk via the Nachtigall bridge. **Bus 378** from Bochum-Langendreer to "Witten-Bommern Bhf." then ca. 20 mins walk.

Car: A 43 Exit "Witten-Heven", follow the signs

I must confess to being pretty ignorant about night-life in Witten. But I can recommend a first-class Portuguese fish restaurant. **Casa Portuguesa** is a family restaurant in an unassuming building at no. 81, Breite Straße. The prices are very reasonable considering the range and quality of fish, which is bought in regularly from the Paris fish market (Tel: 26826).

✳ Heveney Leisure Bath
(Freizeitbad Heveney)
⛄ ⛄ ☺

This is on the south side of the Kemnade Leisure Park (→ Bochum and ch. 11). The very pleasant complex has heated indoor and outdoor baths and a toddler's pool. There's also a large new outdoor sauna complex on a grassy slope which includes a cold waterfall, two pools, an earth sauna, a sauna designed like a mine gallery complete with coal wagon (in this case containing hot coals), an indoor solarium, fitness and rest rooms, a café-restaurant and gardens. The open-air pool (summer only) has a giant water chute.

Open: Mon-Sat: 9.00-23.00., Sun and public hols: 9.00-21.00. Day ticket: 13 €. Children (to 16): 6 €. Family (2 adults + up to 3 children): 31 €. Cheaper rates for 2 and 3 hour tickets. Querenburger Str. 29, 58455 Witten. Tel: 02302/56263. www.kemnader-see.de

Bus: 339 to and from Bochum Querenburg and Witten (once an hour) or **350** from Herbede and Witten Centre, **to 'Freizeitbad Heveney'**.

By car: Motorway **A43, exit Witten-Heven.** The very first thing you'll see is a sign to the 'Freizeitbad'. Free parking.

✳ Haus Herbede
is situated on the south-west edge of Lake Kemnade and dates back to the 11th century. There's a small museum here, and you can also eat and drink in the mediaeval vaulted cellars. In the afternoons they serve café and cake. (**Restaurant:** 02302/72258) In the summer there are occasional concerts and open-air events in the courtyard. Von-Elverfeldt-Allee 12, 58456 Witten-Herbede.

✳ Indoor Beachsport Center
This is just over the road from the 'Freizeitbad'. Here you can play in the sand all the sports you'd normally play on grass – just add the word 'beach' to volleyball, badminton, handball and soccer and you'll see what I mean. On top of that there's a separate fitness club for budding Schwarzeneggers, a beach bistro, beach parties as well as a special kids birthday beach where they can build their sand castles and throw sand and bits of pizza in each others' teeth and eyes.

Open: Mon-Fri: 8.30-24.00. Sat, Sun: 9.00-22.00. Courts cost between 29 and 39 € per hour according to the time of day. Reservations: 02302/580400. Lühnsmühle 2, 58455 Witten. www.beachsport.de

Public and private transport: As for 'Freizeitbad Heveney'

And while we're in Kemnade, Richard Noice, who bought the first edition, e-mailed me to recommend a schnapps distillery called **Privatbrennerei Sonnenschein** in a street called Alte Fährweg about two kilometres to the south of the Kemnade Leisure park, without which he claims, 'a visit to Witten will not be complete'. He tells me that their 'Korn is superb and they'll fill any empties you might just happen to have with you.' So, if you're in the area, watch out for a strange Englishman staggering around under the weight of bags full of empty bottles. It could be Richard, but it might be me. Because I can indeed confirm that the distillery shop has a huge range of schnapps, wines, whiskeys and even olive oil from all over the world. Sho shthanks for the tip(ple), Risch-Risch-Rischard. Whhopsh, thash another typo! www.sonnen-schein-brennerei.de. And if you need to line your stomach well before visiting the Brennerei, several people have recommended a pancake house to me called **'Pfannkuchenhof'** just down the road in Herbede at Meesmannstr. 85. It's in a lovely old half-timbered building. Tel: 02032/79509.

∗ **Hohenstein**

This is right on the other side of Witten to the south of the centre. If you leave Witten and proceed along the banks of the Ruhr eastwards on the B226 towards Wetter you'll pass some tall cliffs on the left. Shortly after you drive under the railway bridge, there's a signpost. Turn left, drive to the top, and you'll find yourself in one of the most popular open-air resorts in the region with extensive walking trails and fantastic views over the valley below.

Continue along the same road and you'll come to...

WETTER and **HERDECKE**, two attractive little towns along the Ruhr, full of half-timbered houses. In the 18th century Wetter was an important coal-mining centre, but after the central mining office moved to Bochum, the empty buildings were taken over by a man called Friedrich Harkort who, in 1819, converted them into an engineering workshop for manufacturing steam engines and the like. Harkort's factory has been immortalised in a famous painting by Alfred Rethels which has become a symbol of early industrialisation in Germany. Nowadays the areas is a mecca for ramblers, cyclists and water sport fans. I took one of the many signed paths (the so-called 'Harkortweg') towards Herdecke. The trail led past the factory remains and steeply up into the wooded hills. The climb almost killed me but the view over the valley from the viewing-platform at the top was worth every thumping heartbeat.

Tourist Information:
Wetter: Kaiserstraße 170, 58300 Wetter. (They've very good walking maps and will tell you where you can hire bikes).

Herdecke: Kirchplatz 3, 58313 Herdecke. Down at the Bleichstein Leisure Centre, you can hire a canoe.

I can recommend two eating places in the immediate vicinity. **Henriette Davidis** (Trienendorfer Straße 8 in Wengern. Tel: 02335/7411) an ideal place for bikers and day trippers. The original Henriette was a preacher's daughter and a very famous cook in her own right. Closed Tuesdays. If you're looking for a decent Italian meal try **L'Osteria** (Hauptstraße 1-5. Tel: 02335/844 8448)

Harkort's factory

HAGEN (pop: 205,000)

Tourist Information:
Bürgerhalle, Rathaus,
Friedrich-Ebert-Platz,
58042 Hagen.
Tel: 02331/207-3383.
Fax: 02331/207-2400.

Hagen is the south-east gateway to the Ruhrgebiet. Bedded between valleys and mountains the town was at its height at the start of the 20th century when it gave its name to the so-called 'Hagener Impulse'. Its moving spirit is recalled by the museum of the same name in the town centre:

✳ The Karl-Ernst Osthaus Museum

Karl-Ernst Osthaus (1874-1921) was the son of a very rich banker and the museum was built to his orders by the Belgian architect Henry van de Velde

131

to house his private collection which included works by Van Gogh, Cézanne, Gauguin, Matisse, Renoir, Rodin and many other contemporaries. As such this could be said to be the first museum of modern art in the world. Osthaus died at the age of 47. In 1921 Germany was still in the throws of poverty and horrendous inflation was round the corner. Since the town of Hagen could not afford to buy the collection his heirs sold it to the city of Essen which, thanks to Krupp, was still relatively wealthy. (→ Folkwang Museum p. 104) What remains here is an extraordinarily beautiful art nouveau building and an excellent collection of works by the German artist Christian Rohlfs and other key works by German expressionists such as Franz Marc, August Macke, Max Beckmann and Otto Dix. There's a magical area in the basement which contains a section of the Los Angeles Museum of Jurassic Technology. In addition there are also several contemporary works and a section reflecting the museum as museum. They have a very good English language folder which will give you more information. If you're in Hagen, don't miss it.

Open: Tue-Sun: 11-18.00. Thursday –20.00. **Admission free**. Hochstraße 73, 58042 Hagen. Tel: 02331/ 207-3138. www.keom.de
Closed for repairs till Autumn 2008.

Public Transport: Everything which goes to the town centre. It's a short walk away.

Car: Motorway **A1 exit** Hagen-West, head for Hagen-Zentrum, then follow the signs. Or **A45, exit Autobahnkreuz-Hagen** and head for the centre. When you come to the inner ring turn left and follow the signs.

Hohenhof

If that interested you then you must take a look at:

✳ Hohenhof – The Museum
of the Hagener Impulse 🕮 ERIH

I can wholeheartedly recommend this museum to addicts of architecture and interior design. The house was conceived by van de Velde as an *art nouveau Gesamtkunstwerk* to the orders of Karl-Ernst Osthaus. Ceilings, wallpaper, windows, doors, furnishing and fittings all harmonise right down to the last key-hole. Don't miss the Matisse sketches on the white tiles in the winter-garden. 'Hey Henri, I don't suppose you could pop over from Frankreich and scrawl something on one of my walls? I'll make it worth your while of course'. But seriously, should you be wondering about the museum's name, Osthaus intended this house and the adjoining garden suburb to provide a decisive impulse to the development of modern architecture and to restore beauty as the dominant power in life. To achieve this, he brought most of the leading artists of his time to Hagen, including Mies van der Rohe, Le Corbusier and Walter Gropius, in their search for a modern art completely detached from the idea of luxury.

P.S. If you've no idea what an *art nouveau Gesamtkunstwerk* is, steer clear.

Open: Tue-Sun: 11-18.00. Stirnband 10, 58093 Hagen. Tel: 02331/ 55990. www.keom.de

Bus: 527 to Stirnband.
Car: Motorway **A45, exit Hagen-Süd.** Follow the signs to Emst.

Back in town: if you're in any way interested in the history of Hagen from its origins to the present day I can recommend a visit to the

✳ Historisches Centrum /
Stadtmuseum

The permanent exhibition is very attractively laid out with plenty of multi-media films illustrating various historical epochs in a very lively manner. There are seven main sections taking visitors from the Stone Age all the way up to the 1950s, accompanied by plenty of good exhibits. I particularly appreciated the short videos on early industrialisation and the Nazi era.

Open: Tue-Sun: 11-18.00. **Admission free**. Eilper Straße 71-75, 58042 Hagen. Tel: 02331/207-2740. www.historisches-centrum.de (English pages)

Public Transport: From Hbf: Bus: 84 (dir: Halver), 510 (dir. Dahl/ Rummenohl), 512 (Selbecke/Breckerfeld), and 516, 519 (dir Eilperfeld). Alight "Stadtmuseum".

Car: Motorway **A45, exit Autobahnkreuz-Hagen-Süd** and head for the centre/Hagen-Eilpe. This will take you directly onto the Eilper Straße. There is a car park in the Wippermann Passage adjacent to the museum.

✳ Allerwelt Haus

I discovered this one evening when I was invited to an exhibition by two Cuban artists. The "All World House" is a good meeting place for anyone interested in global concerns and intercultural encounters. It has a regular programme of concerts, workshops and lectures, not to speak of yoga, qi gong, African drum courses and the like. Attached to the building is an attractive shop selling "fair trade" goods from all over the world, a library and an archive, and a cosy **vegetarian bistro "Mundial"** that also offers hot home-made dishes. The night I was there I tucked into a tasty New Orleans Jambalaya, followed by a huge bowl of quark and apples, both at very reasonable prices. Best of all it's slap bang in the middle of town, within walking distance of the Karl-Ernst Osthaus Museum.

Potthoffstraße 22, 58095 Hagen.
www.allerwelthaus.org

But the town's top attraction for me (and thousands of others) is...

✳ The Westphalian Open-Air Museum *(Westfälisches Freilichtmuseum)*

✪ ♿ ♿ ☺ ⚑ ⚑ ERIH

Every time I come here I feel I'm entering an old village rather than a museum. The authentic buildings stretch far and wide over a beautiful hillside on the edge of town and feature over sixty crafts and trades from the period between 1780 and the end of the 19th century. In many of the workplaces you can actually see historic working-methods in action: everything from rope-making, baking, paper making, water-driven smithies to a tobacco factory. For these and more, see the excellent free English leaflet/map or buy the catalogue. In short, this place is a perfect, fine-weather, day out for young and old alike. If you don't want to take a

The Westphalian Open-Air Museum

picnic there are plenty of places where you can get snacks or a full meal.

Open: April – end October, Tue-Sun: 9-18.00. Adults: 5 €. Under 6: free. 6-18 yrs: 2 €. Family ticket. 11 €. Mäckingerbach, 58091 Hagen. Tel: 02331/7807-0. www.freilichtmuseum-hagen.de

Bus: 512 from Hbf to 'Freilichtmuseum'

Car: As for Hohenhof above. After leaving the motorway, follow the signs. From the town centre, B54 southwards, follow the signs showing the museum's logo or "Route Industriekultur".

And lastly, on the North-East edge of town you'll find a very pleasant little suburb called Hohenlimburg, with a lovely fast canoeing stream running through the middle. High above you can't miss one of the most interesting castles in the area.

✳ Hohenlimburg Castle and Museum *(Schloss Hohenlimburg)*

This was another tip from Richard Noice who thought it 'a little gem of a "place". He's right about the gem but I wouldn't call it little. It's the oldest extant mediaeval castle in the area and so high up I could only pity the poor workers who had to hunk the bricks up the hill to make the whole thing possible. The building is no longer lived in but serves as a museum of local and regional history stretching right back to the stone age.

Foreigners can get a basic information sheet in English, Dutch and French, but it's the atmosphere of the rooms which give the castle its particular attraction. In another wing of the castle there is a unique museum on cold (steel) rolling. Afterwards you can sit outside in the beautiful inner courtyard and wait for Ivanhoe to come galloping through the gateway.

Open: April to September, Tuesdays-Sundays: 11-18.00. October to March, Saturdays and Sundays only: 11-18.00: www.schloss-hohenlimburg.de The cold steel rolling museum is also open.

Public transport: Train: The most convenient train from the Ruhrgebiet is the **RB 40** (once an hour) from Essen via Bochum and Witten to Hohenlimburg Station. From there you can walk it if you're fit and crazy. Invalids and reasonable people take **bus 517, 518 or 525**. If you're coming **from Hagen** itself **take the CE 77 bus** from the town centre and change at Hohenlimburg station. **From Dortmund** you can take **bus 518** from the Westfalenhallen to Hohenlimburg Station and then change.

Car: Motorway **A45, exit Hagen-Süd** and turn left towards Hohenlimburg. Go straight on until you come to the first main crossroads. Turn right and go straight on to the station. Cross the railway line and go straight up the hill (don't follow the main road round to the left!).

8. North by North Vest
RECKLINGHAUSEN and district. HERNE

RECKLINGHAUSEN (pop: 125,000)

Tourist Information:
Öffentlichkeitsarbeit, Rathaus,
45655 Recklinghausen.
Tel: 02361/50135-1. Fax: -3.
www.recklinghausen.de
English info.

This pleasant little town was for centuries an important station on the north-south trading route from Cologne to the north coast, but only really grew with the arrival of coal-mining in 1869 under French and Belgian management, the railway in 1870 and the opening of the Rhine-Herne canal in 1914. As a result, in the course of thirty years, its population increased over tenfold from 5,000 to 55,000. Now there are no working pits remaining in the town – the last closed in 2001 – which is the administrative centre for the Northern area of the Ruhr region (the so-called Vestland). The major magnet for tourists in the summer season is...

✳ The Festival Theatre
(Festspielhaus)
   ♿ ♿ All languages possible
Situated on top of a hill in the town park this is the headquarters of the 'Ruhrfestspiele', an annual perform-

ing arts festival which presents world-class (Peter Brooke, Robert Wilson, Alvin Ailey etc) dance, musical, circus and theatre companies from every continent on the globe from the 1st May for six weeks or so. The May-day opening is no accident as the first festival in 1947 was originally presented by theatre workers from Hamburg as an expression of gratitude to their mining colleagues in the Ruhr who had smuggled them extra supplies of coal the previous winter in order to keep their theatres open. During its 50 years' existence it has expanded to become one of

The Festival Theatre

Europe's major festivals – much more attractive than Bayreuth and

There are plenty of interesting little bars and restaurants in the centre of town. The traditional cult bar is **Drübbelken** at number 5, Münsterstraße. Its slick rival **Eckstein** is at Münsterstrasse 17-19. Nearby, along a small street called 'Im Rom', there's a good daytime meeting place cum library for international contacts called Die Brücke ("The Bridge"): Tel: 502011. Peking (Königswall 11. Tel: 02361/181231) is a popular Chinese restaurant. In Augustinessen Straße, right next to the top hotel in town, the Engelsburg, you can spend the night supping home brew in an attractive brewery house called **Boente**. Indeed it's the nearest thing I've seen to an English pub, except that it seems to be open half the night. At the back of the room there are plenty of tables where you can eat. I tried their 'panhas' – a Westphalian speciality which is a bit like a black pudding cake – with fried potatoes and onions. It was great! On fine days they open the beer garden at the back. And as an added bonus they have jazz sessions almost every Sunday morning from eleven onwards. There's a very attractive alternative arts centre in an old smithy called **Die Altstadtschmiede** in Kellerstr. 10. (www.altstadtschmiede.de.).

Just outside town in the village of Bockholt there's a very good place to eat. **Landhaus Scherrer** (Bockholterstraße 385. Tel: 02361/10330) used to be the old school. Now it's a fine mixture of a pub, restaurant and live event venue. (www.landhausscherrer.de. English pages)

137

distinctly less snotty. Don't miss the opening May day festivities in the park with lots of action, bands and street theatre.

Address: Otto-Burrmeister-Allee 1, 45657 Recklinghausen. Booking essential. Tel: 02361/92180. Fax orders: 02361/921818 or travel agencies. www.ruhrfestspiele.de

✳ The Icon Museum
(Ikonenmuseum)

Around 700 works from Russia, Greece, the Balkans and other 'orthodox' Christian countries make this one of the most comprehensive collections of icons and Coptic art in Western Europe.

Open: Tue-Sun: 10-18.00. Adults: 5 €; concessions 2.50 €. Kirchplatz 2a, 45655 Recklinghausen. Tel: 02361/

The Icon Museum

5019-41. It's in the town centre. www.kunst-in-recklinghausen.de

✳ The Vestisches Museum

This is the traditional town museum and here you can trace its history from the earliest times to the present day. There's an old geological collection, and upstairs some interesting rooms on the history of coal-mining and the Recklinghausen Festival. But for me the high point is on the ground floor where you can see a unique collection of "naïve" paintings on miners and their lives, with extraordinary group sculptures, all created by former miners who deserve more recognition.

Open: Fri-Sun: 11-18.00. Adults: 1.50 €. Hohenzollernstraße 12. 45659 Recklinghausen. Tel: 02361/5019-46. To the left of the front entrance there's a car park reserved for visitors. www.kunst-in-recklinghausen.de

✳ Kunsthalle

The "Art Hall" comes into its own right during the Recklinghausen Theatre Festival, when it presents a major international artist. Apart from that there are regular exhibitions throughout the year, many of which are well worth seeing.

Open: Tue-Sun: 11-18.00 only during exhibitions. Adults: 1.50 €. Große-Perdekamp Straße 254-27, 45659 Recklinghausen. Almost right next to the Central Station. Tel: 02361/5019-35

VEW Electricity Museum

✳ VEW Electricity Museum 🏛
(Umspannwerk Recklinghausen)
♿ ♿ ERIH

This brand new museum shows the enormous influence of electricity on industry and everyday life throughout the last century. Developments in cultural, technical and social history are displayed over an area of 2000 square metres. Exhibits include a juke box, a tram, kitchen gadgets and a 50s cinema.

Open: Tue-Sun 10-17.00. Admission: 2 €. Concessions: 1 €. Uferstraße 2-4. 45663. Recklinghausen. Tel: 02361/382216. www.umspannwerk-recklinghausen.de

Bus: SB 20 from Recklinghausen Hbf (ca. 22 mins.) or Herne Hbf (ca. 6 mins.) to 'Hochlarmarkstraße'.

Car: Motorway **A42, exit Herne Baukau** and head for Recklinghausen. It's on the right hand side about 2 kms away. Or **motorway 2, exit Recklinghausen-Süd** and head for Herne. It's on the left hand side about 4 kms down.

✳ The Hoheward Mining Tip

This magnificent new landscaped tip is actually in Herten but it's right on the edge of the suburb of Hochlarmark on the southern border of Recklinghausen. Ideal for a great walk with spectacular views. (for more → pp. 139, 155)

Recklinghausen is on the border of Münsterland and the area contains many pleasant country towns, some of which I shall now deal with – in alphabetical order.

The Hoheward Mining Tip

CASTROP-RAUXEL
(pop: 79,000)

> **Tourist Information:**
> www.castrop-rauxel.de

Mulvany's town. And mine. The town was first mentioned in documents as "Villa Castorp" in 834 and for centuries was a tiny rural administrative centre on a trade route. It only really began to grow in 1867 when the Irishman William Mulvany arrived here with a team of Englishmen to sink the Erin pit. In 1902 the town was given municipal status and 24 years later the two parts of Castrop and Rauxel (further north) were joined into a single administrative unit. The town now has a population of around 80,000 and because of its geographical setting – far enough from large cities but near enough to several motorways – is an attractive place for new businesses, families and commuters. There is no longer any mining in the

Erin Colliery

town but the **Erin Colliery** site with its illuminated pithead tower is now one of the most eye-catching industrial estates in the region and a favourite place for a stroll and a bit of fresh air. From time to time you can even see sheep grazing on the greened Irish-landscaped tips. The panorama point of the town, to the south-east on the Bodelschwingerstraße, is the greened-over **Schwerin Tip**, which is adorned with a huge steel sundial created by a local artist, Jan Bormann. From here you can see all the way to Bottrop on the one side and Dortmund and beyond on the other. Just down the road from here you can visit the Hammerhead Winding Tower (Hammerkopfturm), a relic of the Erin Pit. It's the oldest of its type in the area and is surrounded by a Celtic tree-circle in memory of William Mulvany.

Goldschmieding Park is well worth visiting, especially in the snow when the slopes are full of tobogganers. While you're here you should take a look inside Mulvany's old villa, **Haus Goldschmieding**. It's now part of the neighbouring hotel – the favoured lodging-place of many international football teams – and houses a café called the "Westfalenstube" (open 12 – 23.00) as well as the hotel's gourmet restaurant. The restaurant lounge used to be Mulvany's living room and the hotel manager assures me its open to anyone to look around whether they are guests or not. Here you can see an extraordinary fireplace created

Schwerin Tip

in 1597 and adorned with sculpted reliefs, figures and images from mythology and religion. The two pillars are supported by St. Peter and Paul respectively standing on heathen lions beneath two angels. Above them amongst the frieze stand various gods, including Hercules, Vulcan, Neptune, a naked figure called Mantiqal (assumed to be Bacchus), and Apollo. Mercury, the messenger to the gods stands next to Vulcan holding the baby Dionysius. But pride of place, right in the middle, goes to a figure known as "Antino". This represents a man called Antinous, who was the lover – sorry! constant companion – of the Emperor Hadrian. There's something horribly modern about Antinous because, in order to prove how fanatic he was about his religion,

he committed suicide by throwing himself into the Nile. As a reward he was promptly elected to stand amongst the Gods. Well, that's one way of doing it, I suppose. The individual scenes between the figures begin at the far left side of the fireplace with a scene showing the Earth on a chariot of Time complete with the elements fire, water, air. This is followed by a warning series of processions showing us what man makes of the world: from prosperity, to envy, to war, to ruin, to modesty, finally leading back to prosperity again. At which point, I suppose, the whole round is likely to start again. The motto above the frieze "Soli Deo Gloria" (Honour to God alone) reminds us that the fireplace is not primarily a renaissance tribute to gay liberation or even classical my-

141

Food and drink in Castrop-Rauxel

Should your holiday budget not stretch to a meal at Goldschmieding, there are plenty of other alternative places to eat. A new favourite in town is the **Olivo** restaurant (Tel: 359280) attached to the EuroStar hotel at Bahnhofstraße 50, where you can eat in modern neo-Italian surroundings. Within months of opening it was selected as one of the best in the region by a well-known restaurant guide. I can confirm the fine quality of the Mediterranean style food and wine. (Tel: 358290). Those of you in search of German fare with Hungarian variations will be more than satisfied at **Bei Sandor** (Tel: 24313) on the B235 at Wittener Straße 159. From the outside it looks rather unprepossessing but don't be fooled: inside it's extremely elegant. There are several Chinese restaurants in town. My favourite is **Jade** in Obere Münsterstr. 17 (Tel: 549090) which has good freshly cooked food and makes it really spicy if you want it that way. As a bonus there's a public car park just over the road. The latest addition to international cuisine in the town – and very fine it is too – is the **Himalaya Restaurant** (Tel: 4455100) in the equally fine Raj Mahal Ayurveda Health Centre and Hotel opposite the town hall at Europaplatz 3-11. www.raj-mahal.de. The chef has been brought in specially from India so you can be assured of some authentic dishes. If you're looking for a piece of social history I suggest you call in at **Haus Oestrich**, Frohlinderstr. 35, near the Schwerin Tip. This authentic working-class pub – <u>not</u> a restaurant – is over one hundred years old and the entertainment room at the back (discos and live-music shows at weekends) looks like it's not been changed since the days when it was used for celebrations by miners and their families. On my first visit I was regaled by the locals in the bar, one of whom told me how much he liked Yorkshire Pudding whilst another waxed enthusiastic over PG tips! It's a funny old place, Haus Oestrich! **Hotel Daum**, on the Bochumerstraße has a very popular restaurant and beer garden. From here you can take a delightful walk through the paths in the adjoining wood. And finally Castrop-Rauxel has its very own home brewery. You can sup an authentic local home brew at **Haus Rütershoff** at Schillerstraße 33 on the south side of the Stadtgarten. And there's an extremely pleasant bistro and beer garden in the Stadtgarten itself: see **Semi-Secco** in Parkbad Süd below.

By now you'll be thinking I've eaten and drunk my way through the whole town. Not at all. Those of you in search of the traditional German answer to afternoon tea will find two excellent "coffee and cake" cafés in town. The **Confiserie Café Residenz** in Wittener Straße 34 is very near the old market place in Castrop. Everything is home-made, stylish and very traditional. It's also a very good guesthouse if you're planning to stay for a few days. Up in Habinghorst at Langestraße 76, **Café Harsdorff** will more than fulfil your craving for cakes covered in cream, chocolate or whatever's likely to ruin your waistline. Whoops, I'm drooling as I write this.

thology, but to the triumph of Christianity over the heathen world. If by now you've been taken in by the atmosphere you can always stay and indulge yourself in an extravagant meal. To book a table, telephone 02305/30132.

The town has two new interesting artistic and social centres, both of which came into being with the support of the International Building Exhibition (1989-99). In the north-east in the suburb of Ickern you can find the **Agora** (Greek for 'open space') centre, that is particularly used by the town's Greek community. The site even boasts an open-air Greek amphitheatre which is used for summer celebrations by all sections of the community. The adjoining buildings are used for language and dance courses. Evening programmes include jazz, rock and classical concerts.

Back in the old centre of Castrop you can take a short walk from the market place into the town park (Stadtgarten) and look for the old open-air swimming baths. The **Parkbad Süd** has changed its function completely. The building, pool (no longer in use) and surrounding park are still intact but the complex, which is supported by a grass-roots initiative, now houses the popular **Semi-Secco bistro** complete with beer garden and "boules" area. Boules are available at the bar. The bistro is also used as an arts, entertainment and exhibition centre.

Jan Bormann, who designed the Schwerin Mining Tip is not the only remarkable artist in town. If you're looking for quite outstanding works of pottery, you must visit the **workshop of Ursula Commandeur** at Kleine Lönstraße 58, very near the town centre. She not only makes practical objects but also quite unique works of art that have been exhibited all over the world. Not for nothing was she awarded the major State Prize of North Rhine-Westphalia in 2007. Give her a phone call to warn her that you're coming: 02305/4781. www.uc-keramik.de.

Castrop-Rauxel can boast of having two of the top 50 jewellers in the whole of Germany. Matthias Zimmer's shop can be found at Am Markt 25, right next to the old market place. (www.juwelier-zimmer.de). Just behind the ERIN trading estate, at Karlstraße 20, you can drool at the creations of Kersten and Matthias Grosche.
www.galeriehaus-grosche.de

One last tip for those of you using **public transport**. Castrop-Rauxel has two railway stations: **Castrop-Rauxel Hbf** is in the north of the town and has direct connections to Hamm, Dortmund, Herne, Gelsenkirchen, Oberhausen, Duisburg and Dusseldorf (including the airport) on the **RE3** train. I'm telling you this because most station information signs omit Castrop-Rauxel Hbf from the list of RE3 stops, probably because the name is too long! Take no notice, they <u>all</u> stop here. The other station is called **Castrop-Rauxel Süd**, (= South) next to Münsterplatz bus station. To get here you must take the **RB43** train (Dortmund – Zollern II/IV Colliery (Bövinghausen) – Castrop-Rauxel – Herne – Movie World – Dorsten). It only goes once an hour but will at least drop you right in the middle of Castrop. The best way to the centre of Bochum from Castrop-Rauxel South (Münsterplatz) is to take bus number 353 which stops very near to the German Mining Museum. Alight "Kunstmuseum" and walk through.

DATTELN (pop: 36,000)

For current information:
www.datteln.de

Datteln has a claim to fame as the largest canal junction in Europe. It's not only sited on the river Lippe but is the junction of the region's four canals. Datteln celebrates its watery status every year with **the August canal festival** which attracts thousands of visitors to the streets around the harbour and ends with a lantern procession and firework show. As you might expect the town is an **ideal** starting point **for a cycle tour**. I rode alongside the canal half way up to Haltern, then cut west across country through a wooded region called the "Haard". The trail took me to a modern coal mine stuck right in the heart of the woodlands and past a hotel tucked back in a peaceful oasis miles from the urban roar (for more on the **Landhotel Jammertal** see box). I then headed up and over sandy heath land to a huge reservoir with great views northwards before descending slowly into Haltern and heading for the lake. For more on this go to Haltern below.

Landhotel Jammertal
This exceptional hotel is one of the very few in the area catering almost solely for holiday-makers, especially for anyone looking for a

short break from the stresses of big city life. It not only has a regular programme of sporting activities (free tennis court and bike hire) but a complete wellness programme including heated indoor and outdoor swimming baths, a whirlpool, sauna baths and a massive range of cosmetic and massage treatments. I tried it for just two days and loved every peaceful, recuperative second, not to speak of the excellent food and drink, friendly service and a luxurious suite complete with fruit bowl, free bathrobes and sauna towels. No surprise that the family-run hotel is listed as one of the top ten wellness hotels in the whole country. It may not be cheap – look for special last-minute arrangements on their website – but it's worth every cent of your money. For non-residents there's a good **restaurant**, **Schnieders Gute Stube**, a café and a beer garden. Address. Naturpark Haard, 45711 Datteln-Ahsen. Tel: 02363/3770.
www.jammertal.de

DORSTEN (pop: 80,000)

For current information:
try the information office in the old town hall, Markt 1, 46282 Dorsten or the internet at: www.dorsten.de

Dorsten's history can be traced back to 12 BC. when the Romans set up a camp here. The first written record of a settlement here dates back to 890 AD. "Durstinon" as it was called was officially given town rights in 1251, and for the next few centuries seems to have been a popular place for battles and wars. The Industrial Revolution (iron ore) arrived around 1830, but it was not until 1911 that the first colliery went into production. It can't have been too productive because it was closed down again in 1931. The town has a pleasant old centre, much of which is pedestrianised. But the main focus of leisure is the surrounding countryside which is ideal for cyclists and ramblers.

✳ The Jewish Museum, Westphalia (Jüdisches Museum Westfalen) ♿ 🇬🇧

This is not a holocaust museum. It rather seeks to illustrate the important stations of everyday Jewish life (circumcision, bar mitzvah, marriage etc), Jewish religious rituals and their connection to Christian festivities, and the wellsprings of anti-Semitism. A new annexe to the museum opened in 2001 dealing with Jewish life in Westphalia. There's an English language folder to help you round the exhibits. (→ Old Synagogue Essen p. 93)

Open: Tue-Fri: 10-12.30 and 15-18.00. Sat, Sun and Public Holidays 14-17.00. Adults: 4 €. Students 1.50 €.

145

The Jewish Museum, Westphalia

Julius-Ambrunn Straße 1, 46282 Dorsten. It's just across the road from Dorsten Station on the south-east edge of the town centre. Tel: 02362/45279. info@jmw-dorsten.de. www.jmw-dorsten.de (English summary).

✳ Lembeck Moated Castle
(Wasserschloss Lembeck)
☺

This is one of the loveliest old castles in the area. The original castle dates back to the 12th century but it was continually rebuilt and extended until it achieved its present state around 1692. It's constructed on two islands joined by a straight axis, behind which is a large park with a picnic area and children's playground, including two separate trampoline areas comprising ten trampolines. The castle building houses a hotel, a restaurant and café and two museums: a castle museum on the ground floor and a local museum above. The latter is open all the time but the former is opened to the public at particular times of the day for guided tours only.

Open: Daily: 13–17.00. Saturdays, Sundays and public holidays: 11–17.00. Site, gardens and museum tour, 5 €. Children: 4 €. Family ticket: 18 €. Site and gardens only: Adults: 3 €. Children: 2.50 €.
Schloß Lembeck, 46286 Dorsten.
Tel: 02369/7167.
www.schlosslembeck.de

✳ Atlantis leisure baths
(Atlantis Erlebnisbad)
♿ ♿

The German title literally means "experience bath". And indeed it is! This is a large, ultra-modern complex at the heart of which is a sun-flooded dome containing a huge 'fun' bath area for swimmers, non-swimmers and (separately) toddlers. There are various different areas with a whirlpool, a fast-running stream which whips you around and round a circuit, a bubble bath, a relaxing area

Lembeck Moated Castle

with lots of water massage jets and, of course, a reasonable priced snack bar where you can get drinks, sausage and chips or salads. The kids have a choice of four different water slides, one of which you can shoot down on a rubber tyre. Outside there are more swimming areas, a warm salt-water bath and waterfalls. Back indoors, next to the fun bath is a 25 metre conventional swimming bath. For sauna fans there's a specially reserved area containing a huge number of different saunas, inside and out, a steam bath, an inhalation bath, a Moroccan mud bath (!), rest rooms and a drinks bar. To top it all there's a fitness studio within the complex but this can only be used by members. It's all super clean and very attractively set out. A real bonus for locals and tourists alike.

Open: Mon-Fri: 8–23.00. Sat: 10–24.00; Sun: 9–22.00 Admission with sauna, 3 hours: 10 €. 5 hours: 13 €. Day ticket: 15 €. Without sauna, 3 hours: 5 €. 4 hrs: 8 €. Day ticket: 10 €. Children (4-16): 4, 6.50 and 7 € respectively. Family tickets get a rebate. Konrad-Adenauer-Platz 1, (Maria Lindenhof), 46282 Dorsten. Tel: 02362/95170. www.atlantis-dorsten.de

By car: Motorway A31, exit Dorsten **or A52** to "Autobahnkreuz Marl-Frentrop", then head for "Dorsten-Zentrum/Stadtmitte" and turn off at "Maria Lindhof". Those are the official instructions. Since it's so near to the middle of town I advise you simply to take the quickest route to Dorsten ("Zentrum") from whichever way you're coming and when you get on the ring road, head north. As soon as you leave the town centre area you'll cross a bridge. The "Maria Lindhof" turnoff is <u>immediately</u> on the right. There's free parking opposite the baths.

Dorsten is lucky enough to have three exceptional restaurants which are renowned throughout the region. **Henschel,** at Borkenerstr. 47, can boast one of the best women chefs in the country, Eleonore Henschel (Tel: 02362/62670). The **Goldener Anker** at Lippetor 4, can go one better as its chef Bjorn Freitag has just picked up a Michelin star. I tried it. Fantastic! (Book early. Tel: 02362/22553). Lastly **Rosin**, named after its owner Frank Rosin, offers a rich selection of international dishes just outside town at Hervesterstr. 18 in the village of Wulfen. (Tel: 02369/4322). The **Kaffeehaus** on the south side of the town centre serves simple snacks and good coffee in quiet pleasant surroundings (Essenerstraße 19).

GLADBECK (pop: 79,000)

For current information:
www.gladbeck.de

When I'd finished the first edition of this book I took a look at what I'd covered and was more than a little embarrassed to see one small gap in the map of my travels though the Ruhrgebiet. This gap, between Bottrop and Gelsenkirchen, was the town of Gladbeck. In 1975 the State of North-Rhine Westphalia attempted to merge Gladbeck with Bottrop and Kirchhellen (locals maintain it was to have been called Glabotki!) but the residents brought a successful legal action to prevent this and since then it has been a part of the district of Recklinghausen. The first traces of a settlement here go back beyond 1000 BC and the town itself is mentioned in documents dating back to 1019. But as with most towns in the Ruhrgebiet its growth and decline went hand-in-hand with the coal industry. If you approach the town along the A42 motorway it is difficult to see it at all because it is cut off from the road by a high wall. Indeed when you turn off onto the B224 road towards the town centre it still remains walled in. This is not to protect the town from war-mongering hordes of foreigners but rather from the noise of heavy traffic travelling between Essen, Holland and the German coast. Anyway,

Wittringen moated castle

before you get into the town centre –
if you've approached it by the abovementioned route – take the very first
left turn and you'll be thrown back
into rural peace with a flavour of the
middle ages. For the road leads off
to ...

✳ Wittringen moated castle
(Wasserschloß Wittringen)

The original castle was first mentioned in 1263 but over the years it has
been ruined and rebuilt on several occasions. The present impressive building houses two restaurants, one of
which has a terrace overlooking the
water where you can take coffee and
cake if you're not interested in a full
meal. One of the side buildings houses
the local museum (entrance free)
which deals with local history since
the beginning of time (!). There's a lot

of interesting stuff here, especially on
local mining history, and it's well
worth looking around even if you
don't speak German. The castle is surrounded by a huge amount of park
and woodland, which makes it ideal
for ramblers and cyclists. There are
public tennis courts right opposite,
and the local football stadium and a
large open-air swimming bath are
also sited here. Burgstraße 64, 45964
Gladbeck. Wasserschloss Wittringen
Restaurant: Tel: 02043/22323.
www.wasserschloss-wittringen.de

✳ The Zweckel Engine House
(Maschinenhalle Zweckel)

This imposing piece of industrial architecture in the Frentroper Straße on
the north-west side of the town is the
only remains of the former Zweckel
Colliery (1908-63). It has now been

restored and is used for various cultural events. I know this because the first time I came here in May 2001, it was late one evening after a ten hour theatrical mystery tour. I had a very pleasant banquet and film night which lasted so long I was forced to beg a lift home with a stranger. Since then the venue has been used regularly for musical concerts and, most prominently, for stage shows presented by the RuhrTriennale arts festival. Like the Zollern Colliery in Dortmund the building is decorated in art nouveau style and is worth a look if you're in the area. It's run by the same people who are responsible for the Hansa Coking Plant in Dortmund. (→ p. 186) So if you're curious to find out more: www.industriedenkmal-stiftung.de (English pages).

If you're looking for somewhere decent to eat in the middle of town you could do worse than try **Thesings Marktstübchen** at Wilhelmstraße 42.. The fish dishes are supposed to be especially tasty. Tel: 02043/67583. www.thesings-marktstuebchen.com

One last word for literature lovers. The town library (Friedrich Ebert-Str. 8) houses the **Literaturbüro NRW-Ruhrgebiet**. The office awards an annual literary prize to regional writers and is the best place to go to for any information concerning the region's literature and writers. Tel: 02043/992168. www.literaturbuero-ruhr.de

HALTERN AM SEE
(pop: 35,000)

Tourist Information:
Stadt Haltern-Stadtagentur,
Altes Rathaus, Markt 1,
45721 Haltern.
Tel: 02364/933-366.
Stadtagentur@haltern.de
www.haltern.de

This is the northern-most stop on our travels, at the heart of the 'Hohe Mark' nature park on the borders of Münsterland. The town was originally the site of a small Roman settlement. Despite some industrialisation it has retained its rural charm. The surrounding countryside makes it ideal for ramblers and cyclists (rent a bike at the Hbf). **Lake Haltern** (Haltenerstausee), a huge reservoir with boating and bathing facilities and sandy beaches amongst the woodlands, is an immensely popular resort in the summer. Drive out of the town centre towards the east (there are signs to "Stausee") along the Hüllernerdamm. First you'll come to an **open-air swimming bath** on your right, and shortly afterwards on your left to a huge lakeside bath and beach on the reservoir itself. The car park and road get packed on hot days so expect to walk a bit or take a bus: www.seebad-haltern. de. Shortly after the entrance to the second baths you'll come to a smart

Lake Haltern

hotel, the "Seehof", on your right, opposite which there is a jetty for the pleasure boats. 30 metres further on there is a small open-air beer garden besides which there is a path which runs through the wood alongside the lake. Walk all the way through (about 20 minutes) and you'll come out at another car park frequented by bikers. You're now in Stockwieserdamm. Opposite this park is a large brand new café/restaurant called the **Lakeside Inn** which has a kid's playground and sandy area overlooking the water. I highly recommend a stop here, all the more so because the only alternative for toilets is in the bikers' park and these are pretty dismal: www.lakeside-inn.de. On the other side of the road going right from the Inn you'll find a jetty where you can **hire canoes or pedal boats** or get a snack (but no loo!). If you want to

drive straight to Stockwieserdamm, just continue up Hüllernerdamm and take the first left by the lights. Haltern is quite a way from the centre of the Ruhrgebiet but the **S9. RE2 and RB42** trains will all take you to and fro pretty quickly.

✳ The Westphalian Roman Museum *(Westfälisches Römermuseum Haltern)* ♿ ♿

The Romans had a small fortress here until they were driven out in 9 BC by the Germans. Now it's the site of an elegant museum whose eye-catching architecture fills the sky with skeletal tent-like shapes. Within the building there are wonderful models and re-creations of the original fortress, along with a valuable

The Westphalian Roman Museum

151

collection of finds, including coins, pottery and weapons, illustrating the lives, duties and customs of the Roman army around the time of the birth of Jesus. The accompanying texts are laudably concise and informative. Such a pity they're not in English.

Open: Tue-Fri: 9-17.00. Sat-Sun: 10-18.00. Adults: 3 €, children 1.50 €, family ticket 7 €. **Free on Fridays.** Weseler Straße 100, 45721 Haltern. Tel: 02364/93760

Bus: 298 from Haltern Bahnhof to 'Römermuseum'.

By car: Motorway **A43, exit 8, Haltern** and **follow the B58** towards the centre. The museum is on the left as you come into town. www.lwl.org/LWL/Kultur/WMfA_Haltern

✳ Ketteler Hof Leisure Park
(Freizeitpark Ketteler Hof)
♿ ♿ ☺

This is one of the top open-air attractions for families from all over the region – justifiably so. It's not only situated in a beautiful rural environment, it contains a large and imaginative variety of well-maintained playing facilities for kids from toddling age to around 14. (I'm telling you this because older teenies *might* find it a bit babyish). There are sandpits, giant slides, climbing frames, crazy golf, a fairytale wood, a Western fort complete with train ride, gigantic jumping cushions, a peaceful nature trail

through the woods – watch out for the deer – and much much more. There are picnic areas as well as restaurants and snack bars at affordable prices. It's perfect for prams and wheelchairs, but dogs are not allowed in. I spent six hours here and had a great time. The only problem was tearing my kids away to come home.

Open: Late-March to late-October, daily from 9.00 to 18.00. Admission: 10 € per person, (under 2s, free) Ketteler Hof, Rekenerstraße 211, 45271 Haltern-Lavesum. Tel: 02364/3409. www.kettelerhof.de

Public transport: Because it's in the heart of the Münsterland countryside there's just one **bus** route here, the **275** from Haltern Bahnhof. If you're travelling from afar, come by...

Car: Take the **A43** motorway (Wuppertal-Recklinghausen-Münster) **to exit 7 Haltern-Lavesum**. It's about 3.5 kilometres in the direction of Reken. Car-parking free.

If you want a pleasant evening in the countryside, try **Landhaus Föcker** in the village of **Lippramsdorf** just outside the town. The restaurant not only has a large beer garden. There is an additional counter where you can buy their home-made jams, meats and liqueurs. For early birds there's breakfast from 9.30. Closed Mondays and Tuesdays. Lembeckerstraße 12. (Tel: 02360/791)

HERTEN (pop: 66,500)

For current information:
www.herten.de or
Stadt Herten,
Kurt-Schumacher-Straße
45699 Herten.
Tel: 02366/303-0. Fax: -255

Herten, which is twinned with Doncaster, was first mentioned in a tax register in the 10th century and until that time was a part of the Electorate of Cologne. For almost 330 years the moated castle (see below) was a seat of the Counts of Nesselrode who were the governors of the area known as the "Kurkölnisches Vest Recklinghausen". Coal mining began here in the 1870s and the town grew rapidly, finally achieving municipal status in 1936. For a long time the town was regard as the largest mining town in Germany so it was hit very hard by the crisis in the industry which set in during the mid 1950s. The last pit closed here in April 2000 and the town is now in the midst of a large economic upheaval and transformation to future technologies. Being on the edge of the Ruhrgebiet it enjoys a huge network of rambling and cycling trails.

✳ Herten Castle *(Schloss Herten)*
One of my German readers, Bärbel Gross, wrote to me to point out that Herten has more to offer than the Copa Cabackum Baths. She's right!

On her advice I took my wife and mother-in-law along to Herten Castle on a sunny Sunday afternoon in August. The moated castle, which lies to the west of the city centre, was built in a mixture of late gothic and Renaissance styles, but its present appearance dates from 1702. The castle grounds, which contain many exotic trees, were originally designed along baroque lines but re-modelled between 1814 and 1817 as an Eng-

Herten Castle

lish landscape garden. The castle itself was fully restored in the 1980s and is now used for a variety of cultural activities, especially **chamber concerts**. After a walk round the 30 hectare grounds we ended up in the delightful old rooms of the castle café, which is open every afternoon except Monday. Well worth a visit. www.herten.de

✳ Copa Cabackum
☝ ☝ ☺

No. Not 'bana', 'Backum'; which is a suburb to the north of the town containing a park and this large swimming complex. The baths are imaginatively designed in a tropical setting and contain three main sections: the sauna and solarium, the fun baths with a water chute, and a fitness area containing a 25 metre indoor swimming bath for those who like a really good swim rather than a splash-about. In particular they cater excellently for the needs of non-swimmers and small children. In summer you can go outdoors and take advantage of another four large pools and two huge water chutes. (→ ch.11).

Open: Mon: 10-22.00. Tues: 8-22.00. Wed-Fri: 8-23.00. Sat/Sun: 8-21.00. Admission: 16 years and over: 2 hours: 6 €, 4 hrs: 7.50 €, all day: 9 €. Children (4-15 incl.): 4 €. 4.50 € and 5.50 € resp. Family ticket: 15.50 €, 19.50 €, 23 €. 4 hours for the price of two on weekdays before 10 a.m. (Mons before 11), except in the school holidays. Address: Über den Knöchel, 45699 Herten. Tel: 02366/307311. www.Copacabackum.de

Bus: 242, 225 or 217 to 'Copacabackum'.

Car: If you're coming from outside town the easiest way is **motorway A43, exit Herten-Nord** and head for the middle of town. Turn right at the sign for Herne Scherlebeck/Zentrum and head for the cen-tre. It's about 1 kilometre down the road on the right.

✳ The Hoppenbruch Mining Tip

A few days later I decided to try my feet at climbing the Hoppenbruch Mining Tip, the first panorama point on the Industrial Heritage Trail. The tip is in a large wooded area on the south-west of the town tucked neatly in the corner of the border separating Herten from Herne and Gelsenkirchen. I approached it from the A42 motorway (exit Herne-Wanne) and as I drove north over the Rhine-Herne canal I spotted a huge white windmill on a wooded hilltop to my right. From the road it looked as though any view from the top would be blocked out by the trees. I was wrong. I followed the tracks between the trees until, after a good sweaty climb (there are plenty of benches along the way) I finally emerged into clearness just beneath the summit, with the blades of the windmill rolling lazily above me. The windmill itself generates electric power for the town. Directly at its foot there's a small 'wind-sculpture' park and orientation boards identifying the various landmarks in all directions. I was astonished at the amount of different plants, flowers and bushes which had shot up on the old tip – it's a nature-lovers' paradise here – and delighted that those who used to work the pits had received some sort of leisure-time reward for their labour.

The Hoheward Mining Tip

✳ The Hoheward Mining Tip

This is the latest, and one of the most spectacular spoil tips, to be specially greened over and landscaped. It stands almost alongside the Hoppenbruch tip to the south of Herten on the borders of Recklinghausen, with which it will eventually be connected when work is completed in 2012. The motto of the joint project promoted by the two towns is "New Horizons", and the artistic landscaping features elements of water, wind and heaven. The final stage will be a "celestial lake" on the upper plateau joining heaven and earth. As part of the astronomical theme park a magnificent obelisk based on that of the Emperor August in the Campus Martius in Rome stands on a huge new plateau at a height of 140 metres above sea level. A spectacular new red dragon-head bridge leads from the old coal mine, "Zeche Recklinghausen II" (there's a car park here)

over the Cranger Straße to the bottom of the tip from where there are paths to the various plateaus. Needless to say the views are breathtaking. More information at www.horizontastronomie.de (English pages)

Bärbel Gross also recommended I take a look at the **Glashaus** in the middle of the town. It not only houses the town library but also a popular café/bar with a regular programme of evening attractions from jazz to cabaret and book readings. Frau Gross also tipped me off about the following: There's a cult 'party' pub in Feldstraße 71 called **Rheinhousen.** Inside it's a bit like an all-American bar. A must for the late teens and early twenties. Further to the north of town there's a new art exhibition area in the engine house of the **Zeche Scherlebeck** (Open Friday and Saturday afternoons: 15.-18.00 and Sunday mornings: 11-18.00. Scherlebecker Str. 260, Bus:

Historic village of Westerholt

242/224, alight "Polsumer Straße"). Lastly – a real find for bike lovers – if you want to try the latest in cycle technology you can hire prototype **hydrogen driven cycles** at **Hybike Herten** in the middle of town at Ewald Straße 222. They can only be hired as part of a guided tour, but Hybike also have 20 conventional bikes and 10 mountain bikes for hire. 02366/181160. www.hybikeherten.de. Frau Gross should be made an honorary citizen of Herten for all her unofficial publicity for the town.

✳ Westerholt

In 1975, as a result of municipal reform, Herten was amalgamated with the small town of Westerholt, which lies on the north-east border of Gelsenkirchen. Its remarkable 'historic village' consists of about 80 half-

timbered houses, mostly from the 18th and 19th century, embraced by the church of St. Martinus at one end and Westerholt Castle at the other. Just outside the castle there are several restaurants, one of which has an enticing beer garden. The castle itself is now a golfing hotel, whose restaurant and café are both open to the general public. The afternoon I arrived the café terrace was awash with hundreds of golf trolleys and exhausted golfers trying to reconcile the reality of their performance with their illusions of being Germany's answer to Tiger Woods. The golf course is open to non-members. I couldn't find out what the green fee is because the office had just closed. Who cares? If you have to ask the price you probably can't afford it anyway. www.schlosshotelwesterholt.de

MARL (pop: 92,000)

Tourist Information:
Creilerplatz 1,
45768 Marl.
Tel: 02365/990.
www.marl.de (English pages)

For such a small town Marl is admirably active in its support for the arts. The town hosts the country's most important annual television award ceremony as well as supporting its own theatre. Furthermore in the heart of town opposite a modern shopping centre (containing the information office) and next to the Town Hall you can visit...

＊ The Glaskasten Sculpture Museum *(Skulpturenmuseum Glaskasten Marl)*

The town council has been buying up contemporary sculpture since the 1940s and erected a museum in 1982 to house the collection. Nonetheless over 70 exhibits can be found in the adjoining park around and in the middle of the city lake. If you cross the bridge to the theatre you'll see my favourite: a huge upside-down locomotive and tender by the German sculptor Wolf Vostell: mighty power transformed into utter helplessness. Get a leaflet/map from the museum. (→ Duisburg, Lehmbruck Museum p. 41)

Open: Tue-Sun: 10-18.00. **Admission free.** Creiler Platz/Rathaus, 45765 Marl. Tel: 02365/992257. www.marl.de/skulpturenmuseum

S-Bahn: Line S9 between Haltern and Essen to **Marl Mitte**.

For a look at power of a different kind you should visit the town's most recent attraction:

The Glaskasten Sculpture Museum

✴ The Chemical Industry 🖳 Estate *(Chemiepark Marl)*

♿ (Visitor centre) ERIH

Hand on heart, I'm deeply prejudiced against anything to do with chemistry. Probably because I hated it in school. But after touring this gigantic site (109 km of roads, three power-stations, two water-clarification plants railways and a canal harbour) I came away deeply impressed. The guided tour starts with a look around a small exhibition in the Visitor Information Centre. Then it's onto the bus for a 90 min. round-trip. Sadly the exhibition and tours are only in German at the moment. They say they're aiming to cater for English language visitors: ring and check. If you're looking for something to eat and drink try the Feierabendhaus in the hotel directly next door. They have a beer garden.

Open: Tue-Sun: 10-18.00 Tours: April-Oct: Tue and Thur: 11.00. Sat and Sun: 11 and 15.00. (Nov-March, 11.00, Tue, Sat, Sun only). Guided bus tour of the site: 2.60 €.

Paul-Baumann-Straße 1, 45764 Marl. Tel: 02365/499436. Fax: 497375. www.route-industriekultur.de

Public transport: S9 to **Marl Mitte**, then **bus 221** to **Feierabendhaus** (every 30 mins).

By car: Motorway **A52, exit Marl-Zentrum/Rappaportstraße** and follow the signs to the Information Centre. (about one minute away!)

The Chemical Industry Estate

MARITIMO

OER-ERKENSCHWICK
(pop: 30,800)

For current information:
www.oer-erkenschwick.de

This little town tucked away in the Haard area is notable for its exceptional pleasant rambling facilities. Head for the Stimberg park where there's a large hotel. Immediately below it you'll find one of the very best leisure and wellness baths in the whole region.

✳ MARITIMO – Paradise in Stimberg park
☺

This is an extraordinarily huge complex consisting of two main areas. 1) the sport and fun baths, indoors and outdoors (in summer) and 2) the "sauna and wellness paradise". The latter has a total of eleven different indoor and outdoor baths from steam baths, to aroma baths, Russian and Finish saunas, a whirlpool, an indoor celestial salt-water grotto, outdoor salt-water baths with massage jets, a Cleopatra bath, Hamam, Ayurveda and Wellness massages, a gastronomy area, comfortable lounges and a glorious "peace" room where you can settle down for a good sleep on the waterbeds. Paradise indeed! There are no separate male and female baths. For more on sauna culture in Germany see "the Pleasures of Leisure" chapter.

Open: Daily. There's a huge range of prices and times. It's not expensive, and much cheaper of course if you only want to swim. Check out their website for more details.
Stimbergpark 80, 45739 Oer-Erkenschwick, Tel: 02368/698-0. Fax: 698-199 www.maritimo.info

In show-business the top-of-the bill attraction always comes last. Appropriately enough, the number one attraction in the area and one of the best in the whole region can be found in:

WALTROP (pop: 30,000)

> **Tourist Information:**
> Stadt Waltrop,
> Münsterstr.1,
> 45731 Waltrop.
> Tel: 02309/930237.
> www.waltrop.de

Waltrop was first mentioned in 1036 as "Waltorpe", which is Early German for Walddorf, "the village in the wood" (I bet that impressed you!). It's still pretty green and sits astride both the Dortmund-Ems and the Datteln-Hamm canals, both of which are flanked by cycle tracks. The centre still has a few old half-timbered houses, an old church and at least one very good restaurant which I shall mention right away. **Gasthaus Stromberg** (Tel: 02309/4228) is an old half-timbered building at Dortmunder Straße 5. Here you can get excellently cooked local and international specialities at reasonable prices in unpretentious surroundings. They have their own car park and beer garden at the back in Isbruchstraße.

But most visitors head west to...

✳ The Old Henrichenburg Shiplift (*Altes Schiffshebewerk Henrichenburg*) 🛗
✪ ♿ 🇬🇧

On 11th August 1899 Kaiser Wilhelm II officially opened the largest and most magnificent construction on the Dortmund-Ems canal to a jubilant crowd of thousands. The Henrichenburg shiplift was necessary to offset the considerable difference in water-level between the Dutch coast and the canal harbour in Dortmund. This was partially accomplished by a network of locks, but at this point it was necessary to try something more ambitious. There were similar works to the shiplift in England, France and Belgium, but their lifting capacity never exceeded 400 tons. Henrichenburg, on the other hand, was able to lift ships of up to 800 tons

up and down a height of 14 metres. How? The solution was as simple as it was elegant. A system of five floats provided a counterweight to the ships which enabled them to be raised or lowered with comparatively little effort. (If you still can't picture it there's a good working model in the museum). The shiplift is not only a feat of engineering, it has an expressive elegance which emanates pride, stability and confidence in a future which was to be so cruelly destroyed by the events of the Great War. It was in use for 71 years before it was finally replaced by a more modern one about a kilometre away. After many years of neglect it was saved from disrepair by the local authority and re-opened in 1992 as a museum. The museum houses a permanent indoor exhibition, after which visitors can go aboard the trough in the lift or climb the steps to the top from where they can look over the canal onto the museum's ships, one of which – the Franz Christian – contains a fascinating exhibition on everyday work and life on board a canal boat. In 1995 the museum was awarded the 'European Museum of the Year Award', and in 1999 it increased its attractions by opening the upper waters to visitors with a further series of canal ships, cranes and a lifting bridge. And best of all you can now take a 60 minute trip on the water on the "Henrichenburg" which is moored in the lower harbour. What I particularly like

about a visit to Henrichenburg is that you can combine it with a visit to the more modern sluice and shiplift just up the road where you can

watch the ships going up and down at regular intervals. (Don't confuse the disused sluice here with the old shiplift!). Both shiplifts are joined by a landscaped park containing the upper waters. Many visitors, however prefer to take the winding path along the canal banks from one to the other. If you're like me, however, you'll take the road between the two sites and end up in **Papa Christo's Greek restaurant** and beer garden. Here I can sit outside on the terrace beneath the setting sun and bore my family with yarns about my days as a sea-scout back in Merrie England.

Open: 10-18.00 (except Mondays). Adults: 3.50 €. Children over 6 and students: 2 €. Family ticket: 8 €. An English pamphlet is available. Furthermore the museum offers leaflets in Spanish, Portuguese, French, Dutch and Polish. If you want to visit both **old and new shiplifts** the cheapest way is to buy a **combined ticket**. This'll set you back 4.10 € (adults), 1.80 € (children), 2.10 (students), and 7.80 € (family ticket) respectively. Am Hebewerk 2, 45731 Waltrop. Tel: 02363/ 9707-10. Fax:-12. www.schiffshebewerk-henrichenburg.de

Bus: Take the **231** from Recklinghausen Hbf. to 'Kanalstraße'. (every 30 mins. Journey-time: 30 mins.). Or bus **C58** from Castrop-Rauxel to "Datteln Wittenerstraße" from where it's a five minute walk.

By car: Motorway **A2** to **exit Castrop-Rauxel/Henrichenburg**

and follow the signs to 'Schiffshebewerk'. There are car parks at both shiplifts. But the most appropriate way to visit Henrichenburg is...

By water. In the season you can get a pleasure boat from Dortmund harbour (details → p. 192), and also occasionally from Duisburg and Oberhausen.

✳ Waltrop Colliery Park *(Zeche Waltrop)*

On the other side of town, to the north-east is a remarkable new park and trading estate which is a model of how the industrial past can be preserved and given a new lease of life. The Waltrop Colliery was erected at the start of the century but is now no longer a working pit although the main buildings, which have been cleaned up and renovated, still exist. One of these houses a classy mail order firm, **Manufactum**, whose goods make IKEA look like a jumble sale. Since it's open to the public (Wed – Fri: 14–20.00; Sat. 10–16.00) take your credit card and enjoy a stroll through the beautiful old building which contains a dreamy food shop – oh those cheeses! – and everything from games to clothes to garden tools and vintage kitchen equipment. Not content with mail order Manufactum have now moved into the gastronomy business with a new high quality **restaurant,** the **Manufactum Lohnhalle Gasthaus**. It's open Monday to Friday: 11-19.00 and on Saturday from 10-18.00. Tel:

Spurwerkturm

02309/608884. Another building next door houses a made-to-measure bike shop and a high class garden furniture boutique, whilst the centre of the site itself has been greened over and dotted with sculptures. Crowning them all on the nearby tip is the so-called **Spurwerkturm**, created by Jan Bormann, the artist responsible for the sun-dial on top of the Schwerin Tip in Castrop-Rauxel. The tower, conceived in 1993, is an artistic tribute to the mining industry and is constructed from wood used to guide the miners' cages as they travelled up and down the mining shafts. There's a great view from the top.
Hiberniastraße 4. 45731 Waltrop.

Bus: line 284 to Sydowstraße. It's five minute walk from here.

By car: Motorway **A2** to **exit Dortmund/Mengede** and follow the sign to Waltrop. Drive straight on for around 4½ kilometres. When you come to the Hirschkamp Stadium on your right, turn right at the main road into Berlinerstraße. There's a sign to Manufactum here, but crazily enough there is no sign two kilometres later to tell you to turn right into Sydowstraße. Hiberniasstraße is about one kilometre down Sydowstraße on the left. You can park on the site.

That brings us to the end of our tour through Recklinghausen and district. Directly adjoining the southern border of Recklinghausen you'll come to:

HERNE (pop: 170,000)

Tourist Information:
Stadtmarketing Herne GmbH,
Kirchhofstraße 5,
44623 Herne,
Tel: 02323/919050,
info@stadtmarketing-herne.de,
www.herne.de.

Although it was first mentioned in the 9th century Herne remained little more than a village until 1847 when the railways arrived. Nine years later the first pit was opened by William Mulvany. The Shamrock Pit had an English-style wooden pithead gear and was one of the most modern and productive in the area. Mulvany built a housing settlement here specially for his miners, forty of whom were British and Irish. For the next century mining dictated the economic life of the town. If you want to know more why not visit...

The Emscher Valley Museum

* The Emscher Valley Museum (*Emschertal-Museum, Schloss Strünkede*)

Situated in an early baroque moated castle, the museum has an extraordinary range of exhibitions on the area, from the ice age till the present day. Watch out for the skeleton of a giant stag. I've never seen such antlers! The cellars contain many early industrial and agricultural equipment including a reconstruction of a 19th century smithy. The first floor has some great exhibits on industrialisation and 20th century social history. There are no English texts but since **admission** is **free** give it a try, if only for the building and the surrounding park.

Open: Tue-Fri and Sundays: 10-13.00 and 14-17.00. Sat: 14-17.00. Karl-Brandt-Weg 5, 44623 Herne

Public Transport: U-Bahn U 35, Busses 205 and 343 to 'Schloß Strünkede'

Car: Motorway **A42 exit Herne-Baukau** and drive north. Look for the sign to 'Schloß Strünkede' almost immediately on your right.

* The Westphalian Archaeology Museum (*Westfälisches Landesmuseum für Archäologie*)

This ultra-modern museum has over 4,000 metres of exhibition space and gives visitors an insight into life in the region over the last 250,000 years. The permanent exhibition is conceived in the form of a huge un-

The Westphalian Archaeology Museum

derground excavation area where visitors can follow the progress of humanity from an imprint of the first footstep of the oldest-known human being through to Neil Armstrong's footprint on the moon. The exhibition uses multi-media shows and activities in preference to traditional glass cases stuffed full of broken pots and old coins. So, although there is no special children's section, there is plenty for the kids to experience and get their hands on. In the central, greened-over area there are installations in four closed tent-like cubes dealing with the existential areas of "Climate", "Time", "Communication" and "Sexuality". Everywhere there are concise texts in German and English and, as might be expected from a new building, it's ideal for wheelchair users. Afterwards you can relax in the café, next to which is the museum shop.

Open: Tue-Fri: 9-17.00 (Thur – 19.00) Sat, Sun, Public Hols: 11-18.00. Adults: 3.50 €. Children (6-17) and usual reductions: 2 €. Family ticket: 7 €. Europaplatz 1, 44623 Herne. Tel: 02323/946280.
www.landesmuseum-herne.de
archaeologiemuseum@lwl.org

Public Transport: U-Bahn line U 35 between Bochum and Herne **to Herne "ArchäologieMuseum/ Kreuzkirche".** This is by far the most convenient way to get here as the museum is right next door and there are very few places to park if you come by car. If you arrive at Herne Hbf it's quite a walk through the main shopping thoroughfare, but the way is signed by red and white striped posts. **Buses:** 303, 311, 312, 323, 333, 362, 367, alight ArchäologieMuseum/Kreuzstraße.

Car: Motorway **A42 exit Herne Baukau** or **A43 exit Herne-Eickel** and head for the centre/south. Bahnhofstraße is the main shopping thoroughfare. The museum is at the south end.

✳ Revierpark Gysenberg

Situated on the border of Bochum and Castrop-Rauxel this is a lovely old hilly, woodland park with minigolf, tennis and beach volleyball courts, bowling alleys, boat-hire, an ice-skating hall and an open-air swimming bath in the summer. The **Lago thermal baths** (♿ ♿) have indoor and outdoor heated pools, a toddler's pool, sauna and solarium facilities, mineral water baths, fitness and rest rooms, one of which has water beds! The Lago is particularly popular with kids because of the 112 metre long water chute which will keep them happy for hours on end while you're lazing in the sauna. (If you're like me, you'll get a kick out of the water chute too). This is my local. See you there.

Open: 8.00-23.00 (Sat: -24.00. Sun:-22.00). Adults: 2 hrs: 10 €, 4 hrs 11.50 €. All day: 13.50 €. Kids (4-15): 6,50. 7,50 and 9 € resp. There are two

sorts of family tickets: for one adult with two children, and two adults with two children up to the age of 15. These work out much cheaper. Get there before 10 on a weekday morning and you can have four hours for the price of two. Between 1st May and 31st August entrance is roughly half the above prices if you just want to swim (indoors and out) and laze around in the sun. Am Revierpark 40, 44627 Herne. Tel: 02323/9690. www.gysenberg.de

Bus: 321 from Castrop-Rauxel, **323** and **333** from Herne Bahnhof to 'Gysenbergpark/LAGO' or 'Gysenberghalle' (for the park).

Car: Motorway **A42 exit Herne-Bornig** or **Herne-Horsthausen** and follow the signs.

You can get a map off their internet site.

✳ Akademie Mont Cenis

Just five minutes away from the Revierpark Gysenberg in the suburb of Sodingen you can find one of the most interesting and revolutionary buildings in the region. For anyone remotely interested in architecture and renewable energy the Akademie Mont Cenis is a must. Built on the site of a disused colliery of the same name – the original pit architects were so impressed by the technology involved in building the Mont Cenis tunnel they decided to name the pit after it – the solar-heated glass structure is now a community centre and advanced training centre for senior

Akademie Mont Cenis

civil servants. It houses a local library, social centre, café/restaurant, the academy itself, and a hotel reminiscent of decks on an ocean liner, which is used by the visiting civil servants. All sorts of natural materials have been used including huge wooden beams, the buildings are surrounded by beds of rock, and a water stream running from one end to the other helps to keep the air cool and moist. The rest of the building's heating requirements are supplied by methane gas from the old tip. In the evening it's lit up by a magical circle of blue lights designed by the artist Mischa Kubal. For more on **solar power** go to nearby Gelsenkirchen: Science Park (→ p. 87).

Bus: 311 from Herne Hbf to Mont-Cenis-Platz. www.akademie-mont-cenis.de (English pages)

Herne's main night-life centre is the **Flottmannhallen** (Flottmannstr. 94). Everything from dance shows and exhibitions to cabaret, café and concerts. www.flottmann-hallen.de

There are one or two restaurants in Herne worth trying. North-west of the Gysenberg Revierpark baths is the **Forsthaus Gysenberg** (Tel: 02323/64447) which specialises in Mediterranean dishes and has a beer garden. This is especially attractive in the summer as the park is just over the road. Not far away, also in the suburb of Sodingen, there's an equally rural atmosphere at **Trattoria Ferone** at Wiescherstraße 156. (Tel: 964200) The elegant Italian restaurant has a spacious beer garden with a children's play area looking out over the fields, from where you can go for a great walk up through the woods and through the greened-over site of the former Constantin Colliery. Ideal for working up an appetite in advance or walking of the meal afterwards. Gourmets drop in at **Julius Weinrestaurant,** a bistro and wine shop which presents a range of thematic culinary evenings every month with wines to match. (Bahnhofstr. 62. Tel: 55305). Opposite the new Archaeology Museum, next to the Kreuzkirche you can eat and drink French at the **Elsässer Stube** (Tel: 10580).

The best city centre cafés are in the Behrenstraße, west of Bahnhofstraße near the Town Hall. Here you'll find the **Caféhaus** at number 4, and further along on the corner, **Nils.** Both serve hot food. Lastly, a new development in Wanne-Eickel, the hugely popular American-style, open-all-day, out-of-town **Café del Sol**, a large sunny restaurant cum bar cum beer garden, packed with music and the breathless mobile young. It's at Holsterhauserstraße 190 next to the Decathlon building. Take the Herne/Eickel exit from the A43 motorway and head for Holsterhausen. You'll see it straightaway. Right at the other end of the scale, you can banquet in style at the **Parkrestaurant** in the Park Hotel at Schaeferstraße 109. Tel: 955333.

And whilst you're in Sodingen you should take the opportunity to have a walk round the **Teutoburgia** park in the suburb of Börnig just across to the west. The nearby colliers' settlement has been given a face lift and the park redesigned to house a so-called 'sound' park. Look for wooden platforms and go and listen. Afterwards you can walk back onto the Castroper Straße 322 and take advantage of the largest portions of ice-cream I've ever seen at a very unprepossessing ice-cream parlour called **Il Gelato**. My kids were full after only two scoops. My wife, who visited it later, told me the coffee was magnificent. If you're really hungry there's a good pizza house next door.

Now let's go west to the suburb of **Wanne-Eickel,** originally two suburbs which were amalgamated into one in 1926. They were subsequently swallowed up into Herne in 1975 but the thought of having a town called Herne-Wanne-Eickel was too much even for Germans who love to stick-wordstogetherinanunendingproces-sionuntilyouvenoideawhattheymean-anymore. Anyway, if you're based in the immediate vicinity and touring the area you're very lucky because Wanne-Eickel Hbf seems to be one of those stations which has direct trains to every town in the area.

∗ **Wananas fun bath**
I was told there was a great family fun bath near Wanne-Eickel Hbf so I took along my two daughters to investigate. True! This compact bath is above all excellent for parents with toddlers as there are many pools specially designed to meet their needs, including a large pirate boat with water cannons. That said there is also a great chute for elder kids, a 'proper' swimming bath and a heated outside pool, a bistro with a terrace, and a grassy area for you to picnic and play on. To round things off nicely there's a mixed sauna and steam bath area with its own rest room, outside plunge bath and deck chairs.

Open: Daily 9-22.00. Mondays 14-22.00. Admission: starts at 2.50 € for one hour and rises to a max. of 5 € per day for under-sixteens and 6.50 € for over-sixteens. Family tickets, 10.50 € (2 hrs), 12.50 € (4 hrs) and 16.50 € (day). A sauna and swim will cost an adult 8.50 € (two hours), 9.50 (four hours) and 10.50 (all day). Am Freibad 30, 44649 Herne.
Tel: 02325/926023.
www.herne/kultur (and click on Wananas)
    Bus: 398 from Wanne-Eickel Hbf.
    Car: Motorway A42, exit Herne-Crange, turn left, then first right (traffic lights) into Berliner Straße, then second right into Am Freibad and drive almost to the end. There's a car park on the right.

Since we started our visit to Herne with a museum, let's end with one too. Pitt Hermann, the editor of the Herne "Sonntagsnachrichten" tipped me off about this one in Wanne-Eickel, which is an adjunct of the Emschertal Museum in Herne. Swallow a town, swallow its museum.

∗ **The Wanne-Eickel Museum**
(Heimat- und Naturkunde Museum Wanne-Eickel)
The museum is housed in a lovely old school building in the suburb of Crange near the Rhein-Herne canal. As you enter the grounds you are met by three figures, a railwayman, a miner and a canal boatman; figures

which signal the focus of the museum. Although these are the main themes – coal-mining is especially well covered on both floors, with detailed information on all the old collieries in Herne (including Mulvany's "Shamrock" pit) – visitors can also see a good section on old bakeries, look round granny's sitting-room, inspect cases full of old cam-

The Wanne-Eickel Museum

eras, gaze in wonder at a life-size installation of an original art deco drug store, wander through a room full of decorative stoves, inspect collections of stuffed animals and butterflies before moving on to look at the bones of ancient mammoths. Yes, this is one of those great old jumbled museums which seems to have something for everyone. The back garden is even packed with locomotives and tram cars amidst a lovingly repainted kiosk (Trinkhalle) where the workers used to get their booze at the end of the day's shift. This museum, like its partner above, is also **free** and there are also no English texts. Further down the road on the disused site of the Unser-Fritz colliery you can see the 30 meter high old Malakow tower which has been put under a preservation order.

Open: Tue-Fri and Sundays: 10-13.00 and 14-17.00. Sat: 14-17.00. Unser-Fritz-Straße 108, 44653 Herne. Tel: 02325/75255 www.herner-netz.de (and click on "Museen").

Public Transport: Bus 328 from Wanne-Eickel Hbf (every 30 mins) to 'Museum Wanne' It's a 12 minute ride.

Car: Motorway **A42 exit Herne-Wanne.** Drive north to the traffic lights at the first main crossing, Dorstener straße. Turn left, then first left immediately into Gahlen straße. This leads down to Unser-Fritz-Straße. Turn right and its about 400 metres further on.

9. 100 % Black and Yellow (and 49 % Green)
DORTMUND (pop: 591,000)

Tourist Information:
Verkehrsverein Dortmund,
Königswall 18a
44137 Dortmund.
Information in English, Italian,
Spanish, Dutch and French.
Tel: 0231/5025666.
touristinfo@dortmund.de
www.dortmund.de
(English pages and maps)

Dortmund is the largest city in the area and the sixth largest in the country. Its origins can be traced back to the time of Charlemagne. Around the 12th century a fortress was set up here at the crossing of the east-west and north-south trading routes (the so-called Hellweg). The town flourished on trade and the local cloth industry and in 1232 the citizens erected the first stone town hall in Northern Germany, which stood until 1955 when it was finally torn down as a result of extensive war damage. After the Reformation Dortmund went into steady economic decline and in 1809 the 4,000 inhabitants (cf. 7,000 in 1350) were predominantly dependent on agriculture. The industrial revolution was just around the corner, Dortmund was sitting on a gold mine and the gold was black. The beginnings were slow but after 1860 every village in the area had its own pit and workers poured in from all over Germany and abroad to cater for the ever-growing demand for coal. The arrival of the railways and the first steel mills (Hoesch) accelerated expansion even more and the population rose rapidly. Accommodation soon became scarce and housing was hurriedly thrown up by the mining companies. Within a matter of decades the individual villages had conglomerated to form what is now the city of Dortmund. Even today, travelling through the town from suburb to suburb each joined by a few green fields, you can get a clear impression of the connected-village structure of the city.

For most of the twentieth century Dortmund was the city of coal, steel and beer. Despite the fact that the last pit closed in 1985 and steel production ended in 2001 it still claims to be the largest beer producing city in Europe: rumour has it, the second largest in the world after Milwaukee. Over the last thirty years the city has undergone a massive transformation which has resulted in a large loss of jobs for working people. New employment opportunities have been mainly in middle-class areas and Dortmund has become a centre for service industries (particularly insurance), communications and logistics. The university campus contains a huge and ever-growing Technology Centre primarily involved in computer research. Even the Japanese come here for information!.

But the city's largest and best known currency earner is the local football team. Borussia Dortmund, a working-class club founded in 1909 in the Northern part of the city, is now a huge capitalist enterprise. The club were European Champions and World Team Champions in 1996 and 1997 respectively and Bundesliga champions for the sixth time in 2002. Its black and yellow colours with the initials BVB are everywhere to be seen in the city. Cynics claim the colours were chosen to match their supporters' necks and teeth, but whatever you feel about football, BVB is embedded deeply in the 'soul' of the town. If the team wins the town radiates happiness, even through the rain. And if they lose, life in Dortmund seems a little heavier. I'll never forget stepping out of the underground in the city centre one evening after a match to be accosted by two little old ladies coming out of the Opera House with the vital question: 'How did BVB get on?'

Enough of football. How are you going to get on in Dortmund? More importantly, how are you going to find your way around?

City Centre

The most convenient way to get around the city centre, which is encircled by an inner ring road, is by foot especially because all the major points of interest are well signposted. **Dortmund Hbf** is literally a cou-

Concert House

ple of minutes walk from the centre. When you come out onto the station forecourt you will see a tall building to your right beyond the car park. This is the **Harenberg City Centre**, a publishing house that stages high quality cultural events. On the other side of the inner ring road, directly opposite the station and next to the impressively modern regional library, is the **city tourist information office** (Verkehrsverein) where you can get all the latest information you want. The city centre itself has a reputation as an excellent shopping centre, not least because of its extensive pedestrian precincts. The main shopping thoroughfare from Ostenhellweg through Westenhellweg leads – as the name suggests

– from East to West. On the north side of Ostenhellweg in Bissenkamp 8-10 you'll find the elegant new **Concert House** which presents a wide range of classy concerts from classics to jazz in an acoustic paradise. The Stravinsky restaurant is open to non-concertgoers. This area used to have a rather seedy reputation, but since the concert house opened, it has become dotted with restaurants and cafés. On the south side of Ostenhellweg there's the Alte Markt (the Old Marketplace). This is the traditional heart of the city – symbolically enough there's a BVB fan shop here – with some attractive cafés and beer-houses. And if you're short of cash, Betenstraße, which directly adjoins the square, is the place

Dortmund after dark

Since the opening of the Concert House the gastronomic centre of the town has moved to the Brückstraße area where you can laze away the evening. On the west side of the centre just over the inner ring road at Humboldtstr. 4 you can find one of the most busy cocktail bars in the region. **La Cucaracha** is open 8 till late and, apart from its huge selection of cocktails, has a biergarten with over 150 tables where guests can while away the summer evening. Just two streets away there is a cosy bar/restaurant where you can literally make yourself at home. **The Liv'Inn Room** (Augustastr. 4a) is furnished with chunky armchairs and plush sofas and a roomy back area with rattan chairs and tables. The ideal place to chill out after a hectic day. There are a number of cafés and bars in the Kreuzviertel, an area much inhabited by students, the media and arts set. At Kreuzstr. 69 you'll find **Cuisina Central** a small friendly bar serving drinks and good fresh food at reasonable prices. You can sit outside if the weather's good. There are a few small cafés and bars in the vicinity of the Ostwall museum. One of the most popular, at Olpe 14, is a very relaxed bar called **Speak Easy** which also has a small outside terrace where you can sit, eat and drink on summer evenings. One of my favourite café/restaurants is **Swabedoo** in Kleine Beurhausstraße right next to the Möllerbrücke S-Bahn station. They've high-quality hot and cold food, a buzzy atmosphere, occasional live music – especially on Sunday mornings over brunch – and in summer you can sit outside. Over the road almost opposite is a disco called **Silent Sinners** (Ritterhausstr. 65). The very best **jazz** spot in the region is **Domicil,** conveniently in the middle of the city at Hansastraße 7. The club's has an international reputation – and international stars. A must if you're at all interested in contemporary jazz. Even if you're not going to a show, the bar is a great place to meet up and chill out. www.domicil-dortmund.de

The 'Nordstadt' (lit: north town) is the traditional working-class area of the city. Because the housing is cheap a lot of students and foreign workers choose to live here too. The Münsterstraße leading from the centre is its main pedestrian thoroughfare, at the end of which you'll find one of the city's two main 'art' cinemas, the **Roxy.** On the corner next door there's a small, lively bar called **Bass** where you can also get hot and cold snacks. **Sub Rosa** not only has occasional live music, the first night I was there they had a wild evening of poetry and cabaret. It's on the corner of Feldherren Straße and Gneisenau Straße, south of the harbour. **Depothek** (Immermannstraße 39) used to be a tramline depot. Now it's one of the most attractive bar/restaurants in the Nordstadt. The new owner must have gone right off the rails for his prices are as attractive as his décor.

There are quite a few discos in the town, most of which are only open Thurs to Sats. One of the largest, mainly for early teenies, is **Soundgarten** in the Lippestraße, to the east of the centre. It's huge, loud, cheap to get into and has a rough, underlit charm – i.e. the sort of place to scare the hell out middle-class parents. Being a middle-class parent myself, I felt much more at home at **Im Keller**, (Geschwister-Scholl Str. 24 just off Schwanenwall). It caters for 20 to 35 year olds and is clearly a big favourite amongst students. No wonder. It's cheap, informal, not too big, has a separate bar/snacks room, good beat music and, best of all, no techno. For 25-60 year-olds who want to dress up in style, the classiest disco in town is **Nightrooms** in the Hansastraße, almost next door to **Café Fluxus** and opposite **Panciera's** (→ City Centre). Much less formally, over 18s can rave the night away in **SIXX. PM.** Next door there's a large cocktail bar with latino music called **Mendoza.** You'll find them both in Hövel-straße just behind the municipal theatre on the site of the former Thier brewery. Most convenient of all you can park your car on the huge old lot where the brewery lorries used to line up for the booze. **Justin's** (Wittekindstraße 32), a super chic venue, caters for almost every taste with R'n'B, soul, funk, black music, classic and salsa. Not to speak of its own free underground garage with parking lots for around 500 cars.

If you're looking for live pop concerts with international mega-stars you'll find them at the **Westfalenhallen.** Dortmund has a spectacular new **Concert House** which opened in September 2002. Here you can experience top-class classical orchestras and musicians, as well as jazz, dance and popular concerts. www.konzerthaus-dortmund.de Lovers of classical music should check out the **Opera House** (Tel: 5027222). The main venue for alternative theatre and cabaret is **Fletch Bizzel** (Humboldtstr. 45. Tel: 142525) which plays occasional host to English groups. And if your German's half way good you might like to try the variety and cabaret shows at **Cabaret Queue** (Hermannstr. 74 in the suburb of Hörde, Tel: 413146).

Finally if you want to round off the evening in 50s Dolce Vita style try a cocktail at **Meyer-Lanskys** at Westfalendamm 166.

Marien church and Reinoldi church

The altar of the Reinoldi church;

for banks. From Betenstraße you'll reach the city's main square, the Friedensplatz (Peace Square) which is next to the new town hall. Continuing on the other side of the town hall across the Hansastraße you'll find the **theatre and opera house**, erected next to the **site of the old town synagogue** which was compulsorily taken over and demolished by the Nazis even before the Night of Broken Glass (November 1938). During the Second World War the centre of Dortmund was extensively de-stroyed by allied bombers. Miraculously the outer walls of the two Protestant churches on the Hellweg survived. The **Petrikirche** (Westenhellweg) contains an impressive carved altar dating from 1520 but, apart from that, the interior has all the appeal of a concrete refrigerator. The **Reinoldi** church is a much more welcoming place of refuge. Directly behind the church on the Willy-Brandt Platz and Kleppingstraße there's a good choice of cafés where you can sit and watch the city goings-on.

If you turn off the Hellweg at Hansastraße and head northwards, you come to the **Museum für Kunst und Kulturgeschichte**. (the Museum of Art and Cultural History) This is one of those grand old museums with a bit of everything for everyone. It's housed in a

City Centre Addresses

Harenberg City Centre ♿ ♿
Pick up a programme for information on their high-class music recitals, readings, cabaret, jazz and chamber concerts.
Königswall 21. 44137 Dortmund.
Reservations: Tel: 0231/9056-166.
www.harenberg-city-center.de

Museum für Kunst und Kulturgeschichte ♿ ♿ 🇬🇧
Opening times: Tue-Sun: 10-17.00 (Thurs till 20.00: on Saturdays it opens at 12.00). Adults: 3 €. Reductions: 0.75 € (except special exhibitions). **Saturdays free.**
Hansastr. 3, 44137 Dortmund.
Tel: 0231/502-5522 (German only).
www.mkk.dortmund.de

Ostwall Museum ♿
Opening times and prices are the same as for the Museum für Kunst und Kulturgeschichte above. Special exhibitions extra. **Saturdays free.**
Ostwall 7, 44122 Dortmund.
Tel: 0231/502-5741. www.museum-amostwall.dortmund.de

Steinwache ♿ ♿ 🇬🇧
Open: Tue-Sun 10-17.00.
Admission free.
Steinstr. 50, 44147 Dortmund.
Tel: 0231/502-5002.
(→ Old Synagogue, Essen p. 93)

Dortmund museums' website
www.museendortmund.de

Auslandsgesellschaft
Steinstraße 48, 44147 Dortmund.
Tel: 0231/83800-0
www.auslandsgesellschaft.de

fine *art nouveau* building and covers pre and early history, the history of Dortmund, painting and artworks from the middle ages to the end of the 19th century, religious art, life styles and living rooms both rural and urban, applied art and design in the 20th century, 19th and early 20th century entertainment in the town, and Dortmund under the Swastika. Attached to the museum but entirely independent is **Café Fluxus**, which is also a pleasant place to meet for an evening drink or a bistro meal. Just over the road at 14 Hansastraße **Panciera's** serves up the best ice-cream in town, and the coffee is as Italian as the decor. (Attenzione! If it's closed or turned into a fur shop you've come at the wrong time of year. In late autumn the Italian proprietors migrate to the south till the following Easter). The area east of Kleppingstraße is the best place for boutiques and smaller more individual stores. Keep walking east towards

Ostwallmuseum

the ring road and you'll come to the **Ostwall Museum.** Founded in 1947 the museum is well worth a visit if you're interested in 20th century paintings, sculpture and photography. It can also boast some outstanding temporary shows, like the Mirò exhibition in 1999. In 2010 it will probably be moving into the renovated Dortmund "U" building near the Harenberg City Centre.

Dortmund has traditionally been a centre of left-wing politics and has an admirable anti-Nazi history. If you want an insider tip, I can wholeheartedly recommend a remarkable exhibition on 'Resistance and Persecution in Dortmund 1933-45' in the **Steinwache**, minutes away from the Hbf (north exit) on foot. The

Steinwache was the building used by the Gestapo for holding, torturing and murdering their opponents, both religious and political. The exhibition, which is housed in the original cell-block complex gives a shudderingly vivid impression of the time. As you come out of the building you'll find yourself right next to the building of the **Auslandsgesellschaft** (Foreigners' Society) which specialises in promoting contacts between Germans and foreigners from all over the world.

Other major Dortmund attractions are all outside the immediate centre but easy enough to reach. First I shall deal with the museums, then the open-air attractions.

MUSEUMS (outside city centre)

Dortmund has two of my Top Twelve highlights in the region so I'll begin with them straightaway.

Starting nearest the centre you shouldn't miss:

✳ DASA
(The German Occupational Safety and Health Exhibition)
✪ ♨ ♨ ☺ 🇬🇧
Russian, Turkish, French

'What's in a name?' said Shakespeare. Everything, say I, when it comes to marketing. In a competition for the worst named museum in the country (world?)'The German Occupational Safety and Health Museum' would win hands down. Only an id-iot or a German civil servant could think up such an unspeakably mind-numbing title as 'Deutsche Arbeits-schutzausstellung'. Whoops! The law forbids me to claim that German civil servants are idiots so of course they can't be! Anyway, when I first heard of DASA I had depressing visions of roomfuls of helmets, gloves and ear-mufflers. At the time I was living nearby, so I thought it best to ask the locals what they thought of it. None of them had been near the place and most had never heard of it, which confirmed my worst fears. It took me two years before my natural curiosity combined with a tidy portion of masochism finally got the better of me. At the time there was no charge for entry (further cause for

DASA (the German Occupational Safety and Health Exhibition)

suspicion!) so I even took my kids along. GOSH, (now that would be a name)! To my amazement I discovered that its supremely boring title was in equal and opposite relationship to the fun to be had inside. Suddenly the reason for the name became clear. It was nothing to do with the deadly hand of Teutonic culture. Nein! A clever clique of insiders wanted to keep the place for themselves. Not any more!

DASA is a huge museum spread over several floors and split into different sections each dealing with a branch of work: the history of printing through to computers, building, transport, steel-production, textiles etc. What makes it so great is that the actual objects are there, life-size and authentic with lots of hands-on activities and experiments. You can wander through sound-tunnels or check your reactions, test your sight and hearing, do simulated racing on bicycles, get into a helicopter or an aircraft cockpit, drive around with a fork truck (simulated) and even go for a ride in a steel wagon. Ask at the info desk for foreign language route plans and guides. Or borrow the mobile headphones for an English commentary as you walk around.

Open: Tue-Sat: 9-17.00. Sundays: 10-17.00. Adults: 3 €, students and children: 2 €. Family ticket: 6 €. Friedrich-Henkel-Weg 1-25. 44149 Dortmund. Tel: 0231/9071-645. www.dasa-dortmund.de (English and French pages).

Public transport: S1 train from the **Hbf.** It's just two stops to **Dortmund-Dorstfeld Süd,** which is in tariff stage Dortmund Centre/West. If you're coming to Dortmund on the S1 from Bochum and other towns to the West, this station is <u>before</u> you reach the Hbf! ♿ beware! There's no lift here.

By car: A40 motorway to 'DO-Dorstfeld/ Universität' between Dortmund and Bochum, and follow the signs through the University campus to the DASA car park (free).

✳ **Zollern II/IV colliery** ⚒
  (Zeche Zollern II/IV)
  ✪ ♿ ☺ 🇬🇧 ERIH

I have to admit I've a vested interest in this one as my wife was responsible for devising the permanent exhibition here. Not withstanding that I'd recommend a visit whole-heartedly as this will confound all your ideas of what a colliery should look like. The mine is now the headquarters of the Westphalian Industrial Museum

(WIM), a complex of eight on-site museums to be found scattered all over the region. The Zollern II/IV colliery was built at the turn of the century for a work-force of around 2,000. It is situated in a small road on the outskirts of the city called 'Pit way' (*Grubenweg*), which conjures up visions of crumbling walls, grit-filled air and grimy shirt collars. Not at all. This extraordinary and, yes, beautiful coal mine is a jewel of industrial architecture. As you wander through the leafy groves of trees amidst red-brick neo-gothic buildings topped with Russian-type onion towers you might be forgiven for imagining this was once the grounds of a university rather than a coal mine. The original owners, the Gelsenkirchen Mining Company (GBAG), were the largest and most wealthy mining company in the region, so when it came to putting up this mine (Zollern I/III was a few kilometres up the road: the numbers refer to the shafts) no expense was spared. The company's aim was to build a colliery which would not only serve its industrial purposes but have an aesthetic dimension. This was primarily art for prestige – 'Let's show the competition once and for all who's top dog in the area!' – for working conditions underground were no better than anywhere else.

The most remarkable building on the site is the engine house whose architecture contrasts strongly with the prevailing style in the entrance

Zollern II/IV colliery

Zollern II/IV colliery – an overview

(The buildings in grey no longer exist. They include cooling towers, chimneys, a benzene factory, coal washing and coking plants, and a second boiler room. The original pithead shafts were also demolished but have been replaced by two similar shafts)

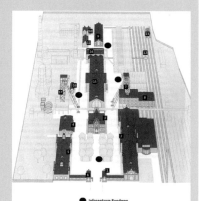

Infozentrum Rundweg

1. Tag checker's office
2. Wages Hall, Warehouse, Washroom, Lamp room.
3. Administration building
4. Stables and coach house
5. Workshops
6. First-aid room
7. Pithead shaft (shaft II)
8. Shaft and sorting house
9. Ammonia Factory
10. Pump and Engine room
11. Coking workshop

12. Colliery station
13. Engine shed
14. Boiler house I
15. Engine House
16. Toilet house
17. Pithead shaft IV (ventilation)

Information centre. Circular walk.

area. Its design was inspired by an iron-trelliswork pavilion from the Good Hope Mill in Oberhausen which had aroused much praise in the 1902 Trade and Industry Exhibition in Düsseldorf. The GBAG had originally planned to build its engine house in Gothic style, but at once abandoned these plans in favour of a similar, liberally glazed, building. As an additional flourish the architect Bruno Möhring added a elegant oval *art nouveau* portal adorned with stained glass windows, oriented on the highly modern entrances of the 'Métro' in Paris. Although the original canopy no longer exists (there are plans to reconstruct it), the stained-glass doorway has become one of the icons of the Ruhr area and was even immortalised on an 80 pfennig postage stamp.

The modernity of the architecture reflected the technical equipment inside the engine house, for the pit was one of the first to exploit the modern energy source, electricity. Two huge electrically-driven winding machines were put into operation to power the transportation of men, material and coal to and from the surface. In the middle of the building electrically-driven compressors produced the air which was necessary to operate the pneumatic picks, drills, engines and lights underground. Between the compressors and the winding machines were two large transformers, and the whole area was controlled from a raised podium in the middle.

The pit closed down in 1966, a victim of the structural crisis which was to continue in the region for the rest of the century. In those days the idea of industrial heritage was practically unheard of and the site was scheduled for total demolition. Thankfully, due to a hard-fought campaign by local inhabitants and industrial preservation enthusiasts, it was saved and subsequently taken over by the regional government who decided to turn it into a museum. And no wonder! The engine house is a palace of electric power (all the levers on the white-marbled wall put me in mind of Charlie Chaplin's 'Modern Times'). The wages house with its tiled floor and walls and carved wooden ceiling looks more like a public school dining hall. Add to this the floral wrought-iron staircase in the administration building, the huge pithead baths, the unloading area and the sorting belt

at the top of the pit head tower and you'll begin to see why I'm so enthusiastic. In one of the cellars there's a long mock-up pit for your kids to crawl around in, and with a bit of luck they might even get a ride on 'Anna', an old steam locomotive.

art nouveau **portal**

But the museum is not primarily about machines and technology. It aims to highlight the miners themselves, their families, working-conditions and culture. The exhibition units deal with leisure, training, health and hygiene, lamps and lighting, hazards, safety and accident prevention. Texts are kept to a minimum and emphasis placed on films, videos, sensory experiences and hands-on activities. (Don't miss the film on underground explosions if you want to get an idea of the horrific risks involved). To top it all there's a short comprehensive guide in English. You should plan for a two hour visit and whilst there take the opportunity to buy an English catalogue or pick up a general English-language leaflet

Westfalian industrial museum

giving you details of this and all the other on-site museums belonging to WIM, including the **Henrichenburg Shiplift** (→ ch. 8 Waltrop), the **Hannover Colliery,** the **Nightingale Colliery,** and the **Henrichshütte Steel Works** (→ ch: 7 Bochum, Witten and Hattingen resp.).

Because of the nature of the site wheelchair visitors will not be able to visit one or two areas (e.g. the pithead tower rooms) but general facilities are good, including excellent toilets and lifts. Unfortunately, contrary to the information I received from the site director, I failed to find any wheel-chair toilets next to the café, so after 18.00 you're stuck.

Open: Tue-Sun: 10.00-18.00 Adults: 3.50 €. Children and students: 2 €. Under 6: free. Family ticket: 8 €. Free guided tours in German 11.30 Sundays. **English and French tours** by arrangement. Grubenweg 5, 44388 Dortmund, Tel: 0231/6961-111. Fax: -114. www.zeche-zollern.de

Public transport: The station you're looking for is **Dortmund-Bövinghausen**, which is in tariff area "Dortmund Centre/West". The train you want is line **RB43 from Dortmund Hbf** (destination Wanne-Eickel/Dorsten). There is only one train an hour (on the half hour at the time of writing) from the **Hbf**. So check departure times before you start or you might have an unpleasantly long wait. Having said that, the 20 minute ride gives you a good idea of Dortmund and its past. As you travel out of the Hbf there's a huge disused steel factory on one side, and on the other side, with the canal harbour in the distance, miles of rusty railways sidings with wagons that don't seem to have been moved for the last fifty years. A little further on you chug past the green countryside on the edge of the Wischlingen Leisure Park. (see below) From here on the ever-changing vistas from town to countryside give

The engine house

you a good idea of the 'multi-village' nature of the city. Shortly before you arrive – 25 minutes from the Hbf – the train passes through idyllic woodland only to halt at a weed-stricken, deserted station which has clearly seen better days. It's difficult to conceive now but the Böving-hausen station was once the largest goods station in the city, with trains from nearby mines unloading their coal on the many sidings for delivery all over the country. Leave the station in the direction of the train (i.e. away from Dortmund). As you come out onto the road, turn diagonally right into a small housing settlement which was formerly reserved for mineworkers. Follow the road through the settlement and it's a pleasant five minute's walk until you arrive at the gate.

If you're **wheel-chair bound or starting** your journey **from the Eastern side of Dortmund,** take the **U47** which goes via the Hbf **to Huckarde Bushof**, and then the **462 bus**.(see below).

If you're travelling **from Duis-burg, Oberhausen, Gelsenkirchen Hbf,** take the **RE3 to Wanne-Eickel** and **change** onto the **RB43** in the direction of Dortmund Hbf. Alight **Dortmund-Bövinghausen.** From **Recklinghausen S2, change** at **Herne RB43 ditto.**

Bus: Route no. **462** runs every 20 minutes (weekends 30 mins) be-tween **Do-Huckarde Bushof** (U47 connection) and **Do-Marten Süd**

(S4 connection*)*. Either way, alight **Industriemuseum Zollern.** If you're travelling back into Dortmund and want to see a bit of the northern suburbs take the 462 to the Huckarde Bushof terminus. You're off the bus and onto the station platform in five steps. From here the U47 will take you back into town – and further on to the east of Dortmund.

Why am I telling you all this when it's far more convenient…

By car: Take the **A40 motorway to exit 'Dortmund-Lütgendortmund'**. Follow the signs to the museum in the direction of Castrop-Rauxel, ca. 2 km.

✳ The Hansa Coking Plant 🔳
(Kokerei Hansa) ERIH

The plant went into production in 1928 as part of an integrated system with the nearby colliery and the Dortmund Union Steelworks. It took coal from the colliery, transformed it into coke by heating it at high temperatures in hermetically sealed

The Hansa Coking Plant

The Hansa Coking Plant

chambers, and delivered the finished product to the steel mill. (Because of its higher carbon content, coke is a better fuel for industrial purposes than coal). The colliery ceased production in 1980 and the coking plant followed in 1992. As I wandered round the site, over iron galleries and through blackened halls I was struck by the eerie stillness – broken only by an occasional bird-cry – in what had once been a deafening and scorching environment. Within a few years nature has taken its revenge and there is an amazing amount of plants and exotic bushes growing wild between railway lines and out of the brickworks. Nonetheless the ghosts of bygone labour refuse to be extinguished.

Open: The Information Point is open from April to October: Tuesdays-Sundays: 10–18.00. And from November to March: Tuesdays to Fridays, 10–16.00. Saturdays: 13.30–16.30. Sundays and public holidays: 10.30–16.30. Parts of the site can be visited individually with audio guides in English, Dutch and French. If you want to visit the whole site you can only do this with a guided tour. See "Führungen/Preise" on the website. Emscherallee 11, 44369 Dortmund. www.industriedenkmal-stiftung.de For current information, ring: 0231/93112233. (→ Zollverein Coking Plant p. 101)

U-Bahn: Line **47 from Hbf** in the direction of Westerfilde, **alight 'Parsevalstraße'**. (5 mins. walk).

Car: Motorway **A2 exit Dortmund-Mengede**. The plant is in the suburb of Huckarde. Or **A45**, exit "Dortmund Hafen", head towards Huckarde and follow the "Industriekultur" signs.

✳ **Natural History Museum**
(Museum für Naturkunde)
ㅎ ㅎ

My kids loved this when they were younger. It contains a large aquarium and two gigantic life-size mammoths. At the other end of the scale there are plenty of fossils, insects and creepycrawlies to keep them happy.

Open: Tue-Sun: 10-17.00. Adults: 3 €, Children (7-16), students, handicapped: 1.50 €. Family tickets: 4 (with 1 adult) and 7 € (with 2 Adults). **Saturdays free**. Münsterstr. 271. 44145 Dortmund. Tel: 0231/5024856.

Public Transport: from Hbf, U45 (direction Fredenbaum) or U49 (direction Brechten or Brambauer) to "Fredenbaum"

Afterwards you can take the kids over the road to the **Fredenbaumpark** where they can play inside one of the largest wigwams in the world. The **giant tipi** is 35 metres high and was brought in from the Expo world exhibition in Hanover in 2000. Here they can ascend to dizzy heights and climb around rope ladders and bridges to their heart's desire whilst you wander over to the lake and hire a rowing-boat for an hour. All things being unequal, you can pick them up again in the city hospital which is conveniently just a few yards away. You can find it on the Eastern edge of the park at Lindenhorsterstraße 6. For current information on opening times try: www.bigtipi.dortmund.de.
Which leads us seamlessly into...

Natural History Museum

OUTDOOR ATTRACTIONS:

* **Westfalen Park**
      ♿ ☺

If you're staying in Dortmund this is a sunny day must for the whole family. The park has a wonderful selection of flowers and bushes, especially the rose garden and there's plenty to keep the kids happy too. As you wander through the park there are spinning wheels, games and crazy mirrors hidden along the way, not to mention sandpits, an adventure playground, a lake and other ponds for them to fall into. Two of the exhibition rooms have been put together by Greenpeace. In the summer the park presents special activities at weekends, open air theatre shows and evening concerts. To make things more pleasant, the park has an internal railway, an overhead cable-car system, restaurants, cafés and the Florian tower

Westfalen Park and Florian tower

Westfalenhalle

with good views of the city. Florians Turm restaurant is well worth a visit if you're looking for a really good meal: 0231/138 4975.

Open: Daily 10-18.00 (longer with evening events). Admission: March-October: 2 €, one parent and kids, 4 €, two parents and kids 6 €. A trip to the top of the Florian tower costs 1.70 (Families: 3.40 €, or 5.10 €). Nov-Feb: cheaper. The Florian tower is inaccessible to wheelchair visitors.

U-Bahn: U45 or U49 to 'Westfalenpark'.

The park forms a threesome with the nearby **Westfalenhallen,** (www.westfalenhallen.de) which stages trade fairs, mammoth rock concerts and indoor sports events, and the **Westfalenstadion,** the impressive home of BVB 09, **Borussia Dortmund** (→ ch.11)

U45, U46 to **Westfalenhallen,** resp. **Westfalenstadion**.

A little to the south of the Westfalen Park on the B54 road you'll find the...

✳ **Romberg Park Botanical Gardens**

Do I feel at home here because of it's very English feeling? Who cares! A stroll through the park is always a great pleasure because of the huge variety of plants, flowers and theme gardens. And after the kids have found their way out of the maze of paths you'll end up right next to:

189

✳ Dortmund Zoo *(Tierpark)*
♿ ♿

The zoo is very pleasantly laid out on different levels. Here you can find more than 350 different types of animals from giraffes, kangaroos and big game all the way down to baby goats in the cuddly corner.

Open: March-Oct: 9-18.30. Nov-Feb: 9-16.30. Adults: 6 €. Children 6-17: 3 €. Under 6: free. One adult + kids: 8.50 €. Two adults + kids: 14.50 €. www.zoo.dortmund.de

U-Bahn: U49 to the terminus at **Hacheney** (then ten mins. walk).

Car: Take the B54 road south, exit Wellinghofen/Tierpark and head towards Hombruch/Tierpark.

✳ Hohensyburg

This is where Charlemagne set up house a few centuries ago. Given the view I can understand why. It's high up on a steep wooded cliff overlooking the Ruhr valley, and from the terrace by the Kaiser Wilhelm memorial you can see right into the distant Sauerland. But Hohensyburg isn't only for nature lovers. On the edge of the parkland is the **Spielbank**, a publicly owned gambling casino whose profits help to fill the city of Dortmund coffers. Here you can lose your pocket money on one of the 294 one-arm bandits or your life savings at the roulette table, happy in the knowledge that it's all for the public

The Kaiser Wilhelm memorial at Hohensyburg

Revierpark Wischlingen

good. There's a dress code in force for the roulette room and you have to show an ID. www.westspiel.de/content/de/hohensyburg

Bus 444 from the bus station (ZOB) opposite the **Hbf** to terminus **Syburg Spielbank** (Once an hour, pm-23.00 only).

Car: B54 southwards from the town centre. Or **A45 exit Dortmund-Süd** and head south.

✳ **Revierpark Wischlingen**
  ♿ ♿

This park has everything from boating and tennis courts, to adventure playgrounds and an ice-skating arena. The attractively laid-out **Solebad** has a mineral water pool and indoor and outdoor swimming facilities. There are a number of different sauna baths offering different varie-

ties of heat and dryness inside and out. The sauna gardens have recently been extended and modernised with a new swimming pool containing a waterfall, a large Finnish log cabin sauna (Phew!), a log house where you can lie back and relax, and a so-called polar cellar where you can rub yourself down with ice chips. It sounds like torture but I loved it. (→ ch. 11)

Baths open: 8-22.00. Fri-Sat: -24.00. Adults – baths and sauna: Day ticket 13 €; 3 hours, 11 €; 90 minutes 7 €. Get there on Mon-Fri before 11.00 and four hours cost 11 € (but not on bank holidays). If you only want to swim, prices start at 5 € for two hours. There are family tickets in both categories. Höfkerstr. 12. 44149 Dortmund. Tel: 0231/91707140. www.wischlingen.de

Eating out in Dortmund

After a heavy day's sight-seeing you might want to do nothing else but treat yourself to a classy meal. Dortmund has a variety of good quality international restaurants. I've eaten well at **Zum Treppchen** (Tel: 9414140), a lovely half-timbered building which claims to be the oldest restaurant in the city. It's in Faßstraße 21 in the suburb of Hörde (www.zum-treppchen.de). Nearer the centre, in the Gartenstadt, there's a stylish villa in the Lübkestraße 21, on the first floor of which you'll find **La Cuisine d'Art Manger.** It's now made the Michelin guide! So be prepared to pay a little more than the average for food which is way above average (www.artmanger.com Tel: 5316198). If you're looking for good Thai food, try **Tham Nag Thai** at Hoher Straße 13, near the Concert House. (Tel: 144484). For a taste of North Africa go to **Mosaique** at Vinckeplatz 1 in the Kreuzviertel.

This beautifully decorated North African style restaurant offers a real mosaic of classics from couscous, to lamb to rabbit in olive sauce. Evenings only. Closed Tuesdays. (Tel: 122336). If you're looking for a top Italian restaurant **Incontro** should fit the bill perfectly. It's in the centre at Kleppingstraße 22 (Tel: 5330200). The setting is elegant and the prices incredibly reasonable. The ideal place for vegetarians is **Vegetaria**, a gourmet restaurant at Heiliger Weg 60 (Tel: 1388288), which will certainly satisfy any or all of your organic leanings. Lastly, if you're looking for excellent Portuguese food in a no frills ambience at knock-down prices you must try **Tizé.** Everything's authentic right down to the tv blaring out Portuguese football matches in the bar. It's in the Nordstadt at Altonaerstr.2. As might be expected, no credit cards here. (Tel: 7281628)

Public Transport: S-Bahn line 2 from Hbf to Do-Wischlingen. Buses 447 and 465 to 'Revierpark Wischlingen'.

Car: Head for the suburb of Dorstfeld. The 'Revierpark' is generally well signed.

Before we leave Dortmund I must recommend you the ...

✳ **Boat trips**

A cruise along the Dortmund-Ems canal is the most attractive way to visit the **Ship-Lift in Henrichenburg**. (→ ch. 8 Waltrop) The round trip, including 90 mins on land, is 4 ½ hrs. For times consult the tourist information office. Take the **U45 to Hafen** (the harbour). The boarding stage is directly opposite the station.

10. Egyptians, an Elephant and a Brewery with no Beer

HAMM and the district of UNNA

HAMM (pop: 190,000)

Tourist Information:
Verkehrsverein Hamm,
Willy-Brandt-Platz,
59065 Hamm.
Tel: 02381/23400
Fax: 28348.
www.hamm.de/touristik

The town of Hamm was founded in 1226 at the intersection of several trading routes on the River Lippe. In the course of its history it made itself a reputation for cloth-making, metal working and brewing. Around the end of the 19th century its economy was given a fresh boost by coal mining and the wire industry. Nowadays there are few signs of its industrial past and the city has more of a rural feel. It has turned its face towards ecological projects, is a popular health resort and offers excellent facilities for cyclists and water-sport enthusiasts. The city is right on the extreme eastern edge of the Ruhr area and as such is just outside the VRR transport network. To avoid unnecessary expense on the national railway network, do as the locals do: i.e. drive to

The glass elephant

Kamen, park there, buy a VRR Tages-ticket and start your travels through the Ruhr from here. But first of all there are a couple of things in town you have to take a look at.

✳ Maximilian Park 🗺
✪ ♿ ♿

This is the site of probably the least successful pit in the history of min-ing. The Maximilian Pit started production in 1907 and closed within a year because of shaft-flooding and a gas accident. Four years later it was ready to try again but more water, followed by the outbreak of war, put a merciful end to its misery. The city fathers took it over in 1979 and have turned it into one of the most attractive parks in the whole region. It has playgrounds, picnic areas, a lakeside café from which you can watch your children falling in the water from a wooden pirate ship, not forgetting a railway siding with life-size locomotives, a peaceful nature trail and an indoor tropical butterfly garden where you can stroll amongst a myriad of free-flying exotic butterflies. The old pit buildings are now used for cultural exhibitions and events, and the coal-wash house has been turned into the largest glass elephant in the world. So if you've ever dreamt of riding up an elephant and walking around inside it's head, take the lift to the top! No entry for dogs unless accompanying blind persons.

Open: April-Sept: 9-19.00. Oct-March: 10-17.00. Adults: 3.50 €. Children (4-17): 2 €. Family ticket: 9 €. Butterfly House: Adults: 2.50 €. Children 1.50 €. Family: 5.50 €. Alter Grenzweg 2, 59071 Hamm. Tel: 02381/98210-0. www.maximilianpark.de (English pages)

Buses: 1, 3, 6 or 33 from the railway station (Neue Bahnhofstraße) to 'Maximilianpark'.

Maximilianpark

There's a pub/bistro in the Maximilian Park which is open from 11-18.00 from April to the end of October. (Tel: 02381/487400) www.maxi-gastro.de. The park also stages music and cabaret programmes in the evening.

Car: Motorway **A2** to **exit Hamm or Hamm-Uentrop** and follow the signs.

✳ Gustav Lübcke Museum
    ♿ ♿

This elegant modern building houses a large section on local history, Greek and Roman crafts, and European crafts and applied art from the middle ages to the present day. Not content with that it boasts the largest Ancient Egypt collection in the region with two authentic open coffins ('Has anyone seen my mummy?') and many other works of wood, china, bronze and stone. In the library there's a major collection of coins. The new hands-on children's museum has continually changing exhibitions. Worth a visit.

Open: Tue-Sun: 10-18.00. Adults: 2.50 €. Reductions 1.30 €. Under sixes: free. Family ticket 5.50 €. **First Sunday in the month free**. Neue Bahnhofstraße 9: 59065 Hamm. Tel: 02381/175701. www.hamm.de/gustav-luebcke-museum

It's **opposite the Hbf.** Need I say more?

Gustav-Lübcke-Museum

By car: Motorway **A2 exit Hamm**, head for the centre and follow the signs. When you see the Hbf turn right and it's on your right. There's no museum car park.

✳ The Ecology Centre
(Öko-Zentrum NRW)

If you want a look at an alternative future take a trip up to the site of a disused coal mine on the northern edge of town. The centre for biologi-

The Ecology Centre

cal and ecological planning and building is situated in a half-timbered house, itself rebuilt according to ecological principles. Here you can get information and advice on all aspects of ecological planning. It's also a congress and exhibition centre and stages occasional concerts.

Open: 8-16.00. Sachsenweg 8. 59073 Hamm (suburb of Heesen). Tel: 02381/30220-0. www.oekozentrum-nrw.de

By car: Head north on the Münsterstraße from the centre (B61). It's signed.

✳ Sri Kamadchi Ampal Hindu Temple

This remarkable new building is the largest Hindu temple in the whole of Europe. The portal is 17 metres high and the richly decorated temple 27 by 27 metres. Visitors are very welcome provided they respect the Hindu traditions by removing their shoes (you can leave them in a ante-chamber), not bringing meat or alcohol into the temple and generally behaving quietly. It is open from 8.00-14.00 and 17.00-20.00, and there are daily services at 8.00, 12.00 and 18.00. The name means "the Goddess with the eyes of love".

Address: Siegenbeckstraße 4/5, 59071 Hamm-Uentrop. Tel: 02388/30222-3. Fax: 02388/30222-4. www.kamadchi-ampal.de

Car: Motorway **A2 exit Herne-Uentrop.**

LÜNEN (pop: 92,000)

Info:
Stadtmarketing,
Willy-Brandt-Platz 1,
44532 Lünen.
Tel: 02306/104-1577.
www.luenen.de

Lünen is the largest town in the district of Unna and is situated on the River Lippe on the southern borders of Münsterland. It's one of those towns you tend to drive past on the ring round without stopping. But if you go into the middle you'll discover a rather pleasant old town, criss-crossed by bicycle paths and signposts in all directions. The town centre area contains the protestant **St George's Church** which dates back to 1366. Its altar, showing scenes from the life of Christ, dates back to 1470. Unfortunately the morning I was there it was locked. If you cross

The old town of Lünen

Colani tower

the road and walk into the Roggen-markt (Rye Market) this will lead you into the **Mauerstraße area** which has some very old alleys with half-timbered houses dating back to the 17th century.

Fans of industrial history should head south on the Bebelstraße. On the right hand side you'll come to an old miners' settlement, the Kanal Colony, with an arched entrance adorned by a sculpted relief of miners. For some reason the locals refer to the settlement as the 'negro village on the canal', probably because the miner's looked so black. At any rate it's worth a short drive around the little streets to get an idea of community life and atmosphere. Proceed further down the Bebelstraße and over the canal and you'll see a sign to **Ziethenstraße**, one of the historical settlements on the Industrial Heritage Trail. This really is an eye-opener as it seems to have been preserved in its original state – lots and lots of little brown houses, all in the same pattern and each individualised by its owner. To be honest, I didn't find them particularly beautiful but they really give you a feel for the history of the town and are a million times better than any modern replacement might have been. Now if you go all the way down the Bebelstraße, past the Preußen Bahnhof (bike hire facilities here) and turn left and left again under the railway line you'll be in Preußenstraße which will lead you to the **Seepark** (Lakeside Park). This was the site of a regional garden show a few years ago, and is a popular destination for day-trippers, especially in summer. Amongst its attractions are Lake Horstmar where you can swim, or sunbathe on a long expanse of sand. The nearby kiosk offers snacks and drinks. There are also three separate play areas for the children and, at the far end of the park, a 'Pyramid' on top of a greened-off industrial tip with relics of a former brick-making factory.

Lünen is indelibly inscribed in my memory for this is where I indulged in very first **gliding** adventure. If you want a special holiday experience go to the Lünen Segelflugplatz (gliding airport) on the Moltkestraße and ask for one of the pilots for a ride. Half an hour or so will cost you around 25 €. From the air you'll see a strange round UFO perched on top of an old colliery pithead gear. This is the so-called Colani tower in the technology park. Colani is an Italian designer who specialises in curves and he decided to redesign the pithead gear with this eye-catching result. If you want to see it close-up drive to the south-west suburb of Brambauer. Here there is also a small **miner's house museum** (Bergarbeiterwohnmuseum) at number 10 Rudolfstraße. It's open on Tuesdays (15-17.00), Thursdays (17-19.00) and Sundays (15-17.00) or by arrangement. Tel: 0231/876502.

SELM (pop:26,000)

Tourist Information:
Stadt Selm, Stadtverwaltung,
Adenauerplatz 2,
59379 Selm.
Tel: 02592/690.
www.stadtselm.de

Selm, which was first mentioned in 858 AD, is a small town on the north-west edge of the district of Unna. The area is a favourite place for day-trippers who want to get out into the countryside. This applies particularly to the oldest part of the town, Cappenberg. Here you'll find:

∗ **Cappenberg Castle**
 (Schloss Cappenberg)
This was originally built in 1122 as an abbey. The present-day castle, erected between 1696 and 1739, has three wings, is furnished in baroque style and open to visitors. Since 1983 a part of the castle has been set aside for exhibitions and occasional theatre performances. The nearby Church of St. John the Evangelist (1149) contains a golden portrait of the head of the Emperor Barbarossa. The adjoining castle park was designed in an English style, has a zoo, playground and a café. Cappenberg is well signed on the road to Selm.

UNNA (pop: 66,000)

Tourist Information:
i-Punkt Unna,
Rathausplatz 1,
59423 Unna.
Tel: 02303/1030.
English information. www.unna.de

Unna is an attractive little town which was first mentioned in 1032. It was once an important stopping point on the Hellweg trading route being especially noted for salt and beer. As you come out of the station the information office is on your left. Here you can get a leaflet ("*Historischer Rundgang*") showing you the most interesting walking route around the town which will take you past a myriad of half-timbered

Unna town centre

houses and the oldest church in town which dates back to the 14th century. At Massener Straße 31, near the cinema, you'll find...

✳ The Linden Brewery ⬛ (*Lindenbrauerei*)

This is not, I repeat NOT, a brewing museum. The building used to belong to a brewery but has now been converted into an arts centre featuring dancing, discos, cabaret and concerts. At night the old brewery chimney is lit from bottom to top with the Fibonacci sequence of numbers by the Italian artist Mario Merz, heralding the **International Centre for Light Art** within. Here visitors can walk round beneath the vaulted ceilings of the disused cellars and view a unique, permanent exhibition of lighting installations by international artists. I was particularly impressed by "space-speed-speech", a shooting-stars-in-the-cosmos installation by Mischa Kubal (he's also responsible for the lighting round the Mont-Cenis building in Herne), a weird pink, walkabout room by James Turrell and various aspects of light design in a room by Johannes Dinnebier. The exhibition can only be visited at fixed times in the company of a guide who will also tell you a lot about the old brewery on the 45 minute tour.

Open: It is only possible to visit the light exhibition on a guided tour. Tues-Friday: tours at 14.30, 15.30 and 17.00. Additionally Thursdays at

The Linden Brewery

By car: A1 motorway to **'Unna-Zentrum'**, then the B1 to Unna centre and follow the "Route Industriekultur" signs.

BERGKAMEN (pop: 53,000)

Tourist Information:
www.bergkamen.de

18.30. Sat and Sun: 14.00, 15,00, 16.00 and 17.00. Adults: 5 €. Reductions 3 €. Tel: 02303/103770. www.lichtkunst-unna.de (English pages)

Public transport: Unless its really wet I'd advise you to take a 15 minute walk through the town from the **Hbf.** Otherwise take either **bus C1 or C149** to Lindenbrauerei.

The Lindenbrauerei is the hub of the town's night-life. It houses an alternative arts centre, a bar (open from 19.00) and a restaurant. This is the place to go for discos and live music. www.lindenbrauerei.de On the corner next door I ate in a truly mouth-watering **vegetarian restaurant** called "Himmel und Erde". It's open middays (Monday to Friday) from 12-15.00 and evenings (Tuesday to Sunday) from 18.00. In the same block there's a Greek restaurant and the San Remo Italian ice-cream parlour, and over the road a pizza house so there's no excuse for starving.

Bergkamen is one of those unprepossessing towns you drive past on your way into the heart of the Ruhrgebiet. It must have something, I thought, because the Romans set up the largest camp in Germany here around 11 BC. The site is now one of the most important archaeological sites in the region. The town itself is not a prime address for tourists but it does have four interesting attractions. As might be expected part of **the town museum** is devoted to its Roman history. If you want to know more about the modern history of the town you can go upstairs where, in one of the rooms you'll find a great life-size replica of an old grocery store. Entrance is free and the address is Jahnstr. 31 (near the original Roman camp) in the suburb of Oberaden. Further north you can hit the heights with a walk to the top of the **Halde Großes Holz** (Large Wood Tip). This panorama point on the Industrial Heritage Trail was once the dumping site for all the dead coal dug out of the nearby "Monopol" and "Haus Aden" collieries, but the name recalls the fact that there used to be a large forest of beech trees here. The climb will take you to a height of 90 metres from which you can gaze over the canal to the north and, with a bit of luck, see as far as Dortmund and Unna.

Lastly, in the suburb of Rünthe on the Datteln-Hamm canal boat-lovers will find **a large modern marina,** at one end of which is a restaurant and beer garden. Here you can sit in the sun and watch the activities on the water or the cyclists riding along the opposite bank of the canal. Budding witches might like to know that the **Beversee nature reserve** – almost next door – is supposed to be packed with frogs, toads and other slimy creatures.

Marina Rünthe, Bergkamen

KAMEN (pop: 48,000)

Tourist Information:
www.kamen.de

Kamen is sited almost bang in the middle of the district of Unna and its name derives from an ancient Germanic tribe called the "Charmanen" who were evidently hanging around here in the Stone Age waiting for someone to dig a coal mine. No really! They were called "Charmanen" because this is ancient German for charcoal men.

Anyway a few million years later a local inhabitant with nothing better to do found a lump of black rock in the earth and the place was transformed entirely. Present-day tourists who want to go back into history should drive out to the village of Methler where the Church of St. Margaret (**St-Margarethen-Kirche**) dates back to the 13th century. The town centre has some charming old buildings and it's especially worth taking a look inside the reception office of the Adult Education centre (Volkhochschule) at Am Geist number 1. The building used to be the town apothecary and when you walk into the office you could be forgiven for thinking you've wandered into the apothecary itself for nothing seems to have changed a whit. If you want a good meal at a reasonable price I suggest you try a pleasant old pub/restaurant called **Kümpers** at Bahnhofstr. 1, almost next to the town hall.

201

11. Fun And Games
THE PLEASURES OF LEISURE

The Ruhr area is extraordinarily green and wherever you are you'll find more than enough parks and woodland to relax in. I have listed some of the most interesting in the individual towns and will not repeat them here. I would, however, like to draw your attention to one outstanding leisure feature which I have yet to experience in any other area of the world: the **Revier park**. In the first chapter of the book I told you that 'Revier' was Ruhr slang for 'local patch'. **The Revier parks** (of which there are seven) are scattered around in various local patches throughout the area. Each is publicly owned and

managed and has its own particular features; but what they all offer is a combination of parkland, woods and lakes, with facilities for **cycling, Boating, swimming, skateboarding, ice-skating** or whatever takes your fancy. The diagram below will give you a rough idea of where they are, and you can find more information at the end of the chapter.

The parks themselves are open to everyone free of charge, and you can wander at will, picnic, kick a football around, fly a kite or simply lie on the grass and read that thriller you've been saving for your holiday. But you will, of course, have to pay to use

sporting facilities like swimming baths, tennis courts and the like. Great, you might say, if the weather's fine. But even better if the weather's bad, or if you're at a loss to know where to take the kids. For each park has one particular feature which will make an unforgettable family day-out, even – and especially – in the worst of weather: **the Revier baths**. Before you say you're not interested in swimming, read on. For Revier baths consist of more than just a boring swimming pool. They are huge, modern, admirably clean, leisure complexes which comprise indoor and outdoor heated pools, sauna baths, solariums, salt baths with underwater massage springs to soak away your aches and pains, Roman steam baths, wave baths, sun-lamp areas where you can snooze on

deck-chairs, rest rooms with water beds, fitness rooms, inhalation cabins to clear your head, as well as cafés and restaurants (indoors and out) whose terraces are lined with deck chairs. Some even have water chutes for the kids, and special pools for non-swimmers and toddlers. Whenever I'm feeling utterly exhausted, I head for the nearest Revier bath. And after four hours (you'll need at least four to really feel the benefit) I'm beginning to feel refreshed and ready once more to meet the stresses of everyday life. So if it's wet or you want a break from walking round all the museums I've recommended, pile the kids in the car and go for the day. I deliberately say 'car', because most of the Revier parks are on the edge of town and you might have a lot to carry. Whatever the case I can assure you now that after one visit to a Revier bath you'll be wondering why you haven't got anything remotely as wonderful back home. As an English friend of mine said to me one January, as the snow drifted down from a slate-filled sky to dissolve in the steam rising from the heated outside pool in which we were swimming: "Germany might have lost the war, but this is enough to convince me they won the peace."

So what should you take with you in order to make the most of your visit? A bathing costume of course (two if you want to sit around in a dry one), two large towels (one for the sauna, one for drying off with), shampoo and a hair-brush (they supply hair-dryers), bath shoes for padding around in, a bathrobe for the sauna and a good book. Each bath provides indoor and outdoor picnic areas so feel free to take your own food. It's mostly no-smoking, but a few eating areas are set aside for nicotine addicts.

Each bath has its own price structure. Some have two and four-hour tickets, some are cheaper if you get there early (they might be open from 8.00 to midnight), some have reductions for children, senior citizens and handicapped people, and many offer a family ticket with considerable saving. I've given you a lot of information under the individual venues in this book so study it carefully or check their websites to find out what's cheapest for you. When you get there most of the baths will give you a coded credit-card-like ticket or a plastic chip at the box office. You must keep this carefully as you'll need it to get back out again through the exit turnstile. This is no problem, however, as you use it instead of money to operate the key for your locker. After you've changed you simply deposit your clothes in the locker, slip the card (chip or coin) in the slot inside the door, close the locker and remove the numbered key which you can attach to your wrist for the day. If you're concerned about your valuables you can lock them away in special lockers ("*Wertsache*"). You can return as often as you like to your locker to get food, shampoo or whatever, and the card remains in the slot the whole time for you to close it once again. When you take your things from the locker for the last time, don't forget to take the card (or chip) with you as you're going to need it to get out again. The machines at the exit can read for what length of time your card (chip) is valid and will charge you overtime where necessary.

The highlight of my visit is always a visit to the sauna baths where I can sweat away all my worries and come out feeling physically reborn. Now it might be that you are unacquainted with communal sauna-baths and – especially if you're from England or the USA – feel a little nervous about using them. If it's any consolation, this was exactly how I felt before I tried them. It would be a pity if you visited a Revier bath and didn't try them, so I'm now going to fill you in on the customs and culture of sauna

bathing in Germany. Firstly children under 16 are generally only allowed in if accompanied by an adult. Secondly most establishments have separate baths for men, women and mixed, as it takes your fancy. Thirdly: total nudity. Now the amazing thing about nudity is that it suddenly becomes an irrelevance when everybody is naked. You're also relieved to discover that 99% of your fellow human beings do not look like film stars and top models and that physical attraction has very little to do with conforming to some expected norm. So don't worry about how you look naked, nobody else gives a damn. And if you still feel a little unsure, as many do, you can always drape your towel strategically over the naughty bits. Detailed instructions on how to sauna are hung up in the baths for all to read but only if you understand German. So if you've never enjoyed a sauna bath before, I'm going to outline the normal procedure for you now.

I always enter the sauna area in my bathing costume, bath-robe, bathing shoes and with a bag containing two towels (one for the sauna one for drying off with), a book and my shampoo. Remove your clothes, hang them up or leave them in your bag near the showers. After that have a quick shower, followed by a warm foot bath. This is supposed to be good for the circulation. Now it's time for the sauna cabin, some of which are outside in beautiful gardens, and most lit discreetly to help you relax better. When having a sauna you must take a long sauna towel to lie or sit on in order to prevent you sweating all over the wooden benches. After fifteen minutes at the most, you will be ready to come out again. By now you will be feeling thoroughly warmed through, so stroll around or lie back on a deck-chair until you have recovered your normal temperature. This takes around ten minutes. After this take a cold shower, jump into a freezing plunge bath and relax again on a deck chair with a book or a paper for as long as you like, before starting the whole procedure all over again. Don't sauna more than twice as the strain on the body tends to take it out on you. The secret is to take your time. No rush. (The children will be equally glad to be free of you for an hour or so). And if you can learn that lesson, one visit to a Revier sauna bath will make you a sauna addict for life.

Enough of swimming and sweating; it's time to turn to another favourite outdoor activity, **cycling**. The Ruhrgebiet has an excellent, up-to-date network of cycling trails which cover more than 700 kilome-

Revierrad-Stationen: (cycle hire)

Revier-Rad Headquarters
Mülheim Central Station
Dieter-aus-dem-Siepen-Platz 3.
Tel: 0208/8485720
zentrale@revierrad.de
Mon–Fri: 5.30–22.30
Sats/Suns and public holidays: 8–18.30

Radstation Mülheim
Mülheim-Styrum Station (S1 S-Bahn line)
Hauskampstr 14
Mon–Fri: 5.30–22.30
Sats/Suns and public holidays: 8–18.30

Aquarius Water Museum, Mülheim
Burgstraße 70
Tue–Sun: 10–18.00

Radstation Bottrop Hbf
Am Hauptbahnhof 1
Mon–Fri: 6–22.00
Sats/Suns and public holidays: 8–20.00

North Duisburg Landscape Park
Emscherstraße 71
Mon–Thurs: 10–17.00
Fri–Sun: 10–21.00

Haus Ripshorst, Oberhausen
Ripshorster Straße 306
1st March – 31st October:
Tue–Sun: 10–18.00
1st November – 28th February:
Tue–Sun: 10–17.00
Public hols: 10–18.00 (17.00)

**Hansa Coking Plant,
Dortmund-Huckarde**
Emscherallee 11
1st April – 31st October:

Tue–Sun: 10–18.00
1st November
– 31st March:
Tue–Sun: 10–17.00
or by arrangement.
Public hols: 10–18.00 (17.00)

Radstation Wanne-Eickel Hbf
Heinz-Ruhmann-Platz 1
Mon–Fri: 5.30–18.30
Sat/Sun closed.

Radstation am Hbf Witten
Bergerstraße 35
Mon–Fri: 5.30–20.00
Sat: 8–16.00

All reservations should be made at the headquarters. That said, bikes don't have to be booked in advance. You can just show up and take pot-luck. Then again…

Prices: Adults 8 € per day (2 hours: 5 €), children 5 € (2.50 €). Tandems 14 €, per day only. Group reductions (10 bikes and more)

If this isn't enough, you can also hire bicycles at Castrop-Rauxel railway station, and at the Preußen Bahnhof in Lünen.
If you want a very special experience what about a hydrogen-driven bike? You can hire one for a group tour at Ewaldstraße 222 in Herten.

The RVR publish a range of excellent cycling maps and guides to the area..

tres between the Middle Ruhr Valley in the south and Münsterland in the North. There are cycles trails along both sides of the Rhine-Herne canal: and along the River Ruhr itself further south is the big new attraction, the **Ruhr Valley Cycle Track** that runs for 230 kilometres from the mouth of the Ruhr to where it meets the Rhine in Duisburg: www.rrw. land-in-sicht.com. If you haven't got a bike with you there are plenty of places to hire one, in particular at any of the 'Revierrad-Stationen', where you can get a good quality bike for a very reasonable price.

Water sport enthusiasts are well catered for in Haltern and along the Ruhr valley, but most especially in Duisburg. In the inner harbour, right in the city centre, there is a brand new marina with mooring berths for boats of up to 20 metres, which

makes it the ideal base for touring the area by boat. Should you be planning a motor boat or yachting holiday in the area and can read German, I advise you to get hold of the newly published 'Sportbootführer fürs Ruhrgebiet' from the RTG. This gives tips for tours, maps, details of marinas, harbours, nearby pubs etc. and costs around 29.80 €. In the south of town the Strandbad Wedau is the main centre for **water-ski and wakeboarding** enthusiasts. But if, like me, you're satisfied with an hour or two's rowing on a lake, you can hire a boat in most of the larger city parks – not however the Grugapark in Essen. Even lazier water fans can explore the area with **boat trips** from Dortmund, Essen, Wanne-Eickel, Herne, Gelsenkirchen, Oberhausen, Duisburg, Waltrop and Mülheim, or on the lakes at Wetter,

Herdecke, Heveney and Baldeney. A day out at a **family leisure park** is guaranteed to be a hit with the kids and I have described three of the best elsewhere in the book. They are, in alphabetical order, Freizeit Park Ketteler Hof (→ p. 152), Schloss Beck (→ p. 77) and Movie Park Germany (→ p. 76). Alternatively my kids and I have enjoyed a day at **the zoo** in Dortmund, Bochum, Gelsenkirchen and Duisburg, not to speak of nearby Wuppertal.

And now we come to a new category of leisure which, in Germany, are known as fun sports. I take this to mean that there is so much money at stake in the more traditional sports, like football, that they have to be taken seriously. So before we move on to solemn professionalism, here are a few tips for plenty of fun where the only thing you might be risking is your health. On the borders of Witten and Bochum, almost next door to the Heveney leisure bath there's a new indoor **beach sport** centre (→ p. 129). If **gliding** is for you, see p.

198. Some people of course prefer to climb rather than fall. There's a great open-air **free climbing** site for you to clamber around on at the North Duisburg Landscape Park (→ p. 48), but should the weather be bad you can always go indoors to 'Klettermax' in Dortmund (Tel: 0231/470258) or 'Kletterpütt' in Essen (Tel: 0201/381562). Over in Bottrop you can go **skiing** all the year round at the Alpine Centre (→ p. 74). It also has a rope climbing garden. The best outdoor places for **rollerblading** are around Lake Baldeney in Essen and Lake Kemnade in Witten. Back at the North Duisburg Landscape Park there's a **skin-diving** centre in an old gasometer (→ p. 52).

And now it's time for serious fun: the sort of sport where the fans beat each other up in advance in order to spend the afternoon in a police cell and avoid the agony of having to suffer 90 minutes praying their team is not going to lose because of appalling refereeing or unbelievably bad luck. (Are there any other reasons?).

Football:

Borussia Dortmund (BVB). Tickets go on sale four weeks in advance. The two main methods of getting tickets are online, and personally. Go online at www.borussia-dortmund.de, click on "English pages" and then on "Mein BVB" on the bar on the top. This will get you to ticket sales where you must register your personal details before proceeding to book. (Crazily, it's different if you go on the German pages. Here you should look for "Tickets" on the left hand side and proceed as above). You can pay with a credit card and print out your tickets If you've no printer, visit the main office at Rheinlanddamm 207-209, near the stadium. It's open during the week, and on match days, four hours before the kick-off. All BVB tickets include free public transport to and from the match from anywhere in the VRR region.

If your heart belongs to **Schalke 04**, tickets can generally only be bought online at www.ts-ticketshop. de. Be warned! They are very difficult to come by because most matches are sold out. For Vfl Bochum see www.vfl-bochum.de. Duisburg: www.msv-duisburg.de. The Schalke and Bochum websites also have English language pages.

Up-to-date information:

To find out what's on, where and when in the area (discos, concerts, films, exhibitions etc) there are two monthly magazines which will give you all the info you're after: **PRINZ** and **coolibri** (free). You can get the former at any newsagent. The latter can be found in most bars, cafés and pubs. Natürlich they're both in German!

The Veltins Arena, Gelsenkirchen – home of Schalke 04

Yes, I'm talking about **professional football** and the German Bundesliga. Anybody remotely interested in the game, like me, must not miss the adrenaline rush of a live match at either **Schalke 04** (Gelsenkirchen) or their local rivals **Borussia Dortmund.** These two are the German equivalents of Liverpool and Everton, or Rangers and Celtic. Schalke won the UEFA cup in 1996. Dortmund were European Champions in the same year and world club champions in 1997, and were Bundesliga champions for the sixth time in 2002, the year Schalke won the cup for the second year running. Dortmund's magnificent stadium, now known as the Signal Iduna Park, has recently been enlarged and now has a capacity of 80,708. Not to be outdone, Schalke opened a super new 'Arena Auf Schalke' in 2001. It's now known as the Veltins Arena and has a capacity of 62,000 and a sliding roof which can turn it into a multi-function mega-event hall for rock concerts, opera events and the like. As in Dortmund, tickets are hard to come by. Both stadiums were selected to stage **World Cup matches in 2006**. The teams in Duisburg and Bochum tend to go up and down like a yo-yo so it's impossible to say with any certainty in what league they'll be playing when you read this book. Essen used to have a Bundesliga team, but has floundered in the regional league for years. For **match tickets** see box on page 211.

For **night-life** see my selection of venues, bars and restaurants in the individual chapters. If you want comprehensive details, see **up-to-date info** in the box on page 211.

12. Monumental Enterprises
THE INDUSTRIAL HERITAGE TRAIL

If you've been reading this book sequentially you should have gathered by now that the Ruhr is full of unique industrial sites, many of which are now museums and landmarks. So before I sign off I'll give you one last summary of the network of monuments known as 'The Industrial Heritage Trail' (Die Route der Industriekultur). Wherever you drive in the Ruhrgebiet you will see countless cowpat-brown signs on the roadside pointing the way to the various attractions along the trail, and directly outside each venue you'll be greeted by a long yellow cone-like pole with the words "route **industriekultur**". The trail comprises 19 industrial sites, 6 technical and social history museums of national importance, 12 characteristic housing settlements which have been preserved and restored, and 9 panorama points. The RVR has just produced a "Discovery Pass" in English with all the information you need about the trail. Ask at the anchor points, four of which are also anchor points along the European Route of Industrial Heritage (ERIH). http://en.erih.net (English pages).

route·**industriekultur**·

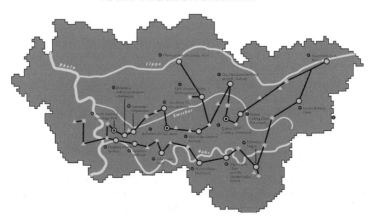

◯ **Anchor points**. The most outstanding industrial venues in the region. (I knew you couldn't wait!)

◉ **Anchor points with visitor centres**. In these three you can get information about the whole route and its attractions.

◆ **Technical museums of national importance**.

M1 German Coal-Mining Museum, Bochum → p. 113
M2 DASA, Dortmund → p. 179
M3 The Westphalian Open-Air Museum of Craft and Technology, Hagen → p. 134
M4 Railway Museum Bochum (suburb of Dahlhausen) → p. 121
M5 Ruhrland Museum, Essen → p. 105
M6 German Inland Waterways Museum, Duisburg → p. 40

▲ **Typical housing settlements** in the area. Here you can get a good idea of traditional living conditions and infrastructures (corner shops, beer gardens etc).

S1 Flöz Dickebank, Gelsenkirchen-Ueckendorf. (*Flöz* means coal-seam) → p. 88
S2 Dahlhauser heath, Bochum-Hördel (next to Hannover Colliery)
S3 Teutoburgia, Herne-Börnig. → p. 168
S4 The old housing colony in Dortmund-Eving.
S5 Ziethenstraße, Lünen. → p. 197
S6 Lange Riege, Hagen-Eilpe
S7 Altenhof II, Essen
S8 Margarethenhöhe, Essen → p. 92
S9 Rheinpreußen, Duisburg-Homberg
S10 The old Friedrich-Heinrich settlement in Kamp-Lintfort
S11 Eisenheim, Oberhausen → p. 68

S12 Welheim Garden Suburb, Bottrop → p. 75

❊ **Industrial Panorama Points**
P1 Hoppenbruch mining tip, Herten. → p. 154
P2 Schwerin tip, Castrop-Rauxel. → p. 140
P3 Großes Holz (Large wood) tip, Bergkamen. → p. 200
P4 'Florian' television tower, Dortmund, in the Westfalenpark → p. 188
P5 Hohensyburg, Dortmund → p. 190
P6 Berger memorial on the Hohenstein, Witten. → p. 130
P7 Pattberg tip, Moers.
P8 Alsumer hill, Duisburg → p. 55
P9 Tetraeder, Bottrop → p. 73

For more information ring: 0180/4000086 and I hope they'll tell you to buy this book! www.route-industriekultur.de info@route-industriekultur.de

There's a very good 88-minute DVD on the market called "Faszination Ruhrgebiet – Route der Industriekultur" with a choice of German or English commentary. It covers the eight most important points along the trail and includes lots of historical film material. It's made by DI-VID-PRO in Bonn. www.divid-pro.de

Now put this book down, get out and have a good time in the Ruhrgebiet.

Keep me informed with changes, updates, tips, endorsements, criticism and differences of opinion, and together we can make the next edition even better!

www.roy-kift.com

INDEX

Major entries are written in **bold** type

Town names, where abbreviated: Bochum (Bo), Bottrop (Bott), Dortmund (Do), Castrop-Rauxel (C-R), Duisburg (Du), Essen (E), Gelsenkirchen (Ge), Hattingen (Hatt), Mülheim (Mü), Oberhausen (Ob), Recklinghausen (Re)

Readers' reactions
TOUR THE RUHR

'... endlich!!!! ist er da!!! ... god bless, you wrote this excellent book ... Thank you very much again ...'
Klaus R., Bottrop

'I am half way through and fully excited. ... I want to make it a present to our... Australian and American friends. ... Your description on how to use the VRR-ticket machines ... and the sentence on how to ride a bus ... are masterpieces of English humour and ... caused loud laughter here as I read them aloud.... thank you very much! ...'
Hermann R., Marl

'Congratulations. ... I wolfed it down. ...It's not only written in a very pleasant and entertaining way ... it is very concise and thorough. Even I, having lived in this area for exactly 50 years ... could learn some things I had not known.'
Axel H., Bochum

'...For me what's great about the book is its accessibility: in style, layout and treatment of subject... My German friends were impressed too, they and went out and got their own copy.'
Richard Noice (England)

'Your new guide is a joy to read and I hope my English friends among whom I'm distributing copies at the moment will feel the same way and laugh as much as I did, maybe even come and visit the Ruhr! ...'
B. Gross, Herten

'Lassen Sie mich zuerst ein großes Lob aussprechen: Ich habe Ihren Reiseführer geradezu verschlungen und festgestellt, dass ich als 'Ruhri' noch eine ganze Menge gelernt habe. Ich bin froh, dass endlich eine große Lücke geschlossen wurde ... Ich möchte Ihnen dazu noch einmal herzlich gratulieren und ich freue mich schon auf die nächste Ausgabe.'
Ingo H., Bochum

Congratulations dear Roy Kift, this is what a tourist guide should be like if you want to have the best possible holiday. It is the best guide that has ever fallen into my hands, not only about the Ruhrgebiet. No, worldwide.
Ursula P.
(Thanks Ursula! I love you, Roy)

Roy Kift is a British writer who has lived in the Ruhrgebiet for over ten years. This third updated edition is the result of years of intensive travelling and research and provides a comprehensive guide for foreigners visiting, touring or living in the area. Every venue in the book has been assessed for its suitability for English-speaking visitors. This book is also available in Dutch.

Other works by Roy Kift include:
Franz, Anna und die Zechengeister
An adventure story for 6 to 10 year-olds
(in German), Klartext Verlag, Essen 1997

The Wupper Valley – Wuppertal, Solingen, Remscheid and the Bergisch Land
Klartext Verlag, Essen 2006

Düsseldorf, Aachen and the Lower Rhine
Klartext Verlag, Essen. 2008

Camp Comedy
A two-act play in "The Theatre of the Holocaust. Vol 2", University of Wisconsin Press (USA) 1999

Stronger than Superman
A play about a handicapped child
Amber Lane Press (GB) 1981

Linienplan Schnellverkehr 2008

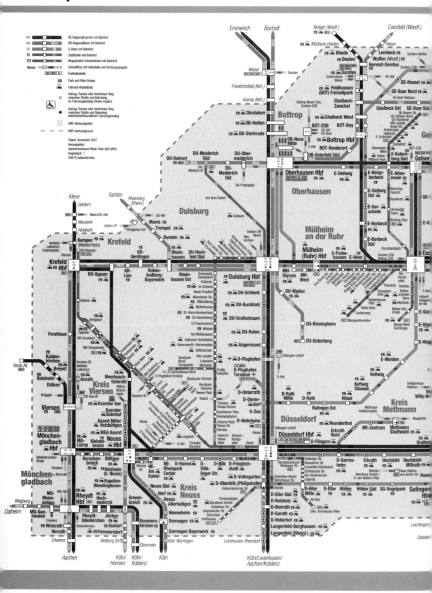

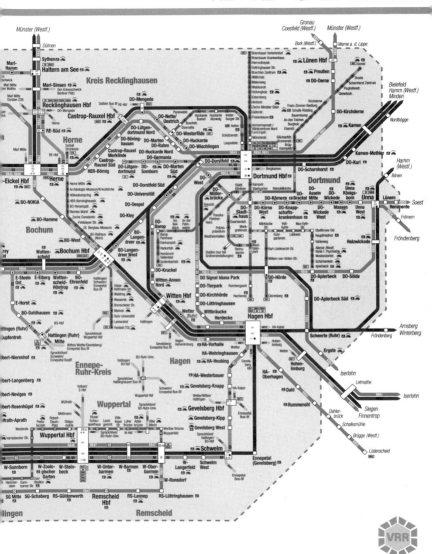

Photos, illustrations, maps and plans

Thanks to:

alpincenter.com AG
p. 75
Bär, Jannis
p. 209
Designbüro Bielefeld
p. 182
Deutsche Arbeitsschutz-Ausstellung, Dortmund
pp. 31, 179, 180
Emschertalmuseum, Herne
p. 164
firo, Gelsenkirchen
pp. 7, 82, 210, 211, 212
Gustav-Lübcke-Museum, Hamm
p. 195
Ikonenmuseum, Recklinghausen
p. 138
Kift, Roy
pp. 77, 88, 100, 101, 109, 119, 123, 139, 140, 141, 147, 149, 155, 161, 170, 186
Konzerthaus Dortmund / Daniel Sumesgutner
p. 173
Kultur- und Stadthistorisches Museum, Duisburg
p. 42
Lehmann, Klaus Michael
p. 13
Ludwig Galerie Schloss Oberhausen
p. 70
Lueger, Ralph
p. 105, 108, 188
Mahlstedt, Olaf
p. 165
monte mare
p. 159
Öko-Zentrum, Hamm
p. 195
Regionalverband Ruhrgebiet (RVR)
pp. 6, 7, 8, 12, 15, 29, 30, 37, 42, 48, 56, 58, 61, 69, 81, 87, 90, 91, 93, 94, 104, 109, 111, 112, 113, 117, 118, 120, 124, 127, 131, 132, 135, 171, 188, 190, 193, 199, 202, 204, 205

Ruhrfestspiele Recklinghausen
pp. 35, 137
Ruhrgebiet Tourismus GmbH & Co. KG
pp. 6, 7, 23, 28, 29, 30, 31, 39, 40, 41, 43, 47, 49, 51, 52, 57, 63, 64, 65, 68, 71, 74, 83, 84, 92, 95, 98, 102, 103, 115, 121, 122, 125, 134, 139, 146, 151, 153, 156, 160, 183, 184, 186, 194, 200, 203, 205, 206, 208, 209
Schlautmann, Rainer
p. 163
Sea Life Oberhausen
p. 67
Schumacher, Joachim
p. 158
Skulpturenmuseum Glaskasten, Marl
p. 157
Stadt Bergkamen
p. 201
Stadt Castrop-Rauxel
p. 14
Stadt Dortmund
p. 191
Stadt Gelsenkirchen
p. 80
Stadt Haltern
p. 151
Stadt Herne
p. 167
Stadt Lünen
p. 196, 197
Stadt Oberhausen
p. 29
Stadt Xanten
p. 11,
Stegner, Birgit
p. 59, 103
Verkehrsverein Dortmund
pp. 176, 178, 181, 185, 187, 189
VRR
pp. 19, 21, 22, 222/223
Zeche Zollern, Dortmund
p. 182
Zeche Zollverein, Essen
p. 99
Zoom Erlebniswelt, Gelsenkirchen
p. 85